HAMMER OF JUSTICE

Molly Rush and the Plowshares Eight

LIANE ELLISON NORMAN

PPI Books
Pittsburgh Peace Institute

Published by the Pittsburgh Peace Institute, Pittsburgh, Pa. 15217
Copyright © 1989, Liane Ellison Norman
All Rights Reserved

Library of Congress Cataloging in Publication Data

Card Number 89–61406
ISBN
hardcover 096 227 6693
paper 096 227 6685

For citizens and pilgrims

CONTENTS

INTRODUCTION

$\mathbf{M}$OLLY RUSH, as another prisoner observed, sounds like someone in history. If history succeeds in sorting out and preserving the essential truths of the human experience, she will be. For somehow Molly saw the blinding fact that humanity was hurtling toward the self-destruction of life on earth. This book tells what she did.

With a fine sense of history, Liane Norman weaves Molly's acts, the family anguish and ordinary daily humdrum happenings into the fabric of the long human struggle for moral life. The effect is startling. From the solemn, compelling history of William Penn, Norman finds a natural harmony of spirit and purpose in the story of Molly Rush in modern-day America. Each confronted the major demons of their moment. With Penn, it was state prohibition of the free exercise of religious faith. With Rush, it was the state pursuit of nuclear holocaust. Each defied authority and stood trial for acts of conscience.

We can hear Judge Samuel Salus of Pennsylvania in 1981 echoing Judge Samuel Starling of England in 1670 muttering that the accused is a person of "cursed principles." Just as Judge Starling told Penn, "You are not here for worshipping God, but for breaking the law," Judge Salus told Rush, "You are not on trial for [conscience arising from religious tradition, reading the Gospels, Hiroshima, Nuremberg], you are on trial for the violation of the Criminal Code of Pennsylvania."

Just as Penn, a lawyer, said, "The question is not whether I am guilty of this indictment, but whether this indictment be legal," Molly, a mother, said, "We're trying to defend life on this planet. . . . We are talking about the morality of nuclear weapons . . . [that is] the heart and soul of our defense." If that is irrelevant, "then this court is irrelevant."

The spirit and purpose of William Penn flourished in Philadelphia, even prevailed for a period, before succumbing to the Practical Man and crushing materialism that ultimately produced Dreiser's *Financier* at its lowest ebb. By the late twentieth century in the wake of despair left by Mammon, the brute force of a Police Chief Rizzo became the

ix

means of controlling the poor without pity or conscience. Whether Molly's spirit and purpose flourish and prevail is up to us.

As a study of the nature and sources of personal heroism in pursuit of moral vision, this book is remarkable. Comparing many creative efforts to capture the essence of Joan of Arc—Anatole France, Mark Twain, G. B. Shaw, Vita Sackville-West—none brings a clear view of the historical, cultural, religious, social, and familial relations that forged the character and created the circumstances in which Joan chose her course. The necessary facts were not available. So we miss the pain of Joan's personal struggle and evoke miracle to aid our understanding.

But Liane Norman has gathered the facts about Molly. Through uses of investigative journalism and oral history, this book powerfully and painfully illustrates the enormous personal sensitivity, courage, sacrifice, loneliness, heartache, patience, and love required to defy authority in mass, urban, anonymous, affluent, technologically advanced America. Molly's family history reveals a people among whom conscience has played a featuring role at times in the past, a people who have made hard decisions often on moral grounds, a people whose lives have been dominated by war, who have known migrations, poverty, alcoholism, separation. An almost wiretap realism in dialogue among husband, wife, children, parents, relatives, and friends recreates the tensions within a family and the awesome strain on the defiant one, caused by a moral decision to contest government conduct.

Here is the hardest kind of heroism. We tend to mistake courage for bravado, for love of violence, for an erratic personality given to risk, danger, death-dealing and defying action, a pursuit of glory, the want of gentleness and compassion. In fact, real heroism is standing gently for principle when it hurts, costs, alienates, and frightens.

Molly saw a tragic wrong, the creation of omnicidal weapons, and she risked everything—her husband's love, her family, her children's care, the anger of relatives and friends, personal security, imprisonment, physical injury, peace of mind—to address it. She did this knowing how powerful the national commitment to nuclear arms was and how unlikely her acts were to alter that commitment. She persevered under constant pressure, in the face of hostile authority and at best ambiguous public opinion.

This book shows how extraordinarily difficult it is for a person to defy authority, an ingrained notion of patriotism, and the economic power of the war machine in a society that celebrates democratic institutions and individual freedom. We are social creatures. We want the affection and approval of others. Few of us dare defy our government when it is tragically wrong. Not many will ever question government on the major questions of war and peace.

Nothing could be more obvious than the fact that weapons of mass destruction are totally unacceptable in moral, legal, and human terms. Yet, in the entire nation only a handful have come forth possessed of the vision, the courage, and the compassion to resist. Molly is among them. The reader is provided an enormous amount of raw material with which to wonder what makes a saint and why so few. With Molly a major factor is clearly the feloniously saintly company she kept.

And for all the courage and sacrifice and love Molly has selflessly given, in this celebrity society, she is barely known. This book can help change that. And perhaps it can help us see the deceit and distortion of Celebrity itself, a lust irreconcilable with democratic faith.

What will happen to a people if they meekly submit to law bent on genocidal ways? History and reason tells us. Governments have produced war as the dominant experience of virtually every generation in viritually every part of the planet through recorded history. Thomas Aquinas told us what had been common knowledge for millennia when he wrote, "War is inevitable among sovereign nations not governed by positive law." World law is essential to life on the planet.

Molly and her friends who ask us to beat our swords into plowshares understand this. They invoke international law to make governments act as they ought. They assume the moral obligation of confronting law when it acts immorally. If we are to end war, feed the hungry, educate the ignorant, employ the idle, and fulfill the spiritual potential of our species, we must establish peace, nonviolence, love as a way of life. And first we must outlaw weapons of mass destruction. Then all weapons. This is Molly Rush's message to the Court of Common Pleas and to you and me.

Ramsey Clark
June 1989

ACKNOWLEDGMENTS

THE STORY that follows is about one woman, Mary Ruth Moore Rush—Molly, as she is known. She is one of the many ordinary people who made an individual decision, took individual action, and bore, individually, the consequences. Her action was something her government called illegal: she disobeyed laws protecting property. She thought she acted legally, in obedience not only to spiritual but also to international legal requirements. Because what she did was colorful and unusual, she became something of a hero, a singularity that dismays her, because she thinks such regard sets her— falsely—apart and above. And Molly Rush is above all things a connecter, a linker, a practitioner of what Riane Eisler calls the "partnership model." Eisler's *The Chalice and the Blade* defines the partnership model as an egalitarian, goddess-centered, social-welfare-minded, nonviolent model of social organization, rooted in prehistory and often resurgent. The alternative is the more familiar domination model, a hierarchical, god-centered, tough-minded, violent way of organizing society, ill-suited to evolution from here on. The latter, says Eisler, has repressed, though not destroyed, the partnership model and now threatens history itself.

Molly did not act alone. Most obviously, she performed the actions recounted here with seven other people, with whom she had collaborated in planning and deciding. There were other collaborators, though not so conspicuous. Molly was and remains deeply rooted in family and community. The needs of family were much on her mind as she decided how *she* would act. The consequences of her decision affected them as well as her. During her absence from home, her husband, older children, and siblings provided for the younger children and for one another in their profound shock and unhappiness. When Molly wrote from jail, it was clear that she knew she could trust her large family to take her place, since one outcome that had to be considered was lifetime imprisonment. She could also trust associates to take up her work at the Thomas Merton Center, a Pittsburgh store-front peace organization. The people she relied on rose to the occasion, as she had anticipated.

There were other partnerships at work. Molly's parents, grand-parents, aunts, uncles, friends, and colleagues contributed to her adventuresome nature, her stability in the face of material hardship, her sense of responsibility, her spiritual buoyancy. And beyond her family and immediate community were partners—male and female—in the historic struggle for social transformation. One of Catholic Molly's predecessors was Quaker William Penn, a piece of whose story is, in this book, linked to Molly's.

Despite the collaborative truth of Molly's story, I've focused on Molly herself, partly because it was by asking why *she*—not why *they*—acted that I came to understand, even to value, this public disturbance of a false peace, and partly because stories are easier to tell about individuals than about collectivities. I have, however, tried to suggest the social density of Molly's life. Nevertheless, I have left out much to make the story move forward rather than (as would be more accurate) every which way.

This book, too, though it bears my name as author, is an immensely collaborative effort. From the very beginning, I have had the support of my husband, Robert, and my children, Andy, Marie, and Emily; they have ungrudgingly put up with my preoccupation and absence, the cost of equipment, copying, postage, and the forfeiture of rewards attendant on writing something more traditionally respectable. To them I owe my deepest gratitude.

Also from the beginning, Molly; her husband Bill; her children, Gary, Linda, Janine, Dan, Bob, and Greg; her siblings, David, James, Joann, Mary Catherine, Barbara, Edward, and Tom; her aunts, Ruth Haines and Catherine Whitcombe, have been generous with their time, privacy, family pictures, and good will. They laid many quite intimate aspects of their family life open without reservation. They are people deeply considerate of one another, profoundly accepting. I appreciate their confidence and hope I have not abused it. Molly's close friend, Cary Lund, provided fresh insights. Some of the people involved in the trial, notably Ramsey Clark, when he might have been too preoccupied for comment, were also generous with their time and courtesy. Even Judge Samuel Salus, though I think he erred judicially in so doing, was generous in providing a midtrial interview. Later, when it was perfectly proper, he responded to several of my letters.

Gloria Emerson was quick to see the possibilities for a book and to offer encouragement. Muriel Bennett and Eleanore Bushnell provided support and suggestions during the first drafting of the manuscript, as did Walter Pitkin. Some of the discerning and helpful readers have been: Montgomery Culver, Angele Ellis, Laurel Everett, Pat Furey, Julie Gustafson, John Krofcheck, Sister Pat McCann, Kate Maloy, Donald McDonald, Marian Norman, Robert, Andy, Marie, and Emily Norman, Marianne Novy, Maggie Patterson, Andrea Richardson, Elizabeth Segel, Mark Sommer. Angele Ellis, with her usual flair, suggested the title. Annette Kolodny was helpful with ideas for trade publication, as were Richard Falk, the late Sidney Lens, Victor Navasky, Marianne Novy and Paul Schrading. Jonathan Pressler and Michael Diamond took some of the photographs, and Marie Norman contributed a drawing. John Krofcheck helped solve some infuriating computer problems. Although we tried our best to find Bill Ternay, to get his permission to use his excellent drawing of the courtroom during the trial of the Plowshares Eight, we were unable to find him. We appreciate and acknowledge his keen eye and astute artistry. In his particular way, which is always gracious and attentive, Ramsey Clark agreed to write the introduction, despite the many demands on his time and talent.

In the winter of 1988, the Pittsburgh Peace Institute's Board of Directors decided to publish *Hammer of Justice* as the first of its major publications. In this effort, the collaboration required to make a book was even more evident than when the usual publishing house takes over. Sondra Zeidenstein, from her experience with Chicory Blue Press, which she established, was lavish with encouragement and counsel. John Burt lent his superb storytelling gifts to the task of editing, his meticulous research to checking out many historical details and incomplete references. Jane Flanders's careful reading prompted immeasurable improvements, both of detail and narrative. She, Rosemary Coffey, Sally Dewees and Karen Cooper combed the manuscript for errors. Jim Kuhn provided legal advice. Frank Moone coordinated production of the book, and Peter Oresick designed the marketing and promotion campaign. A committee led by George Bauman and Linda Schoyer provided leadership for the whole undertaking; other committee members offered a variety of useful skills and energies: Sally Alexander, John Burt, Karen Cooper, Kathy Guthrie, Maggie Kimmel, Priscilla Wahrhaftig, James Welbourne. Bonnie DiCarlo and Sisters Georgine Scarpino, Pat McCann, Grace Ann Geibel, and Sheila Carney helped in formulating fundraising strategy. Bruce Gore provided the beautiful design for the book and promotional materials. Emily

Norman and George Bauman took charge of distribution with energy and imagination. Providing the financial backing, without which no book is possible, were Marian Hahn, Margaret McCoy, the Pittsburgh Peace Institute, Sisters of Mercy, Sisters of Saint Joseph, Priscilla Wahrhaftig. My colleague Kathy Guthrie not only was generous with encouragement, but also did more than her share of work at the Pittsburgh Peace Institute so that I could attend to book matters.

All of these people—and the many more who keep the world running one way or another while the attention of a few people is given to projects that bear their names—made this book. They are not to blame for its shortcomings. In that respect alone I take full responsibility. But they do account for its existence and its virtues, for which I am more grateful than I can express.

PITTSBURGH, PENNSYLVANIA
March 1989

PROLOGUE

O<small>N AN APPARENTLY</small> ordinary day in September 1980, an apparently ordinary woman carrying an apparently ordinary hammer did something extraordinary. This is the story of that woman and what she did, why she did it, and what happened as a result.

This story is not only journalism, though it is that. It is not only history, though it is that, too. It is not only drama, an essay, or an analysis of the intellectual origins of peace activism, though it is also all of these things. It is a story told partly because it is about someone I knew when the events chronicled here happened, someone I know far better now. It is a story told by a narrator who was affected by the events here recounted, told in the way she understands the world, as an untidy mix of narrative genres.

Molly Rush is a native of Pennsylvania. What she did occurred in Pennsylvania. The founder of Pennsylvania, William Penn, might have been pleased by the poetic justice—quite unintentional—of an attempt to begin nuclear disarmament in the state he had established three centuries earlier as a disarmed polity. That spiritually gifted, rebellious, adventurous Quaker man might have felt some kinship with the spiritually gifted, rebellious, adventurous Catholic woman who took a hammer to a nuclear warhead.

The tale told here links two acts of resistance to abuses of two kinds of power, two quite similar legal proceedings in two quite different courtrooms, two unrelated people in two widely divided times and places, two stories that ask the question "Why?"

HAMMER
OF
JUSTICE

In the last days they shall beat
their swords into plowshares and
their spears into pruning hooks,
and everyone shall sit under the
vine and fig trees and none shall
be afraid.

—Micah 4:1–4

For swords into plowshares
The hammer has to fall.

—Charlie King

It's the hammer of justice!

—Pete Seeger

1

"Always put justice above law"

"YOU ARE not brought here for worshipping God," snapped Richard Browne, speaking to defendant William Penn in a London courtroom in 1670, "but for breaking the law." That was also the contention in 1981 when Molly Rush and the Plowshares Eight went on trial in Pennsylvania: that they had broken the law, and that the law was clear, unchanging, and sacrosanct. At issue in both 1670 and 1981 was how fundamental legal principles should be applied to contemporary circumstances.

In 1670, Browne was one of the notables who sat with the judge, Sir Samuel Starling, and a group of local aldermen in London's criminal court, the Old Bailey. Sir Samuel was Lord Mayor of London. To preside as judge was his prerogative and duty. A bailey was originally the outer wall of a feudal castle, the bulwark against attack on whatever order existed inside. The Old Bailey, a gloomy keep, was meant to serve the same purpose. In the late seventeenth century, prisoners were held in Newgate Jail, adjoining the courthouse. Criminal suspects were sometimes tortured, a standard technique of interrogation. In the courtyard of the jail, the heads of executed felons were boiled as a method of preservation so that they might be displayed on poles to warn potential criminals of the wages of sin. Across the road from the courthouse, St. Sepulchre's bell tolled notice of public executions. Next door to the Old Bailey stood the College of Surgeons, ready to receive the bodies of those executed for anatomical experiments.

It was a time between civil war and agricultural-industrial revolutions. The turmoil of the period was both cruel and creative. About a third of the English population barely subsisted, while another third required poor relief just to survive. One writer of the period, estimating the social and economic makeup of merry old England, found the number of "vagrants, as gypsies, thieves, beggars, &c" to be indeterminate. Many of them kept Newgate Jail, the Old Bailey, St. Sepulchre's bell, and the College of Surgeons busy. Despite the poverty of those most often brought before the bar—or perhaps because of the poverty from which they wished to dissociate themselves—judges customarily provided lavish food and drink for their guests during court recesses.

In all probability, Sir Samuel Starling so treated those who sat with him on the bench. They were aldermen Thomas Bloodworth, William Peak, John Robinson, Richard Ford, and Joseph Sheldon. Possibly Richard Browne, who was so insistent about the nature of the crime being tried, along with the recorder and prosecutor, Thomas Howel, and sheriffs John Smith and James Edwards, joined the judge and aldermen in merrymaking.

Sir Samuel Starling almost certainly wore a long curled wig: it bespoke his loyalty to the recently restored Stuart monarch, Charles II, to whom Starling owed his eminence. When the close-cropped Puritans who followed Oliver Cromwell had ridden high, Samuel Starling had been an enthusiastic persecutor of royalists. But when the king was restored to the throne, Starling wore the wig of royal fashion and went after dissenters with a vengeance.

The defendants in Sir Samuel's courtroom were on trial for violating the Conventicle Act, a law passed by a largely Anglican Parliament to prevent the re-establishment of Catholicism, the king's preference, as the predominant religion of England. The law had little effect on Catholics, but it was used with zeal against the relatively new sect of Quakers. The defendants on trial in the Old Bailey were charged with "causing a tumult." They were William Penn, a handsome, twenty-six-year-old Quaker lawyer, and his companion, William Mead, a well-to-do linen draper and newly convinced Quaker. Their crime was having spoken to a throng gathered in the street before Gracechurch Street Meeting House, a violation of the Second Conventicle Act.

The law's stated purpose was to provide "speedy remedies against the growing and dangerous practices of seditious sectaries and other disloyal persons, who, under pretence of tender consciences, have or may at their meetings contrive insurrections."

Such religious groups as the Quakers were feared by the government because of the political implications of religious dissent. And in fact, Quaker belief, which had existed for some twenty years by the time the events recounted here took place, was radically egalitarian. Quakers believed that God resided in each person, that revelation was continuing and available to everyone. These precepts made Quakers both uppity and pacifist. For some time, Quaker meeting houses had been occupied by soldiers whose task was to prevent such conventicles or gatherings. In their armed presence, Anglican ministers performed their services in order to prevent the kind of worship Quakers engaged in, a silent waiting for God's spirit to move among them, perhaps to move one or more of them to provide spontaneous ministry. The high-church clerics might preach love and brotherhood to the congregation, but should a Quaker stand up to offer his or her own ministry, as was Quaker practice, it was considered rebellion against authority and betrayed the fragility of the newly reconstituted Stuart regime. And so, Quakers met outside their occupied meeting houses, their silence and their speaking alike drowned out by the drums beaten for that purpose by the king's soldiers.

William Penn, one of the defendants in the case, was schooled in the law, but he had mixed feelings about his profession, for Quakers objected to practices that set people against one another in adversarial roles. Later on, after he had founded Pennsylvania, Penn came to see the law as a necessary last resort for "the incorrigible class, who failed to agree with their adversaries while in the way with them." Even as a young man, a defendant in Sir Samuel Starling's court, he construed the law as neither fixed nor absolute, but—as Christ had put it to those who chastised him for violating its strictures—an instrument for human well-being.

"Always put justice above law," said Penn, "and when law is unjust, challenge it directly." Penn thought the Conventicle Act was such a law, out of harmony with human need and fundamental law. In earlier times, says Hans Fantel, one of Penn's livelier biographers, "the only thinkable attitude had been that the law must be obeyed because it was the law. Obedience was the chief Christian virtue in the feudal era."

Penn intended to challenge the law, using its foundations as his warrant. This was a somewhat novel intent in the days before Mohandas Gandhi and Martin Luther King, Jr. But there were nevertheless precedents. The fictional Antigone, as well as Socrates and Jesus, had met untimely deaths for heretical teachings or acts. Penn was not averse to setting precedents of his own. Indeed, Quakers, whose egalitarian and pacifist principles offended those in power, were not unused to prison.

William Penn's arrest in London, 1670, as pictured by Violet Oakley, Governor's Reception Room, State Capitol, Harrisburg, Pennsylvania.

Penn had let it be known that he would speak outside the Grace-church Street Meeting House, where soldiers were consequently gathered in advance on August 14, 1670. The soldiers were prepared with a warrant, already drawn up, to arrest the two men for "preaching seditiously and causing a great tumult of people in the said street to be there gathered together riotously and routously." The charges alleged riot and rout rather than violations of the Conventicle Act, because nervous authorities did not want that law tested. Penn, however, intended to call the law itself to account because it protected unjust practices.

Quakers were, as Samuel Starling put it later in a pamphlet, persons of "cursed principles." They refused "hat honor"—that is, taking off their hats before their betters—for if, as they believed, God dwelt in each person equally, there were no "betters" before God. They used the familiar "thee" and "thou" to all equally for the same reason. They refused to take judicial oaths, holding that truth-telling should be a matter of course and not reserved for the courtroom. Nor would they bear arms in the king's service, believing that to kill or injure any person was to kill or injure God. For Christ had said that whatever was done to "the least of these, my brethren," was done to himself. He had commanded his followers to love—not to kill—their enemies and had ordered Peter to put up his sword rather than defend his master. These Quakers, Starling saw quite accurately, were a significant threat to both the form and the content of established power.

Sir Samuel Starling had announced that he, personally, would try this case. Says Fantel, Starling "emerges from the trial record as a man of sufficient narrowness to qualify as anybody's political tool." His conception of the law was not that it served as "the earthly arbiter of good and evil, but merely as an extension of the policeman's club." Fantel describes Sir Samuel as lacking "all concept of the creative function of the judge under English common law. Equipped with civic sense and humane vision, even a conservative judge can deal construc-tively with radical dissidence." But it was Starling's lot in life to go down in history as a barely competent, mean-spirited judge, who, in spite of himself, set in motion events that would enlarge the role of the jury as the independent "conscience of the community."

The trial was itself something of a tumult. The formal proceedings began with the reading of a lengthy and repetitive indictment, naming conspiracy on the part of "the aforesaid William Penn, by agreement between him and William Mead" to "preach and speak" to "a great concourse and tumult of people in the street aforesaid to the great disturbance of many of [the king's] liege people and subjects, to the ill example of all others."

"What say you?" the defendants were asked, "guilty as you stand indicted or not guilty?"

Penn asked to see "a copy of [the indictment], as is customary in the like occasions."

But Thomas Howel, the recorder, who also served as prosecutor, said no. The defendants must plead before they could see a copy of the charges against them.

Penn and Mead, each secured this pledge from Sir Samuel: "No advantage shall be taken against you; you shall have liberty [to make your defense]; you shall be heard." With this assurance, they pleaded not guilty. For if, as Penn intended to demonstrate, the indictment "hath no foundation in law," then indeed they were not guilty.

After considerable waiting while other court business was conducted, Penn and Mead entered the courtroom wearing their hats, in the Quaker fashion. A bailiff knocked them off. Starling ordered their hats restored to their heads, and so covered, they approached the bar of justice. Howel inquired, "Do you know where you are?"

"Yes," answered Penn.

"Do you not know there is respect due to the court?" asked Howel.

Penn said yes, and that he paid it.

"Why do you not pull off your hat then?" queried Howel, and promptly levied a fine on the two men for contempt of court.

At this inauspicious beginning, Penn retorted, "It might be observed that we came into the court with our hats off (that is, taken off [by the bailiff]) and if they have been put on since, it was by order from the bench; and therefore not we, but the bench should be fined."

In his preliminary remarks, Sir Samuel noted that the defendant Penn should be whipped for being Admiral William Penn's son. The admiral, he said, had embezzled funds earmarked for the feeding of his sailors and thus starved them. Penn won the admiration of spectators when he responded, "I could very well hear severe expressions addressed to me concerning myself, but I am sorry to hear abuses of my father, who is not present." So the trial began, the defendants found in contempt for wearing the hats that had been knocked off their heads and put back on and scolded before a word was offered in evidence, and one of them berated for faults alleged against a parent, who was something of a popular hero because he had helped to bring Charles II back to England from his exile during Oliver Cromwell's rule.

Evidence was given by two men, each of whom *saw* Penn speak, but could not tell what he said "because of the noise" made by a crowd of three to five hundred persons. One witness saw Mead speak with Penn. Another did not. And so Howel asked, "What say you, Mr. Mead, were you there?"

Mead replied, "It is a maxim in your own law that no man is bound to accuse himself; and why does thou offer to ensnare me with such a question? Does not this shew thy malice?"

"Sir, hold thy tongue," ordered Howel. "I did not go about to ensnare you."

Penn urged, "We may come more close to the point, and that silence be commanded in the court."

"O yes, all manner of persons keep silence upon pain of imprisonment!" called out the court crier. "Silence court!"

Penn began the serious business of his challenge to the law. "We confess ourselves to be so far from recanting, or declining to vindicate the assembling of ourselves to preach, pray, or worship the eternal, holy, just God, that we declare to all the world, that we do believe it to be our indispensable duty, to meet incessantly upon so good an account; nor shall all the powers upon earth be able to divert us from reverencing and adoring our God who made it."

It was at this point that Richard Browne exclaimed the words that open this story: "You are not here for worshipping God, but for breaking the law."

Penn's civil disobedience had created a crisis for the law. Penn, like civil disobedients before and since, harkened to a large view of the law. He intended an articulation of the principles upon which the law was founded so that appropriate adaptations could be made. But first he had to flush his prosecutors from the underbrush of pretense in which they had hidden their real purpose. "I affirm I have broken no law," Penn said. "I desire you would let me know by what law it is you prosecute me, and upon what law you ground my indictment." Penn wanted the Conventicle Act named and its provisions specified so that he could challenge them.

The court, aware that religious unanimity no longer existed, did not want to spell out the law that tried to enforce conformity. Howel would say no more than that the indictment was grounded "upon the Common Law," and when Penn demanded the precedents, Howel answered, "You must not think that I am able to run up so many years, and over so many adjudged cases, which we call Common Law, to answer your curiosity."

Penn prodded. "If it be Common," he urged, "it should not be so hard to produce."

Howel grew impatient. "Sir, will you plead to your indictment?" and Penn answered, "Shall I plead to an indictment that hath no foundation in law? If it contain that law you say I have broken, why should you decline to produce that law, since it will be impossible for the jury to determine, or agree to bring in their verdict, who have not the law by which they should measure the truth of this indictment, and the guilt, or contrary of my fact?"

Penn insisted, "The question is not whether I am guilty of this indictment, but whether this indictment be legal."

"You are an impertinent fellow," opined Howel. "Will you teach the Court what law is, that which many have studied thirty or forty years to know, and would you have me tell you in a moment?"

"Certainly," Penn said, "if the Common Law be so hard to be understood, it's far from being very common." But, said Penn, "if the Lord Coke, in his *Institutes,* be of any consideration, he tells us that Common Law is Common Right, and that Common Right is Great Charter privileges," and he cited a number of precedents.

"Note," wrote Sir Samuel Starling later in a pamphlet defending his conduct of the trial, "how Mr. Penn plays upon the word *common.*"

Penn made reference to the Magna Carta, extorted by the English barons from King John at Runnymede in 1215. Although the Great Charter redressed specific wrongs rather than declaring sweeping principles, principles were nonetheless established. One was that there were certain things a ruler could not do, that even the king was subject to common law. Another was that there were public rights and liberties the king could not violate. Taxes, for example, could be levied only by "common council for our kingdom," a principle that found its way into the American patriots' cry, over five hundred years later, "No taxation without representation!" Another principle was that "No free man [later construed to mean citizen] shall be taken or imprisoned or disseised or exiled or in any way destroyed except by the lawful judgment of his peers or/and the law of the land." Penn argued that the liberties and property of Englishmen were guaranteed by the Magna Carta and could not be taken from them merely by passing new laws or issuing decrees

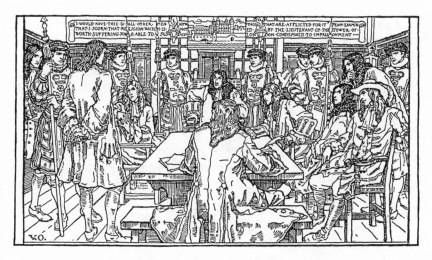

William Penn's trial in London, 1670, as pictured by Violet Oakley, Governor's Reception Room, State Capitol, Harrisburg, Pennsylvania.

for reasons that suited those in power at the moment. Sir Edward Coke, the sixteenth-century English jurist, had compiled legal decisions bearing on particular issues so as to reduce the chaos of old legal authorities into comparative order.

Penn's judge and prosecutor were intent on keeping the charges as narrow as possible. They wanted no talk of Magna Carta privileges nor of Sir Edward Coke and his *Institutes*. "Sir, you are a troublesome fellow," said Thomas Howel.

"I have asked but one question and you have not answered me," Penn pointed out.

To which the recorder responded, "If I should suffer you to ask questions till tomorrow morning, you would never be the wiser," adding, "Sir, we must not stand to hear you talk all night."

"I design no affront to the Court," apologized Penn. But he insisted that refusal to spell out the law he was accused of violating constituted "evidence to the whole world [of] your resolution to sacrifice the privileges of Englishmen to your sinister and arbitrary designs."

Penn's argument was certainly political, part of an effort to reduce the arbitrary authority of the monarchy. Common law, based on precedent-setting legal decisions, was itself a form of resistance to absolutism. Coke, whom both Penn and Mead cited as their authority, and whose name was no doubt a red flag to those behind the bench, was not only intensely involved in the complicated politics of early Stuart England, but was also considered the great champion of the liberties of subjects as against the despotic claims of whichever king occupied the throne. Coke had asserted that the king "hath no prerogative but that which common law allows him." The common law prevented either king or Parliament from changing the fundamental rights and duties of English citizens. The common law position, naturally, was feared and resented by those who made despotic claims. A similar contest was apparent three centuries later, in the trial of Molly Rush and the Plowshares Eight, about who should determine military policy—the national security establishment or ordinary citizens. In Molly's case, claims of international law infuriated the court as much as Penn's claims of common law infuriated Sir Samuel Starling, and for much the same reason.

Howel appealed to the judge, "My Lord, if you take not some course with this pestilent fellow, to stop his mouth, we shall not be able to do anything tonight." Sir Samuel ordered, "Take him away, take him away, turn him into the bail-dock."

The bail dock was a small area in the corner of the courtroom, walled but open at the top, in which malefactors were sometimes held during trials. Penn wondered aloud, "Must I therefore be taken away because I plead for the fundamental laws of England?" Knowing full well how to plead his case—and to infuriate the judge—Penn spoke directly to the jury. "This I leave upon your consciences, who are of my jury (and my sole judges) that if these ancient fundamental laws, which related to liberty and property (and are not limited to particular persuasions in matters of religion) must not be indispensably maintained and observed, who can say he hath right to the coat upon his back? Certainly our liberties are openly to be invaded, our wives to be ravished, our children slaved, our families ruined, and our estates led away in triumph by every sturdy beggar and malicious informer, as their trophies. The Lord of Heaven and Earth," he declared, "will be judge between us in this matter!"

The trial was something like a tennis match. Each side maneuvered to set up the decisive shot. Game point, match point, it was a long and tiring contest. One side had nearly all the muscle; the other, nearly all the wit and agility.

Over and over during the trial Penn reminded the jury that, no matter what Starling said, they were the true judges. Over and over he reminded them that conscience, the inner working of mind and heart, was their legal province. Penn believed that divine inspiration was the basis of conscience, the ability to tell right from wrong, and that, to seek truth, conscience must be free. This conviction was at the heart of his willingness to test a law which his contemporary, the poet Andrew Marvell, called "the quintessence of arbitrary malice."

With Penn in the bail dock, Mead took over. He too wanted the specific law he was accused of violating to be cited. Refused, he told the jury, "If the Recorder will not tell you what makes a riot, a rout, or an unlawful assembly, Coke tells us [that] a riot is when three, or more, are met together to beat a man, or to enter forcibly into another man's land, to cut down his grass, or wood, or break down his pales." Riot had not been his or Penn's intention. They had merely tried to worship as conscience directed.

"You deserve to have your tongue cut out," said Starling.

Mead protested, "Thou didst promise me, I should have fair liberty to be heard" (no doubt further offending Starling by addressing him familiarly as "thou"). Mead too was taken away to the bail dock and Howel charged the jury.

From across the room in the bail dock, out of sight but not out of earshot, Penn shouted to the jury, "who are my judges, and to this great assembly, whether the proceedings of the Court are not most arbitrary, and void of all law, in offering to give the jury their charge in the absence of the prisoners. I say, it is directly opposite to, and destructive of, the undoubted right of every English prisoner." A similar issue arose in the twentieth-century trial of the Plowshares Eight, whether the constitutional right to a public trial was abridged when the judge refused to admit the public during part of the jury selection process.

An "observer" who published an account of "The Tryal of William Penn and William Mead for Causing a Tumult at the Sessions Held at Old Bailey in London the 1st, 3rd, 4th and 5th of September, 1670," commented, "The Recorder, being thus unexpectedly lashed for his extrajudicial procedure, said with an enraged smile, 'why, ye are present, you do hear, do you not?'"

Penn was not finished. "You of the jury take notice, that I have not been heard, having at least ten or twelve material points to offer, in order to invalid their indictment."

Howel ordered the defendants taken even farther away, "into the stinking Hole," where Penn and Mead awaited the jury's verdict.

The drama was far from over. At this point, however, the Penn-

Mead trial, for violations of a law that preserved momentary peace by restricting religious practice, became the Bushel case, named for Edward Bushel, the foreman of the jury. Of Bushel the alderman John Robinson said, "You deserve to be indicted more than any man that hath been brought to the bar this day."

Bushel's offense was that he led the jury in refusing to find Penn and Mead guilty of anything more than speaking in Gracechurch Street. The jury would not add to their verdict that Penn addressed an unlawful assembly, or that he spoke to a tumult of people there. Mead they acquitted altogether.

When he heard the verdict, Starling lectured and threatened. Howel snarled at Bushel, "Sir, you are the cause of this disturbance, and manifestly show yourself an abettor of faction." He said, in effect, that the jury's decision undermined good order and expressed a political bias. In our time, Bushel might have been accused of communist or leftist sympathies. Alderman Thomas Bloodworth, echoing Howel, said darkly, "Mr. Bushel, we know what you are." Starling addressed him with contempt as "Sirrah," and called him an "impudent fellow."

The jury were sent out again with instructions to find a more acceptable verdict. As the observer put it, "After some considerable time they returned to the Court" with the same verdict, "at which the Recorder, [the] Mayor, Robinson and Bloodworth took occasions to villify them with most opprobrious language."

Again the jury were sent out. Again they returned with the same verdict. Again Starling scolded them. "Will you be led by such a silly fellow as Bushel? An impudent canting fellow? I thought you had understood your place better."

Howel decreed, "You shall not be dismissed till we have a verdict, that the Court will accept; and you shall be locked up, without meat, drink, fire and tobacco; you shall not think thus to abuse the Court. We will have a verdict, by the help of God, or you shall starve for it."

Penn burst out, "My jury, who are my judges, ought not to be thus menaced; their verdict should be free and not compelled."

"Stop that prating fellow's mouth!" roared Howel.

After the jury's verdict had been returned several times, Sir Samuel spoke in exasperated instruction to the jury. "You have heard that he preached," said the lord mayor and judge, "that he gathered a company of tumultuous people, and that they did not only disobey the martial power, but civil also." His instructions were, in effect, that the jury must find Penn guilty.

Penn responded. "*We* did not make a tumult, but they that interrupted us. The jury cannot be so ignorant as to think that we met there with a design to disturb the civil peace, since first we were by force of arms kept out of our lawful house, and met as near it in the street as their soldiers would give us leave; and second, because it was no new thing but what was usual and customary with us. 'Tis very well known that we are a peaceable people and cannot offer violence to any man."

As the court prepared to send the prisoners back to jail and the jury back to their deliberations, Penn reminded them, "You are *Englishmen,*" he said. "Mind your privilege; give not away your right."

Bushel replied sturdily, "Nor will we ever do it."

One of the jurymen, saying he was ill, asked to be dismissed. Starling refused. "Starve with them," he sneered, "and hold your principles." The observer noted that the jury "had not so much as a chamber pot, though desired."

The jury returned early the next morning to report, "We give no other verdict than what we gave last night. We have no other verdict to give."

Sir Samuel was frustrated. Sir Thomas Bloodworth said in disgust, "I knew Mr. Bushel would not yield."

"Sir Thomas," protested Bushel, "I have done according to my conscience."

Sir Samuel grumbled, "That conscience of yours would cut my throat."

Bushel was firm. "No, my Lord, it never shall," he answered, to which the judge replied, "But I will cut yours as soon as I can."

There followed more discussion. If Mead was not guilty, then Penn could not be guilty of conspiracy, since, he argued, "I could not possibly conspire alone."

The judge insisted that "not guilty" was no verdict at all and threatened Bushel again. "I will cut his nose."

Penn was moved again to lofty appeal. "It is intolerable," he said, "that my jury should be thus menaced. Is this according to the fundamental laws? Are not *they* my proper judges by the Great Charter of England? What hope is there of ever having justice done, when juries are threatened and their verdicts rejected?"

Starling ordered, "Stop his mouth. Jailer, bring fetters and stake him to the ground."

Howel said, "Till now I have never understood the prudence of the Spanish in suffering the Inquisition among them. And certainly it will never be well with us till something like unto the Spanish Inquisition be in England."

The jury protested against being sent out again. They had agreed, the foreman said, "and if we give another [verdict], it will be a force upon us to save our lives," as they had been repeatedly threatened with violence. Bushel had been told he would be a marked man from that time forward. But again the jury was led away, held without food, water, fire, tobacco, or, presumably, chamber pot. This time the jury, its members being polled upon their return to the courtroom, brought in a verdict of "not guilty" of any charge.

"I am sorry, gentlemen," said Howel, "you have followed your own judgments and opinions, rather than the good and wholesome advice, which was given you." The court imposed fines on the jurymen and imprisoned them in Newgate Jail until the fines were paid. Penn and Mead were also to be imprisoned until they paid the fines imposed for not removing the hats Sir Samuel had ordered put upon their heads.

Eight of the jurors paid their fines. The stubborn Bushel and three other jurymen refused to pay theirs and appealed to a higher court on a writ of habeas corpus, challenging both their imprisonment and fines. A writ of habeas corpus is a common law principle whereby inquiry is conducted into the lawfulness of imprisonment. Two months later, a panel of judges to whom they appealed found, ten to one, that a jury could not be punished for its verdict. This was an important precedent.

In its commentary, the court that heard the Bushel appeal upheld Penn's reasoning. For a judge to threaten a jury rendered the right of trial by jury meaningless, the Lord Chief Justice John Vaughan reported, for "the jury find not the fact of every case by itself, leaving the law to the court, but find for the plaintiff or defendant upon the issue to be tried, wherein they resolve both law and fact complicatedly, and not the fact by itself; so although they answer not singly to the question what is the law, yet they determine the law in all matters, where the issue is joined."

Penn was both visionary and practical. Religious and civil liberty, the opportunity for full and free discussion of every issue of concern to citizens, he saw as great safeguards against both tyranny and violence. He had confidence in the good sense and moral stature of ordinary people.

Sir Samuel Starling did not share that confidence. He was an authoritarian and, like most authoritarians, doubted the good sense and moral stature of anyone who did not outrank him. He wrote a pamphlet, as was common in the seventeenth century, when robust debate took place by this means, "An Answer to the Seditious and Scandelous Pamphlet Entitled The Tryal of W. Penn and W. Mead." In it he abused Penn, all Quakers, and the jury, and defended his conduct of the trial.

"It's no wonder that [Penn], who could daringly blaspheme the Holy Trinity should not blush to villifie and to contemn the King's Court, and falsely scandelize and reproach the King's Justices, and revile all methods of law." The blasphemy to which Starling referred was Penn's pamphlet, "The Sandy Foundation Shaken," in which he questioned the concept of the Trinity, and for writing which he was imprisoned for a time. In his own pamphlet, Starling accused Penn of trying "in a popular way to subject the fundamental laws of the land, impudently asserting that the jury were the proper judges both of law and fact." For, he said, "if the law be as this youngster would have it, that the jury is both judge of law and fact, and that the King's justices cannot fine for contempt of court, nor correct the corruption or misdemeanor of jurymen, nor inform their ignorance, nor rectify their mistakes; the justices in [courts] have that name for nothing, and justices will be but cyphers, and sit there only to be derided and villified by every saucy and impertinent fellow."

Starling asserted that the "Light, which is (as they say) within them (by which they are acted and speak, as they pretend) is the spirit of the devil, the father of lies." Quakers, he said, had nothing better to do than "to asperse our religion, laws, and all men that are not of their cursed principles."

By contrast he lauded the "justice, candor and integrity of the Court towards the prisoners," compared to "the scornful, abusive and un-becoming behavior of the prisoners toward the Court." The only problem with the trial, said Starling, was Penn, who "made such an uncivil noise."

Penn had asserted, comments another of Penn's biographers, Mary Maples Dunn, "that the jury should be used to safeguard the liberties and property of the citizens," for they were citizens themselves. The jury's role had evolved through time. Once upon a time, disputes were settled by armed combat, or by torturous ordeals of drowning or walking over hot coals. The earliest English juries, devised to replace such dubious methods, were modeled on French practices. The Magna Carta upheld the legal right, established in the twelfth century by King Henry II, of trial by jury. At first juries combined several roles, being investigators, witnesses, and judges. Eventually these roles became

separated and the jury was a group of men, drawn from the neighborhood of the crime alleged, whose job was to render a verdict
(literally, a true saying), once they knew the facts. They were advised by
the judge what the law said, but they were also to keep in mind what
verdict would best serve the well-being of the community. The higher
court's decision in the Penn-Mead-Bushel case made it clear that the
jury's job was to be "the conscience of the community," which might
bear a different witness from the judge's conscience, owing, as it might
be, to political power.

The wisdom of Penn and Bushel case was affirmed not long afterwards across the Atlantic in the New World to which many English
men and women had taken their notions of common law. Penn was one
of these, having been granted a commonwealth by the king. The grant
served the dual purpose of paying a debt to Penn's father and getting
the trouble-making son to use his energies elsewhere than in England.
Penn wrote new and liberal constitutions for several colonies, advanced
the idea of separating government powers, articulated the rights of
citizens, bought rather than seized land from the native inhabitants of
his Holy Experiment, and designed a polity that got along without the
use of military force for three-quarters of a century. Violet Oakley, a
twentieth-century artist whose murals decorate the state capitol of
Pennsylvania in Harrisburg, characterized the Holy Experiment, which
she illustrated in her paintings, as "a Message of Love to the World from
PENNSYLVANIA."

Penn's commonwealth, like the common law he had cited in Samuel Starling's court, would establish a model. "For the nations," he said,
"want a precedent."

Sixty-five years after Samuel Starling had tangled with Penn in the
Old Bailey, the precedent in the matter of the jury's role figured in a
crucial case in American law. In the colony of New York, printer John
Peter Zenger was put on trial for libeling the royal governor. Old
Andrew Hamilton, a distinguished Philadelphia lawyer who had sometimes served Penn's family in Pennsylvania, traveled to New York to
defend Zenger and make American legal history.

The judge ordered the jury to find Zenger guilty—as, by the strict
application of the libel laws of the time, he was. But Hamilton urged the
jury to overlook the judge's instructions. "For I must insist that where
matter of law is complicated with the matter of fact, the jury have the
right to determine both." He told the jury about the Penn-Mead-Bushel
case, explaining "that jurymen are to see with their own eyes, to hear

with their own ears, and to make use of their consciences and under-
standings, in judging of the lives, liberties or estates of their fellow
subjects." According to Blackstone's *Commentaries,* a compilation of
legal decisions that served as Coke's had done earlier, the jury "pre-
serves in the hands of the people that share which they ought to have in
the administration of public justice, and it prevents the encroachments
of the more powerful and wealthy citizens."

Both Penn and Hamilton conceived of the jury as a body of active
and independent citizens who could aid in adapting law, by its nature
conservative and backward-looking, to present reality. Hamilton explained to the jury that when "a free people are made sensible of the
sufferings of their fellow subjects, by the abuse of power in the hands of
a governor, they have declared (and loudly too) that they were not
obliged by any law to support a governor who goes about to destroy a
province or colony or their privileges."

It is the right of a free people, explained Hamilton, "to complain
when they are hurt; they have the right publicly to remonstrate the
abuses of power, in the strongest terms, to put their neighbors upon
their guard, against the craft or open violence of men in authority." It
was, he argued, "a duty which all good men owe to their country, to
guard against the unhappy influence of ill men entrusted with power."

Hamilton spoke with great eloquence of such power, which "may
justly be compared to a great river, [which,] while kept within its due
bounds, is both beautiful and useful; but when it overflows its banks, it
is then too impetuous to be stemmed, it bears down all before it, and
brings destruction and desolation wherever it comes." Wise and free
people, Hamilton argued, are "the only bulwark against lawless power,
which in all ages has sacrificed to its wild lust and boundless ambition,
the blood of the best men that ever lived." Those in power, he concluded, "injure and oppress the people under their administration
[and] provoke them to cry out and complain; and then make that very
complaint the foundation for new oppressions and persecutions."

The jury, moved by Hamilton's appeal, ignored the judge's instructions and found Zenger not guilty. The liberty that Penn and Bushel had
insisted on, that the jury must find according to their consciences, a
right exercised by Zenger's jury, expanded the law to fit the need of the
community. Though the decision in the Zenger case predated the U.S.
Constitution, it has ever since had the standing of a constitutional legal
principle.

John Adams said in 1771 that it was the juror's "right, but [also] his duty to find the verdict according to his own best understanding, judgment and conscience, though in direct opposition to the direction of the court." American juries before the Civil War often refused to convict violators of the fugitive slave laws. Because the law was drawn and interpreted by those in power or those with vested interests, it had to be mediated by those affected.

At one time, the issue that ran afoul of the law was what religious practices were to be permitted; in another what could be said in print about governing authorities; in another whether human beings could be treated as property; in still another it was whether nuclear weapons and nuclear policies were outside the law's purview, or whether a more fundamental law than that considered by the courts applied to such weapons.

2

"Challenge it directly"

TO THE WORKERS, the morning of September 9, 1980, seemed like any other. They had to wake early to arrive between 6:45 and 7:00 A.M. at the anonymous-looking Building Number 9, General Electric's Re-Entry Division, a part of the large industrial park at the intersection of the Pennsylvania Turnpike, the Schuylkill Expressway, and state highway 202. There G.E. has its Space Division headquarters, a complex of buildings numbered 7, 8, 11, 12, 13, A, B, C, and also its Re-Entry Division buildings numbered 9 and 10.

To get to their numbered buildings, the workers left their homes in towns with names like Conshohocken, Plymouth Meeting, Phoenixville, Flourtown, Bridgeport, Swedeland and Norristown—names that suggest particular histories, as does King of Prussia, the town where the G.E. plant is located—to travel wide, smooth, fast roads that give no hint of the place or what its history might suggest.

King of Prussia is in Montgomery County, about twenty miles west of Philadelphia, where William Penn first saw his gift from the king in 1682. He sailed up the Delaware River in the autumn, when the heavily forested river banks were aflame with color. The English king had given to Penn what was not the king's, really, to give, and Penn moved energetically to establish a new kind of civil order, free of wars, governed by the will of its members in a spirit of love and nonviolence. Believing that the Delaware Indians were animated by the same divine spirit as he was, he insisted they must be dealt with as equal partners, that land must be bought from them rather than taken by force and

21

fraud. The settlers went unarmed and, for three-quarters of a century, were safer than settlers in other states who seized and defended land by violent means and provoked answering massacres. The settlement thrived, and before long a rough track ran west from Philadelphia, Penn's City of Brotherly Love. Settlement was slow and difficult in the heavily timbered hinterlands west of Philadelphia, though the soil was abundantly rich for farming. Eventually the narrow westward path became a rutted road leading toward and across the Allegheny Mountains to the distant confluence of three rivers in the wilderness three hundred miles to the west.

There, by the middle of the eighteenth century, the struggle between England and France to dominate the "new" world merged with the intention of non-Quaker settlers to dominate the native inhabitants. Imperial excursions resulted in a succession of forts and later the development of industries that eventually made the smoky city of Pittsburgh into the "arsenal of democracy." Still later, when empire and military technology took other forms, those industries declined and the steel mill towns clustered around Pittsburgh lay devastated beneath clear skies. Penn's vision had disappeared from political and economic life and was remembered merely as the name of breakfast cereal and automotive oil.

Twenty miles outside Philadelphia, on the rough road west, by a splendid oak tree that predated any western settlement, an inn was built in 1709 of tan and gray stone from local quarries. A painted sign that showed Frederick I, the king of Prussia, mounted on his horse, proclaimed the Prussian landlord's allegiance. The oak-beamed kitchen featured a fireplace big enough to roast a whole ox. Upstairs there were rooms where tired travelers could refresh themselves and spend the night. Twice a year the Mount Joy Society for the Recovery of Stolen Horses and Detection of Thieves met upstairs to ponder problems of law and order.

By 1980, the oak tree was long gone. The old King of Prussia Inn still stood. Someone had saved it from encroaching highway, frontage development, industrial park, and shopping malls. It welcomed no more tired and hungry travelers, however, standing isolated on a narrow island of unmown grass, protected from two roaring rivers of traffic by a chain link fence. There was no way to stop there, no place to tie up a horse, nowhere for an animal to graze. Down the road, surrounded by parking lots, a Howard Johnson's motel and a Holiday Inn provided hospitality for travelers. Along the highways were the

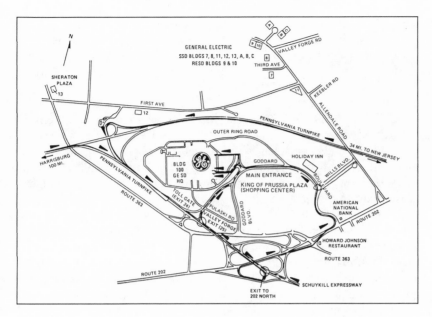

King of Prussia shopping center and General Electric buildings, including Building Number 9.

Valley Forge Inn, Ron's Eatery, King of Prussia Antiques, and a Mobil service station. When I inquired about the old inn across the highway, the Mobil station attendant ventured, "Somebody's supposed to slep' there." Perhaps it was the young surveyor, later, General George Washington, who wintered miserably with his troops at nearby Valley Forge. On the grassy island around the inn, a plaque identified a "Blue Star Highway, Tribute to the Armed Forces who Defended the United States of America." Traffic went too fast to read which wars were commemorated or even to look twice at the small stone building, which was nowhere identified.

The same road that took adventurers west to establish their forts at Pittsburgh, which eventually undermined the disarmed commonwealth named Penn's Woods, brought Molly Rush east from Pittsburgh to King of Prussia. There, on that ordinary morning of September 9, she astonished the employees in Building Number 9 with an act of disarmament. Though she didn't know Penn's story, her act was part of a tradition she helped to recover and revitalize.

The usual routine at Building Number 9 was for the fifty-four-year-old sergeant of security, Robert Cox, to open one door out of the four in the front lobby and one door out of four in the rear lobby. He had worked for General Electric for twenty-two years, thirteen years in his capacity as sergeant of security. When he opened the doors, he marked the end of his night shift. But he often stayed an hour overtime to see the morning workers in.

Cox's job was to watch the entrances, to oversee what he called the "ingress of personnel," to make sure employees wore proper identification badges, to check packages and parcels the workers brought in with them and carried back home. During his night shift, he walked around in the building to make sure everything was undisturbed. When he left in the morning, other security guards took over for the day.

Cox, a small, diffident man who wore his grizzled hair closely trimmed, had not finished high school. He answered to Captain Chester Drobek, but other employees, like Leon Simmons, answered to Cox. Simmons was a balding black man who began his career at G.E. as a janitor but rose to the rank of patrolman. Simmons spent his days guarding the doors, walking rounds, and taking the regular breaks G.E. provided for him and his fellow workers.

It wasn't exciting work; in fact, the security guards were in charge of making sure that it wouldn't be. The normal and desirable condition for the business conducted in Building Number 9 was predictability.

So Cox was disconcerted when, just after he had opened the back door, a tall man "dressed like a father" came in. The priest was accompanied by a short, thin, bookish-looking woman. "She told me she was a sister," said Cox, "but she had plain clothes on."

The two entered the building despite signs barring unauthorized personnel. The priest gave Cox "some literature, telling [him] he was peaceful." Cox remembered the title "Swords into Plowshares," but had no time or inclination to read what he was handed. "They were saying they were peaceful and nonviolent. I did hear that," he recalled. Although he heard the words, "I couldn't understand what [the father] was actually saying," he explained. This was a crisis for Cox, the sort of thing he was employed to prevent. To him as to other employees, what was happening was an enormous shock.

Cox informed the intruders that they were "unauthorized to enter," and he asked them to leave. When they did not, he turned to the phone that hung on the wall behind him, a direct line to Captain Chester Drobek's front-lobby office.

The woman, who was smaller and slighter even than Cox, put her hand on the phone to keep him from calling. It was Cox's impression that the priest grabbed his arms and pinned him against the wall. The priest, however, recalled that Cox held him in a sort of bear hug. "I asked them to leave me go," said Cox. "I tried to get away from them."

As this scramble about the phone was going on, six other people, none of whom was authorized to enter, filed through the back door and crossed the lobby quickly. Another employee heard Cox cry out, "You can't go in there! Stop! Stop!" Cox remembered speaking more formally, telling them that they were "unauthorized and not to enter the building. But they just kept on walking."

The group went through the double doors on the far side of the lobby and disappeared into the building. The woman who had briefly kept Cox from using the phone followed the others. "As soon as she left, the priest left go of me and he went in."

Cox was free to call his boss, Captain Drobek, to whom he reported the unlawful entry. Cox followed the eight interlopers through the lobby's double doors, where he found the priest kneeling in prayer, a hammer on the floor beside him. Cox picked up the hammer and later put it in his desk drawer. The priest remained where he was, continuing to pray.

Then the sound of "banging of metal" went through him like electricity. It was, he said later, "very unusual." Word began to spread through the plant that something out of the ordinary was going on.

About the time Cox unlocked the rear door, Robert Hartmann, a large florid man of forty-eight, had drawn into the parking lot behind Building Number 9 in his truck. He had noticed a car with a priest and some other people in it. "I remember thinking, that's rather odd at this time of morning." Hartmann, manager of shop operations, went around to the front door, wondering about the car with the priest in it. He decided, "Well, they're probably demonstrators, and they'll probably be around. I'd better warn Captain Drobek." Demonstrators around the General Electric building were nothing new to Hartmann.

When Hartmann entered the lobby, he heard Captain Drobek say into the phone, "They what? They're where?"

Drobek, a small man of sixty-two, wasted no time. "Someone just forced their way in the back of the building," he reported crisply to Hartmann. "I need your help." Drobek had been in charge of the security patrol for a quarter of a century. He acted with dispatch to find out what was going on.

As the two men went through the front lobby's double doors into the building's interior, they "heard this clanging, like metal against metal." It sounded to Drobek "like fifty-gallon drums being beat on." Hartmann's first impression was of "a very large, loud hammering, as if someone was hitting a bell."

Other employees had entered from both front and back. One tool maker, who said he was anxious to check a drill assembly he'd been working on when he left the evening before "to see how it was," saw strangers come through the rear lobby, "burst through the door and race up the side aisle." He too heard the sound of hammering "on barrels or trash cans or something like that." Another tool maker heard the noise and followed it "right into the tool inspection area." There he saw "six or seven people using hammers to destroy the material that was in the room, a group of people banging on hardware, government hardware."

The two objects he called government hardware he also called "a midshell assembly and a bonded shield and shell assembly." They were about four feet tall, open at both ends and hollow inside. They had been removed from their boxes, or, as Hartmann called them, their "protective handling devices," and set on end on a workbench. The first was an aluminum cone, honey-gold and finely tooled in tiny spiraling grooves. When hit, it sounded like fifty-gallon drums or trash cans. The second was another aluminum cone that had been coated with a coal black carbon material with a velvet sheen. When hit, it sounded like a bell.

The tool maker didn't stay to watch. He left to get help and met Hartmann and Drobek rushing toward room 1650, the Tool Inspection Area, also called the Non-Destructive Test Area. The room was as brightly lit as a stage when Hartmann, Drobek, and the tool maker rushed in. What they saw astonished them. Seven perfect strangers were hammering on the warheads they manufactured day in and day out.

As he entered the room, Hartmann recalled, "in front of me there was a woman, slightly off to my left, and three men directly in front of me. The woman was pounding, using a hammer with both hands, what we commonly call a masonry hammer. The men were smashing hardware with hammers." They were, observed Hartmann, "really laying into it."

Captain Drobek too was impressed by the "young lady who had a hammer. With both hands, she was really beating on this metal structure." To his wondering eyes, "It looked like a bunch of crazy people, beating on metal in this room." He immediately lay hold of the person nearest him. He grabbed the man's "left hand, which was holding a hammer," and then his right hand, which he put behind the man's back. He knew his duty and he did it decisively, though it was, he said later, "quite taxing" and left him breathing hard, his chest hurting "like running five mile." Drobek had only recently recovered from quadruple bypass heart surgery.

Hartmann, used to giving orders, shouted, "Now you've gone too far! Stop! Everything's over!"

When the men from General Electric later described what had happened, it seemed something like a dream in slow motion, though in fact the whole incident happened very fast. As Hartmann remembered, he crossed the room rapidly until he neared one of the strangers, a tall bearded man wearing a beaded necklace. He turned, Hartmann thought, "with his hammer up. And I was coming at him. I was about two, maybe three feet away. And I told him, 'You swing at me and I'll break your neck!' I thought he was going to swing at me, I really did."

The woman who had attracted Hartmann's and Drobek's attention by hammering so vigorously remembered standing between Hartman and the tall intruder. She recalled Hartmann saying, "Isn't there a better way to do this?" She answered, "Well, can you tell me a better one?"

"Were you afraid?" I asked Hartmann months later. Earlier he had told a policeman who asked the same question, "I thought he was going to hit me, yes." But his answer to my question was, "A man of my courage is never afraid." His job was to keep things running smoothly in this room, and even after the fact he seemed to feel keenly the affront to his authority.

Drobek murmured, "Better call the police." He noticed as he said it that the strangers had laid their hammers down and were doing something still more mystifying. They had plastic baby bottles and were pouring what Drobek called "this red liquid" all over the desks and workbenches. "And the paperwork was laying there," said Drobek, plainly distressed. He didn't recognize the liquid as blood, though it was indeed human blood that was being dribbled and splashed on the dented cones and the plans and blueprints that lay where they had been left the night before.

The tool maker who had worried about his drill assembly was dazed. "I couldn't understand why anybody was in the building, because it was a closed area," he said, struggling to express his disbelief.

The intruders moved to the side of the room, joined hands and began to sing, pray, and chant. Hartmann thought he had "herded" them together and "kept them in this area" at the side of the room. And then "we gathered them up," he reported, "and led them back the way they had come. They went toward the lobby where Sergeant Cox had stayed with the prayerful, kneeling priest.

On the way out there was a scuffle. The procession of General Electric people and the intruders passed some four-foot steel drums lined up on the right side of the hallway, invoices on top of them (Hartmann called them "documents"). The tall bearded man, who Hartmann thought had menaced him with a hammer, reached for one of the invoices and tore it in half. Drobek said the tall man had "lunged" for it and that he too had "lunged" to take it from the man's hand.

"That's private property," said Drobek.

The tall man answered, "That's people's property."

Drobek was perfectly clear. "That's private property. You have no business with that."

Hartmann, with two years of college education, claimed that he was "cleared to handle top-secret information, to handle, read, understand and work with that information." He said there were no secrets printed on the torn scraps of paper, though the invoice had been clearly stamped SECRET, according to the tall stranger.

Cox reported that he "had secured the post at 7:30, 7:35," when six of the unwelcome visitors were back in the rear lobby. Two priests, the one in clerical garb who had knelt to pray just beyond the lobby, the other in civil dress, had just been escorted onto the outside stair landing, a locked door between them and the lobby. There, rather than escaping, they had waited, "repeating different Bible verses," according to one of the security guards, while the other six remained in the lobby.

Drobek called the police after he had escorted the "culprits" to the rear lobby. He told the police, "We had a near riot."

The Upper Merion Township police told of receiving a phone call from their police dispatcher. "We responded to the report that there was a riot in progress, that people were inside the building with hammers and clubs. All available personnel were sent to G.E. Number 9 facility."

As they drove up, one officer said, "I noted some people that didn't appear to fit. One in particular was handing out a gold-type leaflet." There were, outside, members of the nearby Brandywine Peace Community, who had known ahead of time what was going to happen at Building Number 9 and had arrived shortly after the unauthorized eight went in. To avoid hitting the leaflet distributors, "we had to slow down," said the officer. "We were directed by a person in a security uniform to the rear of the building. We didn't stop to talk to the people or secure one of the leaflets," but drove around to the back entrance.

"Upon pulling up and exiting the patrol wagon," said the officer, "I noticed two gentlemen standing on the upper deck on the top of the staircase." These were the two priests, six-foot Father Carl Kabat, a Scandinavian blond with milky blue eyes, wearing his clerical collar, and Father Daniel Berrigan, a slight, silver-haired man in street clothes. As one of the policemen noted, they were "singing some type of song. My impression was that Daniel Berrigan and Carl Kabat were leading the others in song" through the glass of the rear door.

Captain Drobek had reported that "there had been a problem," said one officer, "that he wanted the two people that were standing out-side—he pointed to them on the deck and there were several more inside the lobby—he wanted them arrested as they were trespassing and committed damage inside the property, and they had roughed up or pushed around one of his men. I am not sure that's the exact statement, but one of his men had been shoved around," he said.

Drobeck was prepared for danger. "I went up the steps and spoke to the two individuals that had been pointed out to me," he noted. "Both gentlemen had their hands at their sides. I believe it was Father Kabat who said, 'Look, I want you to understand now and for the rest of the day, we are nonviolent. We will not resist you in any way. Do you understand that?'

"I said, 'All right. I understand what you're saying,'" he continued. "I looked beyond him and contained in the lobby were six other people, two females, four males. I placed them under arrest, one by one," and "while walking them down the stairway, I advised them of their Miranda rights."

One of the policemen remembered, "As we were taking the people from the police van into the police station, there was a young man walking nearby. And Mr. Kabat stated to him, 'We got them good. We got some of the nosecones!'"

The FBI arrived shortly after the eight had been delivered to the police station. They were among the "other authorities [who] were called in on the case," according to one policeman.

The federal government, on whose contracts General Electric worked in Building Number 9, decided not to press charges against the eight prisoners. It was left to the Commonwealth of Pennsylvania to prosecute those who had committed malefactions against its twentieth-century sense of order, property, and tranquility.

At the time of their arrest, the two charges against the eight were criminal trespass, which had to do with entering the premises of G.E.'s Building Number 9, and criminal mischief, which had to do with damaging the two warheads, a drill fixture, and papers. More charges were added to the indictment during the day.

When the eight trespassers had been hauled off, Robert Cox got his first look at the Non-Destructive Test Area, which had been "in normal condition" when he had made his rounds earlier in the morning. He saw "blood all over the floor and paperwork, and one piece of hardware [with] holes punched into it." This was the gold-colored aluminum "shield." "They had the area roped off," said Cox.

When the details of the harrowing morning had grown somewhat dim and inconsistent, Drobek, then retired, still remembered his impressions vividly, though he had reflected on them as well. "I thought it was kind of silly of them to come in like that," he said. "G.E. had the contract, but it was government property. They had no right to rush in and destroy what wasn't theirs." John Schuchardt's claim that they had destroyed "people's property" rankled. "It reminded me of the Russian state," he said. "I'm a retired navy man. God and country, that's my attitude." He remained puzzled. "Their credence is against violence. But they had caused violence in themselves."

Molly Rush was the woman who had attracted the attention of both Hartmann and Drobek by hammering so vigorously. A short, compact woman of forty-four with a mass of thick, dark curls, she told me how, after several hours in jail, she and her seven companions were taken back to the G.E. plant. "They led us from the police station out to the paddy wagon without saying where we were going. They drove us along and somebody said, 'Come on, you're going inside,' and we said, 'We certainly are not.'"

The police had taken the eight prisoners back to Building Number 9 to ask employees to identify them. It was an unusual procedure. Identification sometimes occurs, if it is feasible, right at the scene of a crime immediately after it happens, while a victim's memory is still fresh. But, said Norristown attorney Michael Shields, this identification was in the nature of "an illegal line-up. A line-up is not supposed to focus on particular people as guilty."

Some of the eight, refusing altogether to cooperate with the police, went limp and were carried up the back steps to the lobby of the plant into which they'd walked earlier in the day. But "I walked up the steps," said Molly, "and they put me in a wheelchair and took me right back to the scene." She didn't know where the wheelchair had come from, but in it, one after another she and several of her colleagues got a ride back to the scene of the early morning's events. "There was a little security guard that I didn't even remember seeing, and [the police] said, 'Was she one of the ones?' and he said 'yes,' and then they wheeled me out again," said Molly. But before she was trundled out, Molly was impressed—as perhaps the employees were—by the "incredible scene," the dented gold and the scratched black cones, the dribbled blood, all vivid under the bright industrial lighting in the large, impersonal room. "I got this picture of the whole scene," she said. It was roped off, like a reconstructed room in a historic house. "It hadn't been touched. Employees were clustered around in the doorways and hallways, absolutely awe-struck looks on their faces, absolutely astonished. I don't know what word to use—white faces, and," she groped for the right word, "shock, profound shock."

Philadelphia lawyer Charles Glackin, with a rich silvery mane of wavy hair and impeccable tailoring, showed up at Building Number 9 as this unusual identification procedure was taking place. He protested so vigorously that before the rest of the prisoners could be escorted into the building for identification, they were taken back to the police station.

For a good part of the day, the eight were held together in one cell. The two notables among the prisoners were Father Daniel Berrigan, poet-priest, and his brother, former priest Philip Berrigan. During the Vietnam War, the Berrigan brothers had poured burning homemade napalm over draft files, making the point that burning paper was considered a crime but that burning people was not. By their acts of civil disobedience, they had developed considerable reputations and followings, raising issues not presented for consideration by politicians or the news media. Philip had married, fathered a family, and established Jonah House, a community of activists in Baltimore. Carl Kabat, another priest and former missionary in Latin America, had committed a number of acts of antinuclear civil disobedience and spent many months in jail. Anne Montgomery, a nun and daughter of a navy man, worked with street kids in New York City. Dean Hammer, the youngest of the eight, had recently been a student at the Yale Divinity School. Elmer Maas, a musician who had been active in the civil rights movement in the South, had taught in a small religious college before involving himself deeply in antinuclear activism. John Schuchardt, trained as a criminal lawyer, had turned on the law and, searching for another way of defining truth, had joined Philip Berrigan's Jonah House. Molly Rush, a small, earthy woman with a ready smile and a low voice, was a Pittsburgh activist and the mother of six children.

One by one, as the long day slowly passed, the eight were taken out to be fingerprinted and photographed. The police took the shoes of all and the trousers of some of the eight to match with the blood spilled on the warheads and papers, as if they were murdered corpses. Thus, some were wearing borrowed pants when they were all led into the courtroom for the arraignment "with just our socks on," said Molly, amused by the recollected scene.

It was, by that time, about 5:30 P.M. The charges had multiplied from two to thirteen, described in the baroque legal language that hadn't changed much since the time William Penn was charged with riot and rout. They were:

- burglary ("did willfully, maliciously, feloniously and burglariously enter without license or privilege a certain building with the intent to commit a crime")
- criminal trespass ("did gain access by subterfuge or surreptitiously remain in the building")
- criminal conspiracy ("did with the intent of facilitating or promoting the commission of the crimes agree")
- disorderly conduct ("did with the intent to cause public inconvenience, annoyance or alarm, create a risk, a hazardous and physically offensive condition which served no legitimate purpose")
- criminal mischief ("did damage tangible property")
- simple assault ("did attempt by physical force to put one Robert Cox and one Robert Hartmann in fear of imminent serious bodily injury")
- aggravated assault ("did attempt to cause bodily injury to one Robert Hartmann with a deadly weapon, to wit, a hammer")
- terroristic threats ("did threaten to commit the crime of aggravated assault with the intent to terrorize in reckless disregard of the risk of causing such terror or inconvenience")
- recklessly endangering another person ("did knowingly and recklessly place another person in damage of death or serious bodily injury")
- harassment ("committed acts which alarmed and seriously annoyed and which served no legiitimate purpose")
- false imprisonment ("did knowingly restrain one Robert Cox so as to interfere substantially with his liberty")

- criminal coercion ("did with felonious intent unlawfully restrict the freedom of action of one Robert Cox")
- unlawful restraint ("did knowingly restrain one Robert Cox unlawfully")

The group charged with such serious misdeeds had formed the way any enterprise takes shape, by people whose work in various parts of the movement for peace and justice had brought them together, whose individual needs had met, reflected, and encouraged the needs of others. The eight had spent considerable time together, thinking through the action they intended, its purpose and its consequences. They were not surprised when the state assembled an impressive list of charges. John Schuchardt said that this was a common practice in Pennsylvania, meant so to intimidate an accused person as to increase the likelihood of plea bargaining. The magistrate, who arraigned the eight, refused bail for Philip and Father Daniel Berrigan. In addition to having burned draft records during the Vietnam War, Daniel had once gone into hiding while out of prison on bail, and Philip had been accused of plots to kidnap Henry Kissinger, one of the early architects of nuclear weapons policy as well as of policy in the war in Vietnam. For the six others, bail was set at $125,000 apiece. All eight were sent to jail. Sister Anne Montgomery and Molly Rush were handcuffed together and taken to the Berks County jail.

A week later, at a preliminary hearing, Judge Donald Riehl dismissed some of the charges—aggravated assault, terroristic threats, false imprisonment, and unlawful restraint. But on the nine other charges, the eight were bound over to Common Pleas Court to be tried almost six months later.

3

"Preaching seditiously and causing a great tumult"

"WHY ME?" Molly wrote to her husband and her six children on the lined stationery of the Berks County jail. It was the question each member of her family asked over and over, "Why *her?*" Molly had not begun as an activist, but she had grown and evolved to the point that she could answer, "Because I know. Because I love you." Loving one's family members was not so unusual. *Knowing,* in 1980, was something else again.

The employees at G.E.'s warhead factory appeared not to know what it was they were engaged in manufacturing.

Patrolman Leon Simmons, the security guard who had started out as a janitor, said his job was "to protect General Electric property. I didn't ask them what the property was. My job is checking people coming in."

One of the tool makers said, "All I know is we make hardware. My responsibilities are to design and fabricate special tooling that fabricates that particular product."

The financial analyst, using purchase orders and vouchers, computed the dollar value of the damage that the eight had done. He said, "I call it a product, the hardware that we ship. That is all I know it as."

Another tool maker insisted, "I work on tooling only. I am a tool maker. I don't work on hardware at all." He said he had no idea whether the hardware was designed to be outfitted with a thermonuclear bomb. "If it does or not, I don't know. It don't carry it in G.E."

Still another tool maker said, "I don't know what you mean by nuclear warhead. I have never seen a nuclear warhead."

Hartmann acknowledged, "I know what a re-entry vehicle is," and he named it with some pride, the Mark 12A, but he said he didn't know how it might be used. "I have no idea whether it is first-strike capability or not. I have no idea what the so-called payload could be or would be."

These men were all testifying in court when they treated the nature of their work, the uses of the product they made, so gingerly. Molly thought it quite likely that, as they did their daily work, they either didn't know what they were making or didn't want to know. Nothing about the building in which they worked, nor the room in which the warhead parts were made, revealed what was made there. It could have housed any manufacture—aspirin, roller skates, buttons. Inside and out, Building Number 9 was architectural Muzak.

When Molly said, "Because I *know*," she didn't mean that she was privy to special information. She meant that information which to many people seemed remote or abstract she understood as a vivid reality too compelling and menacing to be dismissed. "Gut level," she said, laying her hand on her belly as she explained the level of her knowledge.

The employees, Molly said, "come to work every day and disconnect themselves from what they do so they won't know what they're doing." She and her seven companions had meant to disrupt the daily calm, the workaday neutrality of the people who left their homes and families every day to earn their living at General Electric. Their daily bread, Molly thought—unlocking doors, checking workers' badges and bundles, patrolling to insure the customary calm, taking the permitted breaks, making tools to make hardware or equipment or products, packing them, shipping them, tagging them, totting up the dollars and cents—required some level of self-deception. She didn't mind angering the employees; anger might jolt them out of their sense that it was normal to make nuclear weapons. "We wanted to get to the reality, to the truth that these things are for human destruction."

In this nondescript building, at the busy crossroads near the old inn of lapsed hospitality and forgotten history, Molly said, "They're building genocide." The two funnels, like four-foot ice cream cones up-ended, were the outer casings of a pair of Mark 12A thermonuclear warheads. Each began as a finely tooled aluminum shell, which was then coated with the black carbon material so that, when fired beyond the earth's atmosphere by an intercontinental ballistic missile, a Min-

Three Mark 12-A warheads affixed to the "bus" that fires them at various targets, beside a "shroud," or missile nosecone. Drawn by Marie Norman from a photograph by the Department of Defense.

uteman III, or an MX missile, the warhead would not burn up in the friction of re-entry into the earth's atmosphere. The aluminum cone was a "shell" and the coated cone a "shield and shell."

At a later stage of manufacture, each warhead would be fitted with a miniature electronic guidance system that would direct it with great accuracy to its own target. Each warhead would have, as far as could be determined, a fifty-fifty chance of hitting within six hundred feet of that target. Three or more warheads, each with its own guidance system, would be fitted into the "shroud"—manufactured, according to a General Electric floor plan, in a room not far from the Non-Destructive Test Area.

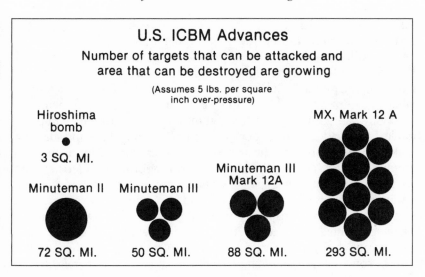

U.S. ICBM Advances
Number of targets that can be attacked and area that can be destroyed are growing

(Assumes 5 lbs. per square inch over-pressure)

Hiroshima bomb

3 SQ. MI.

Minuteman II

72 SQ. MI.

Minuteman III

50 SQ. MI.

Minuteman III Mark 12A

88 SQ. MI.

MX, Mark 12 A

293 SQ. MI.

Comparison of destructive capability of nuclear warheads since Hiroshima.

The last stage of the warhead's manufacture would take place in Amarillo, Texas, a town famous for its slaughterhouses. There, at the Pantex plant, a thermonuclear bomb of at least three hundred fifty kilotons would be fitted into each shield and shell. A kiloton is the explosive equivalent of a thousand tons of dynamite. The atomic bomb dropped on Hiroshima in 1945 was twelve and a half kilotons.

It was the precision, coupled with the explosive power of these warheads, that worried and outraged Molly Rush and her seven colleagues, who therefore brought their hammers and their blood into General Electric's Building Number 9 on that autumn day. The warheads would be, when they were entirely assembled, first-strike weapons. They were constructed to be both accurate and powerful in order to be able to "kill" enemy missile silos before the weapons those silos held could be launched. But though the targets the warheads were intended to destroy were other weapons, millions of people—or "soft targets," as they were called in military jargon—would be killed, too, not to mention the "collateral damage," meaning destruction of communities, homes, churches, schools, museums, grocery stores, crop lands, roads, bridges, water supplies, historic monuments, and other records of the generations.

Molly had thought that the part of such weapons that would do the killing, the part designed to be shot out into space, to re-enter the earth's atmosphere, to find the targets programmed into their circuits, and to explode with such force, would be huge and invulnerable. But both she and Sister Anne Montgomery, the slender nun who had kept Cox from the phone for a few seconds, were surprised by the fragility of what the employees called "hardware," "material," or "equipment."

Molly had been sure that "these things would be absolutely impregnable." She had imagined herself "hammering on this thing and not making a dent." But as she hammered, flakes of aluminum flew up around her face, and she later discovered tiny bruises under her chin where they had hit. That a small woman, only five feet two inches tall, hammering with an ordinary household hammer, could render these two warheads forever useless "exploded so many myths in my mind!" Molly exclaimed. She hoped that the vulnerability of the warhead casings and her own unarmed capacity to destroy them had undermined some of the same myths in the minds of General Electric employees and the public.

Molly had thought about the employees at General Electric long and hard before she walked into their building. "Every day, many people go to work, building these weapons that are going to kill their children and my kids," she said, wonder in her voice.

The employees could avoid knowing what they manufactured "because of secrecy, because of psychic numbing." And because, she meditated, the weapons they helped to make "are idols in the Old Testament sense—not golden calves, but golden nose cones." Aloud she wondered, "I don't understand how people can put their faith and trust in nuclear weapons and not trust the God who made this planet." Her usually low voice rose, as I was to learn it often did when she felt intensely.

The phenomenon of psychic numbing is a way of reacting to a fearful or terrible situation or event with absence of feeling, which makes what is intolerable tolerable. Surgeons or police officers, for example, develop enough numbing to be able to function when their feelings of empathy might disable them. Psychiatrist Robert Jay Lifton has used the term psychic numbing to describe the way Nazi functionaries were able to carry out their deadly tasks, and he has applied the concept to the ability of people living under the nuclear threat to disregard it. Jonathan Schell, in *Fate of the Earth,* speaks of psychic numbing as a perverse sign of mental health. "When one tries to face the nuclear predicament, one feels sick, whereas when one pushes it out of mind, as apparently one must do most of the time in order to carry on with life, one feels well again. But this feeling of well-being is based on a denial of the most important reality of our time, and therefore is itself a kind of sickness."

Molly knew that there was no guarantee that smashing a couple of re-entry vehicles, taken from their boxes and set upon a workbench, would have any practical effect. But she had been faithful to her deepest beliefs. Acting together with others who had reached the same conclusions and whose connections with one another had developed out of growing personal need and acquaintance, she had been freed from the myth of her own powerlessness. "If I didn't end the arms race, I acted on behalf of life—and," she mused, "*connected* with a lot of people. We broke through the numbing."

Molly's intention that cool September morning was very simple. It was something like William Penn's intention when he preached seditiously in the street, causing a "great tumult." He thought the way to change a situation he regarded as intolerable was to act as he thought he was entitled to—to worship according to his lights—without waiting for permission from government authorities. Molly intended to do what she thought ought to be done, to disable as many warheads as she could. In her view, merely by existing these warheads violated Pennsylvania law, international law, and God's law. She intended that the two warheads she helped to damage—she could not reasonably expect to dismantle the whole arsenal of around thirty thousand—would never be used. She did not make her plans by calculating backwards from probable consequences. She did what she thought ought to be done, willing to accept the consequences.

As she understood it, the nuclear arms race was her business. She helped pay for it, and she stood to lose everything she cared about as a result of it. She knew she was expected to leave it to arms control and Pentagon theorists to manage the risks of the weapons that were daily manufactured at plants like G.E.'s Building Number 9. She was unwilling to do that, believing that among other things, the arms control and military planners were too attached to the weapons to consider them dispassionately. Therefore, she took it upon herself to begin to end what she saw as an overwhelming threat to herself, her family, and her community. At the very least, she thought, the courts would have to consider the claim she and her colleagues made.

Molly went to King of Prussia from her hometown of Pittsburgh to commit the act in Building Number 9 that left her, wearing the state's shoes, in jail. In all she spent seventy-eight days in four jails—four weeks in the Berks County jail, two weeks in the Lebanon County jail, five days in the Mercer County jail, three and a half weeks in the York County jail. On November 25, in time to be at home for Thanksgiving, she was released on bail provided by two communities of Catholic sisters in Pittsburgh, Sisters of Mercy and Sisters of Saint Joseph.

She knew very well the consternation she left in her wake. Her husband, Bill, her children, who ranged in age from twenty-five to twelve, her seven brothers and sisters and their families, and many friends and associates were, as Molly knew they would be, shocked and horrified. They did not know of her plans. She had told members of her family only that she was going to do something that might result in a long jail term, but she had shared no details, partly to prevent their interference, partly to prevent any liability on their part to conspiracy charges. Therefore, she had to explain from jail.

"Dear Bill, Gary, Linda and Bob [Linda's husband], Janine, Dan, Bob and Greg," she wrote on her first full day of imprisonment. "Missing you all." She spoke of the mundane details of her new situation. "Meals are pretty good. Sleeping in a dorm (curtains on the windows) with two bunk beds and one single. Downstairs is the recreation room and from there is the yard with grass and the volleyball court. Anne and I did some yoga after dinner—she's teaching me. I'm reading Tolstoy stories right now. He was a famous Russian novelist. He wrote *War and Peace*. Will be glad to get some books of my own. They have to be mailed in new. It may be O.K. to bring in my Bible. Otherwise, I can have a pair of jeans, two or three T-shirts, underpants, sox, shoes, nightgown and robe. The place is surrounded by trees, which I can see from the windows. Not bad." She wrote as if she were visiting her Aunt Ruth in Ocean City, New Jersey, or were perhaps in the hospital having a baby. Knowing that her family and friends would think of jail as terrifying and brutal, she was at pains to reassure.

"Please let everyone know," she wrote, "I'm feeling very good about the way things have gone. I feel very strongly that the Holy Spirit has been with us continually as we went about exposing the vulnerability of the powers that seem so strong."

She addressed the younger children. "Dan, Bob and Greg—I need you to be brave and strong and wise beyond your years. Please be good and help Daddy." And to Gary, Linda, and Janine, the older ones, she wrote, "I'm counting on you—and on Dan—to be of help and to stay your own good selves." To her husband, Bill, who had done and said everything he could think of to keep her from going to King of Prussia, she wrote, "I appreciate your love and support. I know I can count on you and I know how rare it is to have that.

"This is a separation that may not be easy," she wrote, having no idea how long it would be, for in jail all decisions are made by someone else and are rarely explained; an inmate is intended to learn or relearn powerlessness. Knowing how exposed and conspicuous her children must feel, with their mother in the news as a criminal, she wrote, "Maybe you're wishing right now that you had a normal mother instead of me. That's O.K. I understand. But don't think I'm a criminal because we tried to call others accountable. After seeing what I saw first hand, the precision and deep care that goes into producing something capable of 35 Hiroshimas in one small two- or three-foot cone—and that's all that those hundreds of workers in that one place do, forty hours a week—you know that it *has* to be stopped *soon* before it's too late."

She knew her family and community well and could predict what the common view would be: wives and mothers belong at home; families belong together. But she reminded them, "War breaks up families while husbands, fathers, brothers and sons go to fight and maybe be killed. People call it sacrificing for their country. And *no one* thinks it's strange or abnormal, even knowing that a war today can kill everyone."

As she had urged, her family shared her letter with the Thomas Merton Center, a store-front "Ministry for Peace and Justice" that Molly had helped to found and for which she worked as director for seven years. When the news media first called the Merton Center on September 9, other staff members did not know how to react. Should they deny knowledge and support? What should they say? When the board of directors gathered that night, they were confronted with an unprecedented policy decision. Some objected to Molly's action at the G.E. plant on grounds that it could not possibly be effective, that it would take Molly away from her peace and justice work for an indeterminate time. Father Jack O'Malley, who had worked with Molly for years, said that he thought Molly had "upped the ante" for all peace activists, forcing them to think more clearly and carefully about their advocacy. After a long and intense discussion, the board decided to hold a press conference the next day to announce support for Molly and what she had done. I was a board member at that time. My first reaction to news of Molly's action was negative. I was profoundly challenged by that board meeting. I was chosen to speak for the Merton Center in support of Molly and what she had done at the press conference, though I was far from having a clear comprehension of the efficacy of direct action. It was in order to find out why she had acted as she did that I undertook to tell her story.

Molly's great hero was the Trappist monk, Thomas Merton, whose vehement writings on nuclear weapons, civil rights, the Vietnam War, and nonviolence had quickened her sense of religious relevance. Merton wrote, "Auschwitz worked because these people [those who cooperated] wanted it to work. Instead of resisting it, rebelling against it, they put the best of their energies into making genocide a success." Though he had written, "Peace demands the most heroic labor and the most difficult sacrifice. It demands greater heroism than war," he said a year later, "I believe we live in a time in which one cannot help making decisions for or against man, for or against life, for or against justice, for or against truth. And according to my way of thinking, all these decisions rolled into one (for they are inseparable) amount to a decision for or against God. Such an attitude implies no heroism, no extraordinary insight, no special moral qualities, and no unusual intelligence." Merton had written that "the most urgent necessity of our time is not merely to prevent the destruction of the human race by nuclear war. Even if it should happen to be no longer possible to prevent the disaster (which God forbid), there is still a greater evil that can and must be prevented. It must be possible for every free man to refuse his consent and deny his cooperation to this greatest of crimes."

Though Molly was a woman and Merton wrote of "men," Molly took Merton's words much to heart. She came to believe that *not* to take action to disarm the warheads she thought threatened the human project was to consent and cooperate with a criminal undertaking.

She tried to explain to people who had not explored Merton. Without special heroism, insight, morality, or intelligence, she had acted as a mother. She missed her home, but wrote to her family, "It may be a good thing for you to have to fend for yourselves for a time. People who have everything done for them end up feeling helpless. People who learn to take care of themselves have a strength they'll never lose. I'm proud to see how Bobby and Greg have begun to pitch in more and more, doing things without being asked to do them." She offered practical advice. "Dishes and laundry done two or three times a day don't pile up and seem impossible. Gary and Dan: please do your part to set the example and encourage the boys without bossing or hassling them."

More than her housewifery, she wanted to share some part of her sense of achievement. She and her companions had, after all, dismantled the only two nuclear weapons in thirty-five years, despite, as she commented later, "the thousands of *man* hours spent talking about it." She stressed the male gender with raised eyebrows. She knew very well that even her supporters would be dazed, wondering what good it would do to make a grand gesture and end up in jail. While faithfulness to her family and her religious belief rather than consequences had been on her mind, she was delighted with the consequences and wanted her delight understood. "I wish you could have seen the faces of the workers—at the time and later, when they brought us back to the scene," wrote Molly. "The impact was astonishing."

From jail, Molly kept up a lively correspondence. "The mail is pouring in," she wrote, and she was "very hungry for news." But "the best thing people can do for me is to step up the resistance to these crackpots who bring us Titan II, Directive #59, and now a radiation leak from [the] Nevada bomb test site."

The Titan II Molly referred to involved a minor mishap that caused a fuel tank to explode in Damascus, Arkansas, throwing a nine-megaton Titan II missile out of its silo and into the nearby woods. A megaton equals a million tons of TNT in explosive power. The missile wasn't armed and couldn't "go off," but had the warhead broken apart as it banged around in the silo and against the silo's lid, deadly plutonium might have been widely scattered by the force of the explosion. The tiniest particle of plutonium, inhaled or ingested, can cause cancer. Presidential Directive #59 was President Jimmy Carter's declaration of strategic policy, the aiming of U.S. missiles at Soviet missiles. This targeting of weapons rather than populations is a first-strike strategy. Since there is little point in targeting empty silos, silos still containing their missiles must be attacked before an enemy can fire them. The leak Molly referred to at the Nevada nuclear bomb test site was not the first, though such leaks were not often reported.

Molly's imprisonment took place in one dreary county jail after another, each, she wrote, "stunningly like the military." What she had done seemed to some to be dwarfed by the consequences to her. Some of her friends wondered aloud, what good can she do in prison?

Her response was that she wasn't trying to do any good in prison. Nor had she acted for publicity. She had pursued neither celebrity nor martyrdom. She didn't want to go to jail. Her object had been to refuse complicity, to act on her conviction. As a wife and mother, a citizen, and a Christian, she felt called upon to do what was consistent with the survival of the people, the places, the ideas to which she was committed. If she seemed buried in the avalanche of consequences, that was something she couldn't control.

To one reporter she said, "This [action] came to me as a gift, something I couldn't refuse, knowing what I know, loving my kids, hoping for grandchildren. I'm patient. I've been working for a number of years. I haven't lost my patience. It's just that the situation demands more of all of us."

What seemed vandalism to General Electric employees and to the Commonwealth of Pennsylvania, and heroism to some of her supporters, was not so much civil *dis*obedience, she explained, as it was obedience to the various legal or spiritual injunctions she felt were binding. Or not so much obedience—she disliked the authoritarian connotations—as it was an act of coherence, bringing her religious faith and her sense of practical accountability together into one fabric. "I think God works through people," she said. "Christ said, 'Love your enemy.' Well, you can't love your enemy with a nuclear weapon. Every mother ought to think about the threat that's hanging over her kids and ask what she's going to do about it."

Her children were the point of connection for her. What was right in this instance, faithfulness to the biblical command not to kill, suddenly—in the light of weapons technology—made practical sense. Her children's lives were linked to the lives of the enemy's children. Hers could not survive unless theirs did. To love one's enemy, the New Testament elucidation of the Old Testament absolute, was newly the condition of survival.

Montgomery County and the Commonwealth of Pennsylvania considered such a conclusion dangerous and illegal. Molly was a criminal, to be kept in jail and out of trouble. And so, like others who have challenged the social order in significant ways, as Penn and other, lesser-known activists had done before her, she reported from jail. Life in jail was new to Molly's experience.

"I ventured outside the walls without handcuffs today," she wrote in early October. She had been taken to a shopping center to get frames for her glasses, which had been broken in a volleyball game in the Berks County jail, mended, and then broken again in the Lebanon County jail. "Our time outdoors—for all of us—was interrupted so that the matron could take me. After I dressed in my own clothes, for the first time in a week, I had to wait nearly half an hour before we left," she wrote, echoing the typical frustrated soldier. "Hurry up and wait."

"Staff is proud of its shiny new building, strikingly similar in architecture to G.E.'s King of Prussia plant—brick, cinder block, concrete, designed to squeeze out any humanity. Technology here, too, is master." To move anywhere, "you wait between double sets of remote-controlled doors for 'control' to wake up, check the TV monitor, and to push the button for door number two. E. says she once waited twenty minutes."

She rediscovered the helpless sense of childhood, how being treated like children reinforced the inmates' irresponsibility and resentment. "The women feel this is like kindergarten. A very boring one, not even finger paints and playdough, just a TV, rug hooking kits and each other, all day, every day. For me, the advantage is having free access to my own private cell. I can read, write, pray, do yoga in relative privacy."

Her sense of irony was aroused. The warheads she had hammered were officially blessed in the name of "national security," though they jeopardized all life. To protect the public from someone who meant to lessen that jeopardy, the commonwealth of which she was a citizen held her in a "maximum security" prison, with other dangerous people: "an eighteen-year-old paying off $600 plus fines from a traffic accident at $10 per day; a twenty-year-old first offender who was with her boyfriend on an attempted robbery; a woman [already] in two months charged with receiving stolen goods—the thieves are out on lower bond, [but] she can't make bail. I told them *I* am the only dangerous criminal here." Absurdity seemed to her to govern the life of the prison, mirroring the larger society. "We were just told to go to our cells for head count. We are six."

In her first jail, in Berks County, Molly wrote some reflections in her notebook, trying to capture her experience. She imagined the rupture she had made in the lives of her family and friends, how it would repair itself during a prolonged absence, such as she must contemplate. Maybe, she thought, it would be as if she had died and were mourned. She visualized "family and friends gathered at the house, bringing meat loaves and comfort to one another." The thought of the family together heightened her desire "to make roast chicken or spaghetti sauce, their favorites." She would miss more than dinner, though. "I want to watch Bob (14) and Greg (12) grow up, as I have the older ones," she wrote of two of her sons.

She found the words and phrases at her disposal inadequate to explain the loss felt, having given up—for an indefinite time—familiar patterns and relationships. Visits from family, who had to travel across

Pennsylvania to see her, were not the same as daily association. "Today I feel my death to all that in its fullest sledgehammer reality," says her notebook. "I saw the boys grow tall, begin to shave, remembering me with fondness, occasional visits or notes, and, perhaps, resentment.

"I've cracked their world open. As time goes on and the ragged edges heal, I'll be left out of their everyday reality." Her mother had died not long before, so she knew that permanent loss. "If I were really dead, they might feel my presence as I do my mother's. Instead, they'll visit and I'll wonder at the changes in them, no longer daily and imperceptible, but visible and startling. Talk won't be free and easy but self-conscious.

"Perhaps I'll become a sort of myth: 'remember when she did this?' or 'we went there with Mom.' But my daily living reality has perished— at least for months, perhaps for years." Molly knew that if the full sentences possible for each charge made against her were imposed, she would spend the next sixty-four years in jail.

But, she noted, "It was my own decision to interfere with the production of nuclear weapons that could kill [my family], not understanding that they may experience the same guilt/anger reaction of a suicide by a close relative." Her syntax tied itself into revealing knots, indicating the complexity of her own emotions, the sense of her surprise, the sense of herself dead—as result of her own decision—to those she loved, a feeling shared by at least one friend, who declined to talk about Molly because, she said, "I couldn't talk about a relative who had just died, either."

"So now," wrote Molly, "I picture a lessening of grief as life goes on without me, as my presence is gradually forgotten, as new patterns of living emerge without my being a part. The pain will numb, then go away." She dreaded being "walled off from the world I love, a world of family and friends; my satisfying, frustrating work for peace and justice; of walks in the country; laughter over a beer; listening to good music; joking with my kids—all the things that bring joy into my life."

Her small fingernails, kept short, grew longer and pearly. "They've never been in such good shape," she laughed. To manicure them, she had to ask the matron if she might borrow a fingernail clipper and an old soft emery board. "You could borrow a needle and thread if you wanted to mend something," she explained with a grimace. "Then the matron would call it right back.

"I've been allowed none of my books here—again," she wrote from the Mercer County jail in late October. She would collect a few books, sent in from outside, and then be moved to another jail, her books confiscated. "You don't have one belonging that hasn't been carefully gone over," she said.

I interviewed her at the York County jail in early November. From the outside, it had the look of a styrofoam cube, too white and glistening, set in the early winter Pennsylvania hills colored like a threadbare Persian carpet. "This place is so disorienting," she had written about this particular jail. "I'm *almost* grateful that Anne [Montgomery] is finding it the same. Hard not to get lethargic. I did a couple of crossword puzzles and was glad to find that I can still do them. You begin to feel you've lost a few marbles. I would not like a long-term stay."

Each day, she had written, was "another day of push-button conformity, beginning with a greeting over the loudspeaker, a siren, the flickering on of fluorescent lights and "the sound of our solid steel doors clanking open," a shower with a mechanically timed stream of warm water in a doorless, curtainless shower stall. The loudspeaker announced breakfast, to which each inmate carried her own used and washed styrofoam cup. Once, when Molly left her cup behind, she had to supply herself with one picked out of the trash.

To go to the bathroom, she wrote, "You must press a button, and wait for the matron to activate the two-way speaker. 'I have to go.' The cell clanks open, then shuts behind the woman. Requests for toilet paper, Tampax, crochet hook, bring an unhurried response from one matron in particular, who smokes a cigarette before responding to the button." Eating, drinking, going to the bathroom—the mechanics of living, normally not worth reporting—absorbed some of the too-plentiful time, but drained energy. "I'd been too stubborn to ask the Warden for my toothpaste, but yesterday, tired of brushing with water, I relented and asked for skin lotion, deodorant, toothpaste and shampoo, which are locked in a room, along with my jeans, shirt, sweater and some personal papers and letters which this place won't allow in."

By standing on her bunk—a breach of the rules—Molly could see a smidgen of the countryside "through the strip of window." Her tiny view was some relief from witnessing the ruined lives of her sister inmates, whose faces "show[ed] the effects of drugs and jail," she noted. It amused her that, to pass the time, they played games like one called "Killer." "One young woman is in for homicide," she wrote, noting the irony that the real killer "plays it no better than the rest of us."

It was like traveling in a new and very foreign country. Weariness struggled with her awareness of the importance of defining these circumstances, out of sight and out of mind for most of the people she knew. "Rehabilitation through sensory deprivation and infantilization—that's my description for this new maximum security jail. Designed to control every aspect of our lives and virtually to eliminate personal contact with the matrons, who themselves are controlled by rigid rules and paperwork, this place typifies the dehumanization of security-minded technology." She found connections between her primary concern about nuclear weapons and some of the human wreckage evident in the prisons.

"The food is bad but sufficient. The female pod is regularly cleaned by the women. Our laundry is washed daily. Our situation is like an infant's whose bodily needs are met, but whose curious nature is confined to a playpen."

Too little activity resulted in "deadly lethargy [that] takes all my energy. My arms and legs get heavy and numb. If they came to release me today, I'd say, 'Come back tomorrow. I'm too tired right now.'"

At the same time, she had reported on her feeling of superiority to her imprisonment. "My mind flies free," leaving the rest of her "to stand for count, remain on the cold, hard, metal seats after meals until it's time to scrape out our trays." Struggling with lassitude, tedium, and loneliness, she was discovering new resiliency, using her imagination in new ways.

Her husband, back in Pittsburgh, worried that she would be brutalized in jail. "I haven't," she wrote, "in over two months, felt one moment of fear as I've lived among the 'hardened criminals,' awaiting trial, usually in here because they can't raise bail or pay fines." Instead, "it's the prison system that frightens me, the incredible arrogance of those who have interfered with my mail, even to the point of returning letters to my attorney and my co-defendants. I've been denied the right to call my attorney during my entire five-day stay in [the Mercer County jail], been transferred on minutes' notice. In here it's taken two days to be given my pen and my legal papers. In another jail, the matron read my outgoing mail. I refuse to be beaten down, but I will leave here angry."

Even in her outrage at the prison system's assumption that security derives from repressing humanity, she noted, "The employees are more victimized than we are, sitting hour after hour in their glass cases, responding like robots to our press of a button or shouted request. Day follows boring day in this airless, sealed-off world. It's like living in a submarine. Robots or rebels are the only possible products."

She wrote many pages of detail and fretted, "Still can't get it down right." At times, she said, "I was feeling such a sense of gratitude to be in here, sharing lives with the women here, some of whom struggle with tremendous odds." She reported having said to one woman, "To me the main message of Scripture was to learn to love yourself. I think that's true: if we are to love neighbors as self, we must love ourselves enough to let God's love pour in." The real danger, both inside the prison and out, she thought, was that official dehumanization in the name of security was absorbed by people who learned to value themselves and one another too little.

As Molly learned about the separation and idleness of life in jail, she had to account for herself repeatedly. There was an outside world in which people were bothered by what she'd done, far more than if she had murdered someone or stolen something. Outside, people worried that anarchy might somehow be loosed upon the world by her action: civil disobedience, unlike other criminal acts, exposes how deeply the law depends on voluntary obedience. Molly had made the possibility of withdrawing that obedience real for others than herself; this created anxiety. Though she was known in Pittsburgh for her years of work in matters of civil rights, peace, workers' rights, women's rights, poor people's rights, human rights, she was also an ordinary person, a working-class mother and housewife.

While she was in jail, controversy animated the letters-to-the-editor sections of her hometown newspapers, the *Pittsburgh Press* and the *Post-Gazette*. Wrote one woman, "I, too, am a mother and have cared for nine children and eleven grandchildren. I, too, am a Catholic, but I cannot see any possible connection between our mutual religion and her wanton breaking of the law."

A man wrote, "I readily admit that the institutionalized Catholic Church is careful of property. However, I find that Jesus wrecked the equipment of the money changers at the temple. Jesus caused devils to leave a man's body and enter into a herd of swine, which rushed into the sea and drowned. We don't know the size of the herd, but certainly it represented a serious loss to the owner."

One man sneered at the "preposterous conclusion that the seedy trespasses and nasty little vandalisms of Molly Rush and her cronies have something to do with peace," and suggested that her sympathies must be with the Russians.

Another wrote that "unless there is worldwide agreement for total disarmament—which is highly unlikely—nuclear war is inevitable. If that happens it would mean the end of civilization as we know it, if not the end, period."

A man wrote, "No matter how reasonable the stand that Mrs. Rush and her board [of directors at the Thomas Merton Center] take on the nation's nuclear strategy and General Electric's involvement with it, and no matter how strong their feelings, they do an injustice to us all when they attempt to impose those feelings by force on others."

And a woman wrote, "War with Russia is almost inevitable." Russia, she said, was the leader in the arms race. "If we do not have war arms, it's just an open invitation for Russia to move in and take over."

"The buildup of nuclear weapons produces what is basically a non-consumable item," wrote a woman. "If it were consumed, it would mean the destruction of much of life as we know it. The more of these we continue to produce, the more likely they will be used. Already our leading statesmen are trying to convince us that we could survive a nuclear exchange. Molly Rush is trying to protect her children and everybody's children and grandchildren, from such a horrendous possibility."

Another woman wrote, "Molly Rush sits in jail for you. Whether you like it or not, whether you agree with her or not, acts like hers affirm your right to speak out."

Yet another wrote, "When all rhetoric is stripped from our powerful defense systems, the fact remains that armaments kill. We cannot dare call ourselves peace-seeking in the shadow of our constantly growing stockpile. Molly Rush had the courage to see and expose this frightening reality."

"Pittsburgh's own Molly Rush and her seven colleagues showed uncommon courage by responding to the biblical call to 'beat swords into plowshares' in the face of certain imprisonment and separation from family and friends," wrote another man.

These letters constituted the first real public exchange, outside of learned journals and books, about nuclear weapons that I had ever heard. It was only in reading them that I realized how little open debate there had been on a matter that ought to have been of pressing concern.

When I first heard the news from King of Prussia, I felt deep dismay. It was, after all, 1980, the beginning of a retreat from the political involvement of the sixties and seventies. Ronald Reagan was running for the presidency, and public apathy was the fashion. "Oh no!" I thought, "Why did she do *that*? Why *now*? Why *her*?" I had worked with her, though not closely, for some years. I sympathized with her opposition to nuclear weapons, but I thought she would be misunderstood. I did not foresee how her action might explode the apathy and alter the agenda. In addition, I wanted her out of jail, working—as she had for so many years—on community efforts to bring about peace and disarmament.

When I drove across the state to the stark white York County jail set in the muted November hills, I was unprepared for her to look so radiant—a look I associated with women who have just given birth. Her sister, Mary Catherine Gorman, told me uneasily of the "intensity" she had noticed in Molly since her arrest. Molly was thin, I thought, sitting alone in her empty gray cubicle behind heavy glass, wearing a clean blue prison uniform, a hospital bracelet on her wrist. But she seemed in good spirits, laughing often and heartily, eager to articulate her thinking.

"It's amazing," she mused, speaking to me by means of a pair of telephone receivers attached through a heavy pane of glass by a stiff ribbed cable. "People have been nurtured from childhood on the notion of security. I lived a very insecure life in my early days, when my family was on welfare. I really tried for years to get away from that. I wanted to have my own house. I went through *all* that. And yet, here I am in a *maximum security* prison, where you can't go to the bathroom or take a shower without being visible. And here I am, living in a world where I don't know if my grandchildren are going to grow up." She shook her head, her heart-shaped face framed in dark curls, and wondered, "How can you call *anything* 'security' when you live in that kind of a world?" One hand made the quotation marks as she spoke.

"I need to talk about the incredible *freedom* that comes from having done everything that you can do," Molly said that day. "Women are so bound up with the notion of security, have been taught—through marriage and everything—to seek security. And that's a myth. Security is a myth." She had rejected the fiction that national security lay in killer warheads and found startling connections in the assumptions that governed her days in prison as they had, once upon a distant time, governed her days outside.

Her voice over the telephone was low. I could see her mouth making precise words through the glass between us. "The notion is that by building up all these things, whether it's insurance programs or weapons systems or jails, that we're somehow providing security. It really is a myth. When you can let go of that and say, 'That's not what provides my security, there's something more than that,' and when you can just act on what you believe—*just act on it!*—let go of all the fears! They've taken everything away from me, privacy, everything. And I've never felt more free in my life. I've never felt more joy in my life. As much pain as I've felt—I miss my kids and want to be home—I don't feel oppressed in the way I felt when all this was burdening my soul and I was not acting in consonance with what I was believing and feeling." Something had mended in her and it confounded the penalty the Commonwealth of Pennsylvania exacted.

What she saw as an achievement of health, a new freedom, also posed a difficult question for family, friends, and those who knew her name. They saw her act of faith and wondered what it meant to be faithful? how was each of them faithful? to what?

Among the hundreds of letters Molly received in jail, there was one written by an old schoolmate on lined loose-leaf paper. "I'm not sure I know you that well anymore. I could probably tell you that I prayed for you, which I did, but I would rather ask you to pray for me and all the other people who go through life wishing they could have done more and didn't."

After three months, because the prisons intercepted their mail, making planning a defense difficult, Molly, Anne Montgomery, and Dean Hammer accepted bail so that they could work together with the other defendants on their court strategy. Daniel Berrigan was already out, bail having been raised by his fellow Jesuits on account of his chronic ill health. Eventually, John Schuchardt, Philip Berrigan, Carl Kabat, and Elmer Maas, having organized some of the inmates at the Montgomery County jail to protest certain injustices, were offered lower bail, which they refused to pay. They were then released without bail.

"Trying not to get keyed up about our hopes for release tomorrow," Molly wrote the day before she went home. When she walked out, the cold air and wind were astringent. "I drove half of the way home," she said. "It felt *good!* I was made to feel incompetent in prison." To feel the winter air on her skin, to drive herself, was like "waking up after a nightmare." Her sister-in-law (Bill's brother's wife) cooked Thanksgiving dinner for the whole family, which had a grand reunion. Molly's

The Rush family during Molly's eleven weeks in jail, 1980. Back: Dan, Gary. Front: Linda, Bob, Greg, Bill, Janine.

son-in-law, Linda's husband, had composed a welcome-home song. Her large extended family all wanted her attention, as did some friends who irritated family members by wanting to be included.

I visited her the Sunday after Thanksgiving in the cheerful kitchen of her small two-story brick house in Dormont, a working-class suburb of Pittsburgh. The thin winter sun poured in as Molly—still wearing a woolen cap, having just come in from mass—ground the coffee beans Bill regularly brought home, and set water on to boil. I studied the bulletin board, cluttered with family snapshots. Around the edges were pictures of Bill as a young marine, in uniform, posing with his rifle. I glanced from the marine photos to Molly, who shrugged and smiled. "Bill put them up while I was in prison," she said. As we waited for the coffee to drip, she wiped the refrigerator doors and handles with a wash rag. "There are a lot of sticky fingerprints," she laughed.

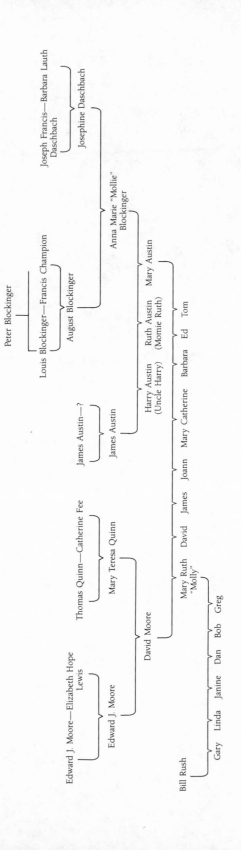

4

"If it be Common, it should not be so hard to produce"

IN 1842, Peter Blockinger and his eldest son Louis brought their families to Pittsburgh from their native Alsace, settling on the south side of the Monongahela River. Three generations of Blockingers arrived in the same year Charles Dickens visited Pittsburgh, comparing it to Birmingham: "[It] certainly has a great quantity of smoke hanging over it, and is famous for its iron works." Pittsburgh prospered by manufacturing guns, ammunition, and other weapons for the Mexican War, an adventure that so offended Henry David Thoreau of Massachusetts that he spent a night in jail rather than pay his poll tax. "We should be men first, and subjects afterward," he opined. "It is not desirable to cultivate a respect for the law, so much as for the right." In the year after the Blockingers settled in Pittsburgh, seven Sisters of Mercy arrived from Ireland to begin their order in the newly established Catholic see in the smoky city. One hundred and thirty-seven years later, the Mercy Sisters would help to bail the sixth-generation descendant of Blockinger lineage out of jail, and nine years after that, would lend their money to the telling of her story.

The Blockingers made their home in warring territory. A traveler in the Laurel Mountains of western Pennsylvania, where French and English soldiers had waged their imperial wars, with native Americans enlisted by the French, reported that he found "great quantity of broken bombshells, cannon, bullets, and other military stores. Found great numbers of bones, both men and horses. The trees are injured, I

"Mollie" and James Austin, Molly's maternal grandparents, in
Atlantic City, New Jersey.

suppose by the artillery." In the next century the Blockingers fought
against the Indians and also in the Civil War. They worked in Pittsburgh's glass factories, iron mills, and stores.

August Blockinger, Peter's grandson, who arrived in Pittsburgh as
an infant, married a Pittsburgh woman, Josephine Daschbaugh. Their
eldest daughter, Mary (called Mollie), married grocer James Austin.
Auburn-haired Mary, their daughter, married David Henry Moore, the
grandson of refugees from Irish famine who had settled on the south
bank of the Monongahela River. The eldest of their eight children was
Mary Ruth—Molly.

Molly's grocer grandfather, James Austin, invented Austin's Carpet
Cleaner "down cellar in barrels," as his oldest daughter Ruth put it

Mary Austin, Molly's mother, in high school.

("Momie Ruth" to her sister Mary's children). Momie Ruth recalled how she and her older brother Harry had bottled and labeled the carpet cleaner. Their father delivered the bottles himself by trolley. As it turned out, there was a small fortune in Austin's Carpet Cleaner, which Pittsburgh women still use.

Molly's mother Mary was a pretty, smart, and well-behaved young woman. A snapshot shows her in late teens with a mop of curly hair, like her daughter's. Mary had perfect attendance at school until she developed rheumatic fever. She was a good student who got high grades, an obedient Catholic girl, Molly said, who loved to tell of her one schoolgirl rebellion. It was during the time in the 1920s when the fashion was bobbed hair that stood straight out at the sides. "It took a lot of work to get it to stick out that way," said Molly, "before they had mousse and everything." The nun who was Mary's teacher ordered all the girls in her class into the washroom, to wet down their outrageous hair. Mary refused, and later, when she told this story with pride,

Mary Austin before her marriage.   Dave Moore before his marriage.

always mentioned that it wouldn't have made any difference; her hair was so curly that it stood straight out no matter what was done to it.

In high school Mary fell in love with handsome David Moore, a "black Irishman" with dark soulful eyes, curly dark hair, a good singing voice, and a dashing way with him. According to her sister Ruth, Mary "never went with anybody else" once she met Dave, her true love. Dave "was just, honest, and fair," according to his sister, Catherine Whitcomb, "and Mary was his only love." He had a "voice like an angel," Catherine said, "and he read a lot." In high school, Dave was voted most likely to succeed. Carnegie Tech offered him a scholarship, but his father thought high school was plenty for the son of a man with a third grade education.

Mary's father, James Austin, objected to Dave. He thought, said Molly, "Nobody was good enough for Mary." Nevertheless the couple were married in 1934. A year later, their first child—Molly—was born. The young couple began with plenty of money from the sale of carpet cleaner, which for a while Dave delivered for his father-in-law. Mary and Dave put their money into a house in the fashionable suburb of Mount Lebanon and filled it with brand new furniture. They moved in when Molly was two, the year her brother David was born. "They spent

Molly Moore at about one year, 1936.

all their money on that house," said Momie Ruth, "and it was beautiful." Dave's oldest son, another David, remembered as a grown man his father's scorn for his neighbors, the "instant millionaires" who lived on "Mortgage Hill," as he put it, "the cheese and crackers crowd." However well-to-do Dave Moore might be, he wasn't at ease with affluence.

Though Mary had been told she wouldn't be able to have children, she belied the prediction with a brood of eight, born one right after the other. They were Mary Ruth (Molly), David Austin, James Henry, Joann Mary, Mary Catherine, Mary Barbara, Edward Joseph, and Thomas Joseph. Dave Moore, the father of this increase, for reasons that no one later could explain, was unable to keep a job. Shortly after Molly's birth he began to drink, and almost immediately, said Molly, "it got out of hand." Dave puzzled everyone. With a fine, beautifully furnished house, a saint for a wife—everyone called Mary a saint—a growing family, why did he take to drowning his sorrows?

His sister Catherine couldn't understand it. He had been "death on drink," she said. "He's a monster," she said to her sister-in-law when Dave's addiction became obvious. Mary replied, "I don't want you

Molly in Ocean City, New Jersey, 1937 or 1938.

Molly on the porch of the Mount Lebanon house, about 1938.

talking about my husband that way." Momie Ruth said, "I got so mad at my sister for putting up with him, though he was a lovable guy and loved the kids." She remembered Mary's answer to criticism about her husband: " 'Well, I made my bed, so I'll lay in it.' "

"There was some sort of split," Molly thought, searching for an explanation for her father's excellence, his love of books, his passion for music—qualities she shared—and his inability to stay sober and work. "I can't imagine what happened to him in his thirties, but that's when he started to drink."

According to Molly's brother David, "I couldn't imagine *how* [my mother] put up with my Dad. He would go out and blow the last dollar on booze and come home, and it was just, 'Hi, Dave. Sit down and have your dinner.' Of course, I don't know what went on behind closed doors, but I'd be surprised if anything went on, in terms of her raising hell with him."

The little fortune from Austin's Carpet Cleaner soon disappeared. Dave took jobs doing one thing and another, keeping none of them for long. Molly recalls the time of affluence, but for David, "We were the poorest people on the street. I can remember being ashamed of being poor. It was like my Dad didn't care. I can remember when I was a little kid, being sent to the store and losing fifty cents. And you'd have thought it was the end of the world. If I didn't find that money, we weren't going to have any bread."

When Molly was twelve, in 1948, her parents finally sold the fine house in the fashionable suburb and moved, just ahead of their creditors, to Ocean City, New Jersey, where they lived near her aunt Momie Ruth Haines and her family. "Oh, my heart ached for them," said Momie Ruth, who had phone calls from angry creditors. She and her older brother, Harry, helped substantially, she recollected. Molly remembers the family finances quite differently. Uncle Harry had offered the family support, but only if Mary would leave Dave. As far as Mary was concerned, the marriage vow, "for better, for worse," meant precisely that.

David recalled a woman who came up to him in church and said, " 'Oh, you're Mary Moore's boy. Your mother is a saint!' I didn't know if she was a saint because she was a good person, or a saint because she put up with my Dad." It must have been hard for Dave, the son of an authoritarian father who had refused to acknowledge his son's gift for learning, to be married to a saint. Perhaps it was hard, as well, to be a saint. Mary Moore kept her troubles to herself. "It was hard to find out what she felt," Molly said. "We learned to look for a little muscle in her cheek, or a little tone in her voice to find out if she was upset or feeling bad about something." Molly's youngest sister, Barbara, said her mother had had two nervous breakdowns, but no one in the family understood why. Molly remembered her mother's refusal to gossip. "My Grand-father Moore terrorized my Dad. One time, my mother was visiting her in-laws before they married, and the old man started to talk about someone. She looked up at a bare light bulb hanging down and said, 'What a lovely chandelier!' It broke my Dad up."

Mary was spunky and loyal and Dave was unhappy. Perhaps Dave had wanted to get ahead in the world by pursuing an education, while his father insisted he not get too big for his britches. Meanwhile his wife's family looked down their noses at their son-in-law. And Mary, uncomplaining, probably made him feel worse than had she nagged and carried on. Molly's sister Joann had no idea why her father drank, but thought that maybe a person of such demanding intelligence might have found it "hard to face everyday life."

"Invariably after meeting my mother," Molly said, "people would say what an extraordinary person she was—and she'd hardly said a word to them. There was something in her that people saw." She wasn't sure how to describe it, "Faith, serenity. She was a real Christian. To me the church has always been filtered through my mother's life. She lived the faith as I've never seen anyone live it."

Momie Ruth was full of admiration for the way her sister Mary managed in practical matters. "Mary would buy a pound of ground meat," she said, "and she would make some sort of filling and put meat over it. She never lost her temper. She was a marvelous mother and never complained."

The family lived four years in Ocean City. Molly's father worked with asbestos for a siding and roofing company. The asbestos, together with smoking, Molly thought, probably caused emphysema later in his life. At school in Ocean City, Molly was voted Queen of the May, a tie vote with Barbara Browne being broken after Mother Rose Mercedes told "the kids to vote for the one most like the Blessed Mother," said Molly. "I won, sixteen to three, and Barbara Browne didn't speak to me the rest of the year."

Somehow Dave managed to line up a job in a Pittsburgh steel mill and the Queen of the May and her family moved back to Pittsburgh. Their poverty was dire. They had nowhere to live in their native city. Dave's cousin, who worked for the county and knew appropriate

Molly about seventh grade.

Molly, Queen of the May in Ocean City, New Jersey, eighth grade.

bureaucrats, suggested that some of the children live as temporary wards of Juvenile Court. So Mary and Dave, Molly, and the youngest, Tommy, moved into an apartment on Forbes Avenue, a few doors from the court's home for homeless and wayward children, where the other six children lived for half of the worst year of their lives. Even as adults, Molly's sisters and brothers expressed bitter unhappiness about that time. Poverty was tolerable, but separation was not.

David remembered the roaches and harsh corporal discipline of the Juvenile Court home. He learned to dislike blacks, who ganged up on his little brothers and sisters. Mary Catherine remembered "having Easter candy brought in and having it taken away from you. My sister, because she didn't eat her carrots or raisins or something, was locked in the bathroom." Barbara, who had been locked in that bathroom "for hours on end," remembered, "Joann used to eat my cooked carrots from time to time" to prevent such ordeals. The children had learned very early to look out for one another. But young Barbara was very hurt when her mother took little Eddie home with her, for he was not thriving. "Why would she get him out and not me?" wondered adult Barbara, still hurt.

The family moved briefly to Edgewood, to the east of the city, where they were able to live together. After that, they moved to a farm Uncle Harry owned near North Park, where they shared a house with a woman who worked for Harry and whose husband was in jail. Molly's memory of her father's sporadic employment is dim. Her memory of poverty and of moving is clear.

Uncle Harry gave the Moores a house on Mount Washington, for which he got tax breaks on the mortgage. It was a disaster, said Molly. "The house was falling apart, no furnace, no plumbing, no water, the walls were falling down. Everything needed done." David Moore inherited some money from his mother's estate—Molly remembered that it

Molly's aunt, Catherine (Dave's sister), and her husband Merton Whitcomb in Moore family orange grove, Florida.

was about ten thousand dollars from the sale of an orange grove in Florida. Molly was afraid, given her father's habits, that he might "blow it," so she spoke to the parish priest, who encouraged her to talk to her uncle. Uncle Harry had inherited the carpet cleaner business and was doing well thereby.

The upshot of Molly's conversation with Uncle Harry was that he persuaded Dave Moore to entrust him with half the inheritance. With the remaining half, said Molly, her father put in a water heater—"because we kids were carrying hot water up to the bathroom from the stove"—bunk beds, and some other improvements. Uncle Harry, said Molly, sent some of his workers to make repairs. They put on aluminum siding, a concrete porch—"an ugly thing, it was a terrible job—nothing like five thousand dollars worth of work. And then [Harry] turned up with a Lincoln Continental!" Molly took him to task, feeling that he had taken unfair advantage of the trust her father had placed in him, and remembered him looking somewhat abashed. Her voice rises in indignation to this day as she remembers the disparity between Uncle Harry's well-being and the desperate straits of her family. The dilapidated house on Mount Washington sold for two thousand dollars in the late fifties or early sixties, bought to be torn down.

During this time of abysmal poverty, Molly recalls, "a woman who owned a restaurant was sending us our meals at one point—mashed potatoes, vegetables, meat in a can. It was leftovers."

Only when the period of separation was over, when the Moores had been able to find a place big enough for the whole family and the struggle to make it habitable had begun, did Dave and Mary Moore apply for welfare. The Moores were proud people and accepting welfare carried its stigma. Welfare investigators came to the house "to see if [the family] was fit to keep together," said Molly. "There was a sense of intrusion and invasion," which she resented, but she also worried that they would not get welfare benefits. It was a heavy load for a young girl. "We were interviewed, asked questions. But we never said anything against our mother," said Molly's sister Mary Catherine. Those years of acute poverty were "very cold," and she hated "taking sugar bread and egg salad sandwiches to school."

"As a teenager," said Molly, "I felt embarrassed and ashamed. It's so much worse having to apologize for your family, your father, his drinking. As a teenager, I just wanted to be like everyone else. It was very painful, living in Mount Lebanon until I was twelve and then having to get Thanksgiving turkeys from the local parish. When we

The Moore children, Mary Catherine, David, Ed, Molly (twelve years old), Joann, James, Barbara.

finally went on welfare, that was a step up." At fourteen she worked as a waitress, making twelve dollars a week for thirty hours' work "to pay the bills," she said.

"I was a worry-wart. I knew what was happening to the other kids." She had always felt responsible for the younger children, mediating battles, trying to make them behave. Mary Moore had paired the children, an older one to take care of a younger one. Molly felt responsible for them all. David, in charge of James, next in line, remembered him as "the scourge of the neighborhood. He'd run out of the house naked. Molly would get all embarrassed."

Molly attended five different high schools in all. As an adolescent, she said, "I was trying to distance myself from all that." She resented her mother's loyalty to her father, "her idea that everyone had a cross to bear. I really thought she should have left my Dad. When she did apply for welfare, they made her put him in jail. That's the only thing I heard her say in her life she regretted." David Moore spent thirty days in jail for his improvidence. It amused Molly later, when she was herself in jail, that father and daughter were both jailbirds at the age of forty-five.

"He was mad about her," Molly said of her parents. "I think they really loved one another. He always spoke so well of her. He must have gone through a lot of self-hatred, but he never put his anger on her." And she, Molly said, "had the kind of psychology with kids—now they talk about positive reinforcement. She just did all that stuff naturally."

Despite her father's failure as a provider, Molly admitted, "We had more of a father than a lot of my friends. We'd talk, do jigsaw puzzles, listen to the opera together. He loved nothing better than to make me lose my temper. He would say just the most outrageous things, till I'd start yelling. Then he'd sit back and laugh." Mary Catherine remembered the arguments. "We knew he was doing it to get her all riled up." Molly and her father both had good minds, well matched, acting as whetstones for one another.

When Molly was a married woman and a mother, she took a course in black history at the University of Pittsburgh. She told her father that they were descended from the Moors, the consequence of Islamic invasions northward. "He was highly insulted," she said. "'But look,' I told him, 'we have black curly hair and dark eyes, and we're called Black Irish.' He pulled out his wallet and took out a carefully folded clipping from the *Post-Gazette*. They'd run a series about different names, with their crests and histories. It was falling apart, the creases were so old. So he gave it to me and I read it to the bottom. And there it was, that the Moore name went back to the Moors. He was infuriated— doubly infuriated, because I had him." With considerable relish, she gloated, "It was the best time I ever got him."

In fact, she may have "got him" better than she knew. The Moores were actually English people of Anglo-Norman descent who moved to Ireland. From the fifteenth to the nineteenth centuries, however, Irish mercenaries served in Catholic armies all over Europe, having plenty of occasion to intermarry with the Moors. When the Spanish armada, sailing with many mercenary Moors, was blown apart in a storm, stragglers landed in Ireland. While the English landlords killed those they found, the Irish people sheltered the Spanish Moors.

But the term "Black Irish" had other origins. During Oliver Cromwell's Protectorate (1653–1658), an Irish revolt occurred. Cromwell quelled the revolt without mercy, and had the children of the rebellious Irish sold into slavery in the Caribbean. These became the "black Irish" because they were slaves like black Africans.

Dave Moore was "a proud man," according to his son David. "He would go up to the bar in a suit and tie and hat, and everyone else would be sitting there in their working clothes, and he didn't have a job." James remembered, "He beat the hell out of us when we were bad, praised us when we were good. He was a tease, kept us alert. He died a very sorry man, who suffered constantly with his pride." James was puzzled. "How do you respect an alcoholic, whose children raised you?"

The youngest sister, Barbara, felt her father was "always head of the family," disabled by alcohol or not. Once, she remembered, when the gas company shut off the gas, "he turned it on again. He was a handy person. He read every historical novel that the library had. And when the children were sick, he was the one that would make sure you took your medicine." Eddie, the next youngest of the Moore children, recalled the Mount Washington house, without heat or plumbing. The "joists and everything was rotten," including the porch, which at last was pulled down and burned for heat. Tommy, the youngest, remembered his father's playing Scrabble with his mother—"Nobody beat *him.*"

"It was very sad to watch what happened to him," said Molly, for he eventually drank himself to death. "I had a lot to get over in feeling reconciled before he died."

Her mother, though, the saintly Mary who suffered two mysterious nervous breakdowns, "was always the one you could go to," remembers David. "I always said she spoiled eight kids." James described "her complete attitude of life: 'God's going to take care, no matter what.' And He did. 'Don't worry about the everyday things. Somehow we'll come through it.' She looked forward to sunrise every morning and said her prayers every night that the sun would rise again for her in the morning. Didn't matter how bad she felt or how good she felt. Sick as she was toward the end," when she had cancer and had broken her hip, "you'd walk in and say, 'Hi, Mom, how you doin'?' and she'd say, 'Oh, I'm fine,'" and according to the doctor's reports, she was suffering greatly. But she'd offer it off for the poor souls in Purgatory."

For the Moore children, the mother of the family was the linchpin. According to most of her siblings, that meant her daughter Molly should stay home and be an active presence in her family; for Molly, the mother's role could be extended to taking part in history. The Moore children survived the ordeal of their family. "Not one of them is a loser," said James. "My brothers are good providers. My sisters are married and raising good families. There's not a loser in the bunch." He laughed. "Except for Molly."

While Dave Moore, the failure, honed Molly's eager mind by baiting her and arguing, Mary Moore once walked with her daughter in a demonstration, remembered their son David. "I looked out the window at *my* office at the bank and saw *my* sister, Molly, and *my* parish priest and *my* mother picketing *my* bank! I think I would have choked Molly if I'd gone out on the streets," said David. His mother's presence "was probably why [he] didn't go out."

Molly and her brother David had some violent arguments. "At one point, I disowned her as a sister. I said, 'I disown you and your ideas! I

Molly at five years old and her oldest brother, David Moore.

never want to see you again!' I got so mad at her!" This was during a discussion of the Vietnam War, which Molly had begun to oppose.

"What happened?" I asked.

"Oh, nothing," said David. "We didn't see each other for a while, and when we did, it was as though nothing ever happened." In the Moore family, no matter what, the family counted on one another, supported one another.

"I suppose," said Mary Catherine, "we were all taught the freedom of our actions." Her mother had left a legacy, she thought, "an inner sense of caring for one another, no matter how much we disagree." Molly had been a sort of second mother for her younger siblings. "At my hysterical moments, there was Molly," said Mary Catherine. "If I had no other alternative, Molly was always the alternative."

Years later, when Molly began to take an active role in public matters, her sisters and brothers thought she ought to stay home instead. "I feel bad that there she is, taking on all this huge thing," said Mary Catherine. By "huge thing" she meant nuclear weapons, the doctrines that governed them, the geostrategic assumptions that required the doctrines, the orthodoxy of warfare.

Molly had decided to take a hand in shaping public policy. And yet she was firmly embedded in the immediate minutiae of family concerns. Her forebears had plenty to do to keep body and soul together; they did not see themselves as actors in the public realm, though of course they were. Like most people, it seemed to them that history, which they learned about from the nuns in school and about which Dave Moore read in library novels, was not theirs to influence.

Somehow, Molly—though she didn't know the entire story that was her warrant—was willing to walk out of her home, away from her family and community, into that larger history. And by doing so, she made clear that the remote figures in history books also come out of the smaller stories of marriages, births, deaths, ascent to riches, and descent into poverty. They are not, after all, separate stories.

William Penn, who acted in consonance with fundamental law in the seventeenth century, provides a parallel to Molly, who acted in consonance with international law in the twentieth century. Both grew up in a world dominated by warfare. Both saw the need for change and found already in existence underlying principles that would make the necessary change coherent. Penn saw the consequences of civil war, which had pitted Catholic monarchists against Protestant parliamentarians. Armed men of both persuasions killed one another, but they killed civilians too. On the Continent, the Thirty Years' War had raged so terribly as to raise the spectre of civilization destroyed. Penn wrote that warfare left "whole families undone, not a bed left in the house, not a cow in the field, nor any corn in the barn, widows and orphans uncommiserated."

Shortly before Penn, the Quaker, decided that warfare was inconsistent with survival, his slightly older contemporary, the Dutch Catholic jurist Hugo de Groot reached a complementary conclusion. De Groot, or Grotius, saw the deadly consequences of the improvement of weapons technology as the contentions of kings wreaked havoc in Europe.

The development of weapons technology was hardly new. Stones were surely the earliest missiles; slingshots would make them go farther than an arm could. Clubs gave way to spears and arrows, which could be hurled farther and with more effect from bows—an improvement in ballistic missiles. Each weapon promoted its own defense. Gunpowder, first developed in the far and middle east, was systematically adapted to weaponry in the early seventeenth century, a quantum leap in ballistic missile technology. Gunpowder reorganized warfare and made it far more deadly.

Medieval wars, compared with those that followed, were civilized affairs. Battles were fought more or less at short range during daylight hours by men, outfitted and equipped, to test their armed strength. When gunpowder was used to propel heavy balls out of cannon, stone towers and earthworks were built in defense. Attacking soldiers, unable to do their work between dawn and dusk, dug in, besieging fortifications with the great cumbersome guns that often blew up in their faces. The point was to prevent people from leaving their fortified areas by threatening them with guns, driving them to desperation.

Soldiers kept long from home, unsupplied and paid little (if anything), lived as they could, by plundering—sometimes even by cannibalism. Their own crops and livestock went untended, while they seized the food supplies of local people. The footloose soldiers took what they wanted, leaving behind both famine and disease. Though the brutality and devastation of warfare were nothing new, the new improved warfare outdid anything known before. By the time the Thirty Years' War had ended and its toll was taken, something like a third of Europe's German-speaking people had died, some seven million souls dispatched.

Long before the development of Mark 12A warheads, capable of multiple Hiroshimas, it was possible to foresee the end of humankind as the eventual result of new weapons and defenses against them. The "crackpot" prophets in the Old Testament had predicted that not until "the last days" would swords be hammered into plowshares and spears into pruning hooks. By the seventeenth century in Europe, it must have seemed as if the last days had arrived. The world was up in arms. Dynasties fought to expand and consolidate their power, each claiming that God seconded their particular claim. In England kings fought with Parliament, both claiming divine endorsement. None of the contestants advertised their craving for power: they all contended for right and honor, though it was death that gained dominion. "Oh what a wretched thing honor is if it must be bought with such an outpouring of blood!" exclaimed Emeric Crucé, a French monk, in 1623.

Those who left a record reacted with alarm. Some, like Grotius, thought it would be possible to limit warfare. Some, like Penn, thought it could be abandoned altogether. We don't know what the thoughts were of such ordinary people as the ancestors of the Blockingers, Austins, and Moores. Ordinary people, however, suffered dispropor- tionately, and probably had views on the matter.

Crucé proposed an international organization to provide for arbitra- tion in lieu of war. Like Penn, he thought religious toleration would remove the pretext of ideology for warring parties. He advocated justice internally and among states to reduce the desire to go to war. The second edition of his sprightly little volume, *The New Cineas,* came out within a year of its first printing in 1623, suggesting that the reading public (which was by no means in the majority) received it with enthusiasm.

Grotius was a weightier scholar than Crucé, though he reacted to the same events. Exiled from his home (he was smuggled out of jail in a trunk), he completed a great treatise in 1625, *De Jure Belli Ac Pacis,* or *The Law of War and Peace.* He accepted the just-war tradition, seeing war as unavoidable. But, he noted, "Even in other animals their desires for their own good are tempered by regard for their offspring and for others of their species."

Just as civil law had developed and was obeyed because individuals saw advantage in the regulation of their affairs, sovereigns, he said, were subject to the laws governing nations. "For as a citizen who disobeys the civil law for the sake of present utility destroys that in which the perpetual utility of himself and his posterity is bound up, so too a people which violates the laws of nature and of nations breaks down the bulwarks of its own tranquility for future times."

Grotius asserted, "Things which are manifestly iniquitous are not to be done, though commanded by the king." Though Molly had not read Grotius, she knew precisely this: that nuclear weapons, no matter how widely accepted, were manifestly iniquitous and their manufacture should not be done. A violation of the king's command, while serious, was not as serious as a violation of natural law, which bound even the king, said Grotius. William Penn, in Sir Samuel Starling's court, spoke of "fundamental law," meaning what Grotius called "natural law." Grotius asserted that it is "true and acknowledged by all good men" that a person has a "right to disobey" iniquitous commands. "If those ordered to go to war," said Grotius, "should believe the cause of the war to be unjust, they ought not to serve." For "God must be obeyed, rather than men."

And furthermore, if there were *doubt* as to the justice of a war, since "disobedience, by its very nature, is a lesser evil than manslaughter, especially than the slaughter of many innocent men," a person should refuse obedience. Nor should a state's desire to keep secret its reasons for waging a war resolve a citizen's doubt in favor of military duty, for "no law must keep to itself alone the understanding of its uprightness, but must impart such knowledge also to those from whom it expects obedience." To invoke "national security" to prevent citizens from understanding why they were to fight would have offended Grotius deeply.

Grotius observed "a lack of restraint in relation to war, such as even barbarous races should be ashamed of." He continued, "I observed that men rush to arms for slight causes, or no cause at all, and that when arms have once been taken up there is no longer any respect for law, divine or human; it is as if, in accordance with a general decree, frenzy had openly been let loose for the committing of all crimes."

Grotius spelled out principles drawn from Roman and natural law. He laid down rules to lessen the destructiveness of war to civilians, to the sick and injured, to prisoners taken in the fighting. He amplified the tradition of the just war, which required the following: the presumption must always be *against* war; decisions to go to war must be made by legitimate authority; the war must be fought for a just cause *not* for revenge, *not* to humiliate a rival, *not* to intimidate or warn, *not* to display power, *not* to protect foreign investments, *not* to dominate); the war must be a last resort, declared only after the failure of all other means to resolve the conflict; and the good to be achieved by armed combat must outweigh the resultant evils.

The principles Grotius established became the foundation upon which all later attempts to limit warfare were built. These principles had to do with containing and limiting the violence of warfare, with protecting the innocent, with keeping war apart from civil society. Some commentators think that international law ought to be observed, although it is not; others point out that, despite violations, international law *is* observed. No nation has ever denied the existence of international law, which is based both on custom and usage—the equivalent of common law in domestic matters—and on rules spelled out and agreed to. Attempts to articulate international legal provisions in the matter of war, peace, and neutrality have been made by way of the Congress of Paris (1856), the Declaration of Saint Petersberg (1868), the Hague and Geneva Conferences (1864, 1899, 1907, 1949, 1977), the League of Nations (1919), the Geneva Gas Protocol (1925), the Kellogg Peace Pact (1928), the London Naval Treaty (1930), the United Nations Charter (1945). The Nuremberg and Tokyo war crimes tribunals, following World War II, were attempts to enforce international legal principles by punishing individual offenders. The Genocide Treaty, formulated in the aftermath of World War II and only recently agreed to by the United States, gave treaty status to prohibiting crimes against humanity, which were among the charges brought at Nuremberg. All of these attempts were designed to secure agreement on international standards of behavior to protect the human race from itself.

Grotius argued, "Just as the laws of each state regard the utility of that state, so also between states certain laws have been established—which regard the utility not of particular communities but of the great aggregate of communities."

Grotius, like Penn, saw the law as an instrument devised not for its own sake, but to promote human well-being. Grotius remains one of the large historic figures—the father of international law, a man whose great work represents him.

William Penn was born in 1644, a year before Grotius died, four years before the thirty-year orgy of European bloodletting ended. An aristocrat trained in the law, he came to his Quaker faith in adulthood. That faith, with its belief that something of God exists in each person, rendered the careful distinctions between civilians and soldiers, the innocent and the guilty—distinctions at the heart of just-war theory and international law—irrelevant.

Questions of guilt and innocence in the matter of war had never been easy. Just-war strictures considered a soldier "guilty" if he put on his sovereign's uniform: at least, he did not qualify as innocent. But if the soldier served at the *command* of a sovereign, how could he be guilty? Soldiers were ordered to violate civil and moral prohibitions, told that to kill under such circumstances would not count against them in God's eyes. As the twelfth-century compiler of canon law, Gratian, put it, "The soldier who kills a man in obedience to authority is not guilty of murder." And yet, according to just-war theory, though soldiers were exempt from blame, they were not innocent. The innocent bore no arms. So soldiers were relieved of moral responsibility yet guilty of violating it. At any rate, the soldiers on either side were considered fair game for soldiers on the other. They wore uniforms, according to the laws of war, so that enemy soldiers would know whom to kill. There was something terribly arbitrary about it—catch-22 as early as the seventeenth century. We don't know whether Penn thought these thoughts, but since Quakers refused to serve the king by wearing swords and using them, and since Penn thought deeply about war as an institution that needed abolishing, it's likely he did.

The effects of England's civil war resembled those of the larger chaos in Europe. Soldiers, having left their plowing and planting to fight against the throne, were afterwards abandoned by their leaders, left stranded to roam the countryside, stealing, murdering, spreading disease and bastards, crowding the cities with unemployed, displaced persons, for whom food, water, sanitation, and housing were inadequate. Some of these displaced persons were no doubt the "vagrants, gypsies, thieves &c" who kept the court system busy at the time of Penn's trial.

Penn hated the suffering caused by people who claimed God's warrant to kill those whose religious views differed. "I abhor two principles in religion," he wrote, "and pity those that own them. The first is obedience upon authority without conviction; and the other destroying of them that differ from me for God's sake."

When Penn designed and planted his colony in Pennsylvania, the central issue was religious and civil liberty. He thought it was the absence of such liberties that had caused such bitter and bloody divisions in England and on the Continent. While European monarchs struggled to consolidate and expand dynastic power among the ruins of the medieval order, the English were struggling with questions of where power rightfully lay. If the king ruled by divine right, then there could be no doubt of the king's authority. He could define truth and right and, as God's vicar, exact obedience. He could order his subjects to kill for him and say he had it direct from God.

But, according to Quakers, God spoke to ordinary people as He spoke to the king. Therefore, the king's subjects might have a say in the definition of truth and right. They might complain of wrongs done them. They might insist that the king himself had to obey the law. Quakers like Penn went so far in decentralizing divinity—believing that it resided in each person, to kill whom was thus to kill God—that the king quite rightly feared such doctrines.

Such theological yeast worked against the restoration of authority, political or religious, and cast doubt on the legitimacy of the new technology of warfare. In Europe too, as the "innocent" perished along with the "guilty," the childbearing women and the gene-bearing children along with the cannon-firing soldiers, the vulnerability of the weaker members of society undermined the idea of strength in arms.

When Grotius wrote, "It is most true that everything becomes uncertain if we withdraw from law," he may have been thinking of the failure of kings and states to obey the law as they wrecked lives and property for their own ends. Perhaps it even occurred to him that the very survival of his species might not be assured. When he wrote of the need for disobedience, he was no doubt thinking of the gap between legal precedent and destructive reality. And Penn, who saw lawless government as far worse than lawless individuals, rejoiced, "By the good providence of God, a country of America is fallen to my lot."

Penn was not only gifted with moral, political, and legal imagination, he also had a very concrete gift in a grant of land from his king in which to try out his Holy Experiment. Its capital, which he named the City of Brotherly Love, was a day's journey from the ancient oak tree where, a few years later, a Prussian innkeeper would provide hospitality for travelers, and where three centuries later, an ordinary woman— housewife, mother, activist—would come to beat nuclear swords, if not exactly into plowshares, at least into scrap metal.

When Penn sailed up the Delaware, he must have thought he had recovered the earth's first days, the unspoiled handiwork of God's busy week. We know now, as Penn did not, that two hundred million years before, Penn's land lay under the sea, was pushed out of the water by a turbulent earth, where plants grew in the humid air. As the land fell and the sea rose, the plants rotted under water and sand, over and over, the mountains folding and buckling, the weight of sand pressing down to make strata of coal, sandstone, slate, and limestone under the thick forests that remained, finally, on the hills, where streams cut out valleys and carried their rich soils to lower land. God's handiwork came complete with its own dynamic laws.

There had been mound-building people on this land long before Penn came, but he met the Delaware, the Seneca, the Shawnee, whose relations to other native nations were as complex as those among white Europeans. He saw and treated the natives as citizens, providing security for new settlers by fair dealings and the new liberties that Penn hoped would take away the occasion for war. Between its founding in 1682 and the French and Indian Wars of 1755 and 1756, writes Brent Barksdale, Pennsylvania was "the only government in the known world that did not maintain a military defense against foreign invasion or internal uprising," and yet its people were safe among the 15,000 native Americans who lived and hunted there. Most white settlers regarded the Indians as a threat to peace; Puritans saw them as naked savages, fleshly allies of the devil, not only a danger but a disease to be eradicated. Penn and his fellow Quakers found among the Indians beliefs similar to their own and were willing to share the land peaceably. In other colonies, settlers took the land they wanted, without regard for Indian custom or use. In Pennsylvania, the colony named at the king's behest for William Penn's father, settlers bought land. Whereas in other settlements, bloodshed was the issue, Pennsylvania experienced seven decades of peace and good relations. Even when the Holy Experiment had broken down, when religious toleration had flooded Pennsylvania with people who were not pacifists, Quakers on the frontier were identifiable by their plain dress and lack of weapons and were safe.

The imperial greed of the great European powers put an end to the Holy Experiment, though Penn left his mark on American institutions with the idea of separating governmental powers and enumerating rights to protect citizens from government. Penn's physical province was large, extending west of the Allegheny Mountains to the relatively uninhabited, rich and wild land of the Ohio Valley. Once the Erie Indians had lived there, but they had been chased out by the Iroquois. In the lands watered by the Allegheny, the Monongahela and the Ohio, Shawnee and Delaware lived and hunted in small numbers. As settlement grew more dense in the east, the Shawnee began their migration

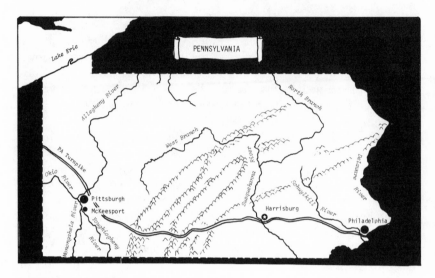

Pennsylvania.

to the Ohio River Valley, arriving in numbers only a little before Virginia speculators sent George Washington to spy out the land.

The young Virginia planter stood on a high point, now called Mount Washington, where Molly Moore spent part of her childhood in a broken-down house. George Washington looked down at the beautiful junction where two rivers formed a third and saw a place "extremely well situated for a Fort, as it has absolute command of both rivers." To look at the clear waters, abundant in fish, bordered by huge stands of trees, and to imagine a fort, made his errand clear. The point of land formed by the rivers, he wrote, was "well-timbered, very convenient for building." Washington's task was to seek good land and to determine ways of taking it.

The Quaker government on the eastern side of the mountains was busy making Philadelphia the most civilized, enlightened, and prosperous settlement in the New World. It had little time for or interest in western affairs. From the English king's point of view, though, Philadelphia was nothing in itself, no Holy Experiment, nothing but an outpost of empire. Since empire, by its nature, must both grow and keep rival empires from growing, however much Penn wanted to set a precedent in peace and liberty for the nations, the English king wanted to beat the French king. The land-speculating gentlemen from Virginia

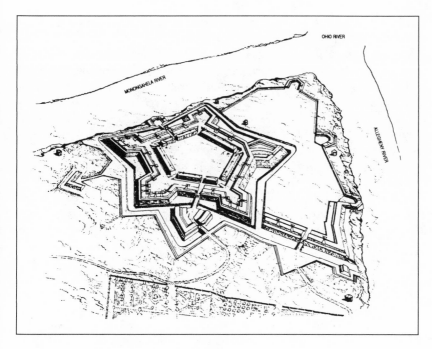

The three rivers at Pittsburgh and the English Fort Pitt.

who employed the young Washington served the royal purpose well. And King Louis, whose imperial outposts lay in the northern region of the Saint Lawrence River, also wanted to control the mouth of the Ohio and all the land beyond. Like most rulers, both kings were prepared to have their way by force, and there were many who were glad to make common cause with monarchs, no matter what the cost.

Washington's intelligence-gathering helped precipitate the Seven Years' War, also known as the French and Indian War. The French seized the chance to build a fort at the confluence of the rivers, holding the English back for a time. Then the English attacked and won, telling the Indians they would leave once they had rid the region of the French. Both sides went after the hearts and minds—and taste for rum—of the Indians, letting them fight their wars for them, dividing and conquering. The Indians, seeing that the English, with whom many had cast their lot, had no intention of returning east, knew the white settlers' presence would ruin their hunting lands. So the Indians attacked the English fort.

From New York, General Jeffrey Amherst wrote to Colonel Henry Bouquet, commander of Fort Pitt, "Could it not be contrived to send the smallpox among those in affected tribes of Indians? We must, on this occasion, use every strategem in our power to reduce them."

Bouquet replied, "I will try and take care not to get the disease myself. As it is a pity to expose good men against them, I wish we could make use of the Spanish method, to hunt them with English dogs, supported by rangers and some light horses, who would, I think, effectually extirpate or remove that vermin."

A trader and soldier, William Trent, wrote about the Indians who had won a battle and had promised the white settlers safe passage from the fort to their homes. "Out of our regard to them, we gave them two blankets and an handkerchief out of the smallpox hospital. I hope it will have the desired effect."

Smallpox was cheap and efficient and the native Americans were even more susceptible than Europeans. Disease was not the only weapon used against the Indians, but it was a new kind of warfare appropriate to imperial assumptions, which reduced those whose land or resources were desired to the status not of persons, but of troublesome insects or rodents. Grotius and Penn would have been appalled by this kind of calculation, which would ultimately lead military strategists to speak of the possible end of civilization in terms of "collateral damage" and "soft targets." What they would call "survivability" meant the ability of nuclear missiles to withstand bombs. According to these strategists, from two-thirds to three-quarters of a population dead might be nothing more than "acceptable levels of damage."

It was to this land of forts wrenched from the wilderness, cleared of trees and people by ruthless technologies, planted with the smoky industries that produced the implements for wars against the latest enemy, that three generations of Blockingers came in 1842. Pittsburgh would soon become a military boom town. And it was from this boom town, at the end of the prosperity brought about by military uses of steel, that Molly Rush would leave to challenge nuclear assumptions.

5

"This I leave upon your consciences"

"I HAD MY OWN SOAP OPERA," said Molly. "It hurts to go through it again, it was so painful."

"She said she *had* to go," said her husband, Bill, a short, round, balding man, "that she would be away for a while, that it was civil disobedience. I knew she was serious." Knowing nothing in detail about her plans, he tried to reason with her. "It was stupid. Someone else should do it," was Bill's view.

The idea of an act of citizen law enforcement in the matter of first-strike nuclear weapons production had been in the works for some months. In fact, an earlier plan had been called off. "She was very relieved," Bill said. To him, Molly's relief meant that she had no real desire to defy the law. And that, Bill thought, must mean that she was under the hypnotic influence of Philip Berrigan and John Schuchardt, tall, good-looking men who lived in a household of religious political activists in Baltimore. As the idea for the Plowshares Eight action had developed, as the members had considered their participation, laid plans, and considered the implications, they had grown to care for and trust one another. Bill resented these men, who "twist[ed] passages" from the Bible. They "used religion to show her she's right to leave her family and going out and doing this thing."

Molly had indeed been relieved when plans for the King of Prussia action had been canceled. "I thought, 'whew!' I knew I didn't want to be a martyr." As far as she was concerned, breaking up the warheads that seemed to her to threaten her children's lives was the important thing. She knew that she would almost surely be arrested and sent to jail, but these consequences were not her purpose. Though she believed that the warheads violated the law, she knew that General Electric and the Commonwealth of Pennsylvania would construe her action as lawless. Going to jail, under the circumstances, "was just an unpleasant task to be done, like cleaning the cellar." She imagined that she might have to do it more than once in her lifetime.

"She's always been religious," said Bill. "If you read the Bible as much as she does—I think she's doing it too much. It gets to her." Too much Scripture could result in brainwashing, he thought. He feared the retreats and meetings the Plowshares Eight held, the deep communion they shared. Planning such an action as Molly and her friends had in mind is an intense, searching experience. To violate the law—even as a way of enforcing a more fundamental law—requires serious scrutiny of motives and consequences and is not lightly undertaken. The Plowshares Eight had met for self-examination, planning, and prayer. To Bill that meant his wife and her companions were "just like the Marines. They separate you. They say the same things over and over again. You're with the same people. You go through the same things, go through suffering together."

Yet, much as he resented what he thought were military techniques being used by her associates on his hot-headed wife, he regarded his military experience as one of the best things in his life. "It gave me pride in myself. I didn't go to war or nothing. Sometimes you felt left out. Some of them didn't come back. That made me feel lucky. But it made me feel disappointed, that I didn't do what I was trained to do."

Unlike Molly, Bill did not think of himself as "a real religious person. I don't like a real religious high. I don't like *any* kind of mind control." Molly was in some kind of thrall, he believed. There was "some kind of commitment. I can't get through to her." What he meant was that he couldn't dissuade her.

"We used to argue about the difference between a fanatic and a patriot. Molly said patriot was worse than a fanatic. But," said Bill, "you can reason with a patriot." By "reason with," Molly said, Bill really meant she should give in to him, do things his way, yield on what was to her a compelling matter of conscience.

"No one in Pittsburgh knew *where* I was going or *what* I was going to do," Molly said. People only knew that she "was contemplating an act that could result in [her] being put away for a time. And that produced *very* hysterical reactions in my family."

On September 1, Bobby's birthday, Bill and Molly gave a party. Molly's sisters Joann and Barbara and some of their children were among the guests. Molly told her sisters of her plans, though only in general terms. Barbara remembered, reliving her puzzlement, "She said that she was going to go and it was an act of civil disobedience. She *told* us that! She did not tell us where she was going or what it was she was going to do, because we asked her. And Joann really laid her out flat. She told her, 'As we were growing up, who held us together in the family? It was Mother. And if the mother's gone, the heart of the family isn't there.' And she told her, 'I don't think you've been a mother to Bobby and Greg from day one!'" All the siblings agreed that Molly had been increasingly away from home as her involvement in peace work grew, though they were not agreed that she had neglected mothering. Barbara recalled that Joann "tried to say as many things as she could to Molly to try to change her mind."

This was the same reliable older sister who had, in earlier days, always been available to the needs and sorrows of her younger siblings, especially her sisters. "It was just like she—it was almost like she was numb," said Barbara. "She had her mind made up. Joann even ended up in tears and walked out of the room! That's how upset she was! And it really didn't do anything to her! She had blocked all feeling out," Barbara said. "It's not Molly to block out feelings like that! And Molly was saying, 'Well, Gary's going to do this and Gary's going to do that.' And Joann said, 'How can you delegate those things off? That's not their job, and why should they have to do that, when you're the mother? It should be with you.'"

Barbara shook her head. The persuasive force of Joann's argument had seemed overwhelmingly clear to her, and Joann's tears were even more persuasive. It struck Barbara as proof that something or someone "had hold of [Molly], she had made up her mind before," that neither argument nor tears had any effect on her.

The next night, a week before she walked into the King of Prussia plant, Molly came home at midnight to find her three brothers sitting on the living room couch, a brotherly posse comitatus in the small, faded living room with its worn furniture and its piles of books. There were James the family joker, David the banker, and Eddie the handsome truck driver. Tommy hadn't come. "He didn't want to talk to me," said Molly. "He was really scared for me."

James acknowledged, "We went to talk her out of it." Mary Catherine, who said that James could never be serious about anything, thought that Molly's plan had "pushed him into reality or something," because he took her announcement more than gravely. As a child he had, after all, been one of his family's troublemakers, running outside without his clothes on, to Molly's consternation. Now she was about to get into trouble and it upset the family ecology.

"I felt bad about it," James said. The brothers argued with her. "Even if [the Plowshares Eight] get in and do what they expect to do, and they don't get hurt—and they *could* get hurt—I don't think it's going to change anything," James recounted. "For the average person on the street, Molly Rush is still a nobody. I agree that we're making too many bombs, but I think she threw herself away on it."

Molly was proof against all her brothers' best persuasive efforts. "It was like yelling up a dead horse's ass," said David in disgust. "She didn't want to hear it. She had her mind made up. There was no reasoning with her." James, seeing that Eddie had decided to back Molly up and that David "sort of withdrew," felt desperate. He knew that Bill had "fought her every inch of the way," and probably knew that Bill's fight was not over.

"They saw that they couldn't dissuade me," Molly remembered, her voice low and her eyes full of hurt. "They were petrified. I think they thought I was totally off my rocker. Did you ever try to talk to someone who thinks you're crazy?" These talks, these struggles, Molly told me in jail, accounted for her unusual thinness far more than the unappetizing prison food.

"Right before they left, they all gave me a hug. James said, 'Molly, if you want to do something, why don't I just put a cross up in the front yard and nail you to it?' And I said, 'But Jamesy, what will the neighbors say?' That's how we left it."

James had the idea that if he told the FBI's Pittsburgh agent what was in the wind, the FBI might prevent at least his sister from her wild scheme—her companions were not his concern. He also thought, Molly said later, "I would be shot." He firmly believed that she would be protected from her own foolishness and the influence of bad companions if only the right officials knew in time to stop her from rash and dangerous action.

The next day, James went to Pittsburgh agent Paul A. Gumto and told him that his sister, Molly Rush, and the Berrigan brothers "were going to be involved in a very big action of some sort. I figured it to be in the Baltimore-Washington, D.C., area. I did not, at this time, have any idea what the action would be, but I did believe it to be of such that possible national security was involved. I felt it to be extremely important." He had the feeling, he said, that there might be hostages taken.

Agent Gumto seemed evasive and uninterested. Keep in touch if you get anything, he told James, and James did, calling him frequently. FBI records, heavily blacked out, show that James made many phone calls over the next few days and that the FBI was anything but uninterested. Even the "Terroristic Section" was alerted.

Like his brother-in-law, James Moore, Bill Rush was beside himself. A mechanical draftsman by trade and good at his work, he loves gadgets and machines—telephones with multiple lines, devices to detect a telephone tap, tape and video recorders. The television is always on when he is in the house. He liked gathering information, keeping track of it and coordinating it—newspaper stories, legal briefs, official forms—in the aftermath of Molly's arrest. At that period, the paper generated by Molly's action was the only thing about her he could control.

"I've always been able to get along with men, admired men," Bill explained. "No luck with women—except Molly. And I caught her young, before she knew what was goin' on." It was a heavy blow to his self-esteem when he could not keep her from going to King of Prussia.

"I come second," Bill said. "I've always known that. She comes first with me, but religion comes first with her." He was "a bit jealous, though it passes," he said. In fact, Molly seemed to inspire jealousy not only in her husband, but among friends and family members too. Bill, however, was more than jealous. He was hurt, fearful, furious. His world, as Molly described it in jail, "cracked open" a few days before September 9.

Bill was convinced that Molly had been coerced by people who had insisted that the event in King of Prussia could not take place without her participation. All eight of the conspirators felt that Molly's taking part in the action would signify that it didn't require "special" people— priests or nuns, or others with vocations that spared them ordinary responsibilty. "She says this one and that one follows their conscience," said Bill, "and when I say 'What are *you* going to do?' she says they have to act as a group." To him it made no sense that conscience was conjoint with collective action. He resented the other seven Plowshares activists, who left him out of the planning of the action and, he said, out of the legal strategy later on. He felt his place in his wife's life usurped by Scripture-quoting outsiders. Molly "thinks I'm suspicious and untrustful," he said, admitting he was both, but partly because he was not included in the group's thinking.

"Two things she knows about me: I'm very impatient, and I'll go out and meet my problems rather than wait for them to catch up with me." But otherwise, "She's never known how to judge me."

Before she left, he said, "I told her I had seven things I could do. I never told her what they were. Could've stopped her. Could've let her go. Could've called the police. A whole bunch of 'em. I could've locked her up. Taken her to the hospital. A couple different things. And I told her I hadn't decided which one I was going to do."

Molly was frightened. "Bill said he had several options," she said. "I thought he could physically stop me."

"Dad could just grab her and take her," said Dan, their nineteen-year-old, "which would make the situation worse in different ways. I think they would've had a bad time."

The day after the Moore brothers tried to talk Molly out of her decision, the day James went to the FBI, "I called her from work," said Bill, "really angry, because I wasn't getting anywhere with her. She asked me what I was going to do." He told her he hadn't decided. "I might just walk right out of here right now. So she took off." He said, regretfully, that he believed he could have "held her" physically. "I thought I could talk to her one more time, reason with her. I didn't get the chance."

Bill saw himself as pitted against powerful outside forces. "I always thought there was somebody she talked to that upset her more about what I might do, or something like that." He suspected her close and longtime friend, Cary Lund, of whom he once said, "She's my biggest threat. A lot of times she's a rival. She loves Molly very much. Molly gets intellectual stimulants from Cary." Molly had, as Bill discovered after she was gone, "left some things with Cary—her car keys, her check-book, my mother's wedding ring," all things she was afraid she might lose in jail. It was clear that Molly trusted Cary, at this point, more than her husband—another blow to his self-esteem.

Frightened of what Bill might do, Molly left town a day earlier than she had planned. "I was with friends. I didn't want anyone to know where I was," she said.

As soon as she had left home, phone calls and visits wove an intricate tissue of emotion and speculation between Molly's sisters and brothers and Bill and the Rush children. One theory was that Molly was leaving Bill for one of the men in the group. Such a theory had, at least, the virtue of a familiar plot. But James snorted at the idea. "If Molly wanted to leave Bill, she'd leave him."

For some time, Molly *had,* indeed, thought about leaving Bill. It had been, for years, said Molly, "an incredibly strange marriage." But "I can think of easier ways to leave your husband than going to jail," she commented. "More romantic ways, too. I'm not that good a Catholic, that I'd have to be so convoluted!" She spoke to me about the complexities of her marriage in an empty cubicle from behind the thick pane of glass at the York County prison.

Bill could have stopped her bodily, Molly acknowledged. "But he couldn't stop me from being where I was." A part of her decision to go through with this act of conscience, she told me slowly, was the decision that she would not, after all, walk out on her marriage, that she would stay with Bill. "I had made the commitment that once I got into this, I was going to battle as hard as I could to make him understand, battle as hard as I could to get him to support me." She had no idea what a battle it was going to be.

When Bill got home from work that day and found that Molly had already left, he took off in his car, driving pell-mell across the state of Pennsylvania, sure that he could get in touch with her by going to Jonah House in Baltimore, the community of nonviolent activists in which John Schuchardt and Philip Berrigan and his family lived.

At Jonah House, Bill was shown a map of the area and told to pick out a motel. Once he had checked in, he was to call Jonah House. Someone would get in touch with Molly and tell her to call Bill at the motel. He followed these instructions, convinced that government agents had followed him and were parked outside. He phoned to announce his arrival there and noted the time it took for Molly to arrive at the motel in the company of Anne Montgomery and John Schuchardt. She was only ten minutes away, he reported to James back in Pittsburgh. James had answered the phone when Bill called home "to check on the kids."

The fact that Molly arrived escorted confirmed his suspicion that she was in a state of psychic captivity, though Molly came with her friends because she feared her husband. They all went to the motel restaurant, Montgomery and Schuchardt sitting at the far end of the room so that Bill could make his final pleas in private.

Molly and Bill talked. Nothing changed. Molly said she was fairly sure that the security guards she would encounter carried no weapons. But Bill, like her terrified siblings, was sure "she feared being killed, the way she said good-bye." Tommy and his wife had heard that there might be a "human sacrifice" involved; Joann thought Molly might blow herself up: "She said she was going to do something serious, and the state she was in—when Molly says *very* serious . . . !" Eddie admitted, "We were afraid she'd be the victim of overkill. Some zealous guard would shoot a couple of women."

The family had no way to know that, in preparation for the action, the eight had prayed, as Molly explained, "for the employees. The security people. We were very much aware that we didn't want to provoke in them a violent reaction. I think I was the one not only concerned about the action coming off, but from early on, I was concerned about the spirit of the action, that it not be a countermilitary sort of thing—not a mirror image of the Pentagon." Later on she worried about such actions undertaken in secrecy, that a startled and fearful eighteen-year-old guard might shoot an intruder "and have it on his conscience the rest of his life." But of course, prayerful consideration was no guarantee that G.E. employees would not react violently.

Bill had gone crazy, said Mary Catherine. And he admitted, "I think I got a lot of people upset by going after her. Cary [Lund] thought I should leave her alone. A couple of her brothers thought, well, it's her decision, whatever she's doing. But others, I could've called home and they'd have been right with me. Tommy would've went right with me. James would've went right with me."

Some time before, using his own shrewd wit, Bill had figured out roughly what kind of thing the eight intended to do. FBI records show that what James passed along to the FBI he learned from Bill. James later regretted his act, particularly since the FBI made no effort to stop his sister.

"More than anything in the world, he wanted her back," said their son Dan. But Bill had failed to persuade her. He thought his marriage was over. He drove back to Pittsburgh, weary and defeated, to find only Dan at home. "He came home after seeing my Mum," remembered Dan, "and he was crying. That's what really plugged me into the seriousness of the situation. Everything just changed from that point. I never seen—Dad's always—pretty much—you know, he doesn't show his emotion a lot. He drove down there and back. That's what the emotion was. He didn't get her."

"I love my Dad," he said. "I tried to comfort him in any way I could, but I knew it wasn't helping." He seemed embarrassed. "I didn't know what to do." He paused, trying to explain. "Little things please my Dad.

Same with my Mum. Like taking out the garbage. That pleases them. I don't know," he grinned, "It flips me out!" Such measures of comfort, however, were for ordinary situations.

Dan felt himself somehow to blame. He thought maybe "they had an argument about me, that my Dad wouldn't say how proud he was of me, or something like that. I used to get into a lot of trouble. And everything I'd do, I'd get caught. And I more or less gave up everything I could get in trouble for. And I think that's what my mother was talking about, where I've come a long way." Dan was right, in a way. When Bill argued that the children needed her, Molly countered that the children were healthy, competent, and self-sufficient. Curly-haired, dimpled Dan, no longer in constant trouble, was a case in point.

Bill then went to Tommy's house, where there was an emergency gathering of brothers and sisters. The hysteria was far from over. Tommy was for going back across the state to get her, tying her up if necessary, and bringing her back, dragging her by her hair if that's what it took.

Meanwhile, Molly and the other seven had retreated to an old country Quaker meeting house in the eastern part of the state. She made and received phone calls from there, she said, from members of her family, "all of whom were hysterical, all of whom were pleading with me not to do it, to come home, afraid I was brainwashed. They were sure I'd been seduced into this. I had my sisters on the phone, crying."

According to Joann, she had been "mesmerized by that Dan Berrigan. He convinced her that it was her calling. But she had a lot of doubts."

Eddie thought not. "I didn't think she was brainwashed," he said, "not after talking to her." He had argued with her, "You can do more on the outside than you can on the inside. Restrain yourself." But, he said, laconic, "She was adamant. She felt that God was leading the way. She convinced me that *she* was convinced."

And so, Molly said, as part of the spiritual preparation for the challenge the eight planned to present to the presumptions of the arms race, "I had to put on the agenda [of the group] the status of my marriage, the status of my *life*." At that point, "It could have aborted."

To Bill, this discussion of their relationship with outsiders was a breach of trust. To Molly, it was essential. She had not only to explain to others the strain she was under, but to be clear for herself. "It was a matter of conscience, something I'd struggled through," not an act of

marital separation. She had to be sure she was going ahead pur-
posefully rather than fleeing a failing marriage. The other Plowshares
members, she said, felt her anguish. "They did everything they could to
help me." The period of retreat, prayer, and melodrama went on, until
Molly said, "I may have to drop out, because I don't know what's going
to happen." At one point, she said to me, "I gave up."

But then, late on Monday afernoon, the day before the action took
place, Bill capitulated. He announced in a telephone call, "I can see
you're going ahead. And I'll support you all the way." Molly said, "From
that time on, the load of everything lifted from me. By Tuesday
morning I was the only one who wasn't nervous." She thought it was
the intervention of God's grace in her life and in Bill's, in their life
together.

Bill said, "I'd decided to support her when I realized I'd lost her. If
she went, I lost her. If I kept her from going, I lost her. Either way, I lost
her." Bill, though in some ways a rough man, is nevertheless both
perceptive and shrewd. He wanted to protect her and suffered because
she didn't want to be protected. "Everything I done," he said later, "I
done for her."

James, Molly's brother, was amazed when, some weeks after the
arrest, he heard Bill say on a radio talk show, "I'm very proud of her
right now." He supported her, Bill said, "one hundred percent." To
James, who knew Bill's inclinations, that meant that he feared that if he
didn't back Molly up, he lost Molly.

"She has everything to lose, as far as I can see," Bill told an
interviewer for the *Pittsburgh Press*. "I'm very proud of her, very much
so. I guess I didn't really want her to take such drastic steps." A
policeman who read the story said to him, "I want to shake your hand
and tell you I admire you that you would support your wife that way.
And I say that with some emotion."

After it was all over and Molly was in jail, James and his wife went
over to the Rush house one evening. As Bill walked them to the car,
James explained how he'd gone to the FBI. "He felt guilty about it," said
Bill, "couldn't sleep at night. I said, 'Forget it,' he did it to help his
sister." But James's troubled confession gave Bill an idea. Maybe they
could prove that the FBI had entrapped the Plowshares Eight by failing
to prevent a crime they knew about in advance. "I took him to Tom
Kerr," said Bill, speaking of a notable Pittsburgh civil libertarian who
had offered his legal services to help in whatever way he could. Perhaps
it would help to get Molly off. And James, angry and betrayed, was

willing to put his story into an affidavit in Kerr's keeping. In spite of the accuracy of the information he had passed on to the FBI, the deed had been done, his sister was in jail, and an impossible bail had been set.

"It was something he did to protect me," said Molly, "and then he felt betrayed. James was anxious to go to court, to testify that the FBI knew. He thought the FBI would look bad, that it might have an impact on the trial."

"I've gone against her," James said, "but I'll back her up." And he did back her up, going so far as to write a letter to the Pittsburgh *Post-Gazette,* which read: "I am Molly's brother and I am not in any way a political activist and most of the time I don't even know where Molly is, as they say, 'coming from.' Many times it was easy for me to say, 'well that's my Pinko sister,' as if she was some kind of a communist. Although I know that she is not one. But now Molly is in jail for what seems to be a long period of time; I thought that I should find out why.

"I do not know where she gets her information from, but she firmly believes that there is a better than 50-50 percent chance that there will be a nuclear war before the end of this century. That's within the next 20 years. I cannot even begin to comprehend this. But I do know that the arms race is for real. If nuclear war should break out, how do we stop it without a doomsday effect? The Russians and the U.S.A. are building these weapons at such a rate and so powerful that total destruction is imminent if total warfare should break out. I would fight in another war to protect our way of life if necessary. But in a push-button war, the only real enemy is the bomb."

James's letter went on, "I believe that not one person, not one politician, not one political party, or that not one of the two governments have the right to decide the outcome of humanity. Building weapons that we cannot use for any reason is wrong. It is a crime against mankind." He concluded, "Molly has chosen civil disobedience knowing full well that she was breaking the law, and is willing to go to jail for a long time, hoping that her cause will be heard. It is like a cry in the dark that no one hears. I miss her."

James, however, *had* heard her "cry in the dark," and had realized that the "authorities" were not interested in his sister's well-being. Out of the "dark" that he felt, he knew one thing without doubt: he loved his sister. As soon as she was out of jail, James told her, "I have to talk to you." He and Molly went to the Eat 'n Park restaurant near Molly's house "and he spilled out the whole thing," Molly said.

Lawyer Tom Kerr thought it was likely that the FBI stood in the next room in Building Number 9, listening to what went on the Non-Destructive Test Area that September morning. While the Plowshares Eight were praying together, when Molly was struggling with the telephoned pleas of her family from Pittsburgh, "There had to be a meeting—G.E., the FBI, the Department of Defense," said Kerr, "at which it was decided to let them in." Molly thought this not entirely unlikely. She had known, she said, that such agencies would be interested in her activities. She had decided not to expend her energy in worry and suspicion.

Bill was again angry and hurt when he heard what had happened in King of Prussia. He had not been kept informed during the day, knowing nothing until Molly was in jail. The people at Jonah House had promised to keep him informed. "I thought Molly was going to get out on bail. I got a couple false imprints, things that they said to me." He would have minded her going to jail less if only she had tried to raise bail. But "she didn't *want* to get out. It was part of the action." And that, he thought, "was what the government wanted. That's what the other side wanted," to keep them "out of action."

He felt torn. "I see good in the government. See, my problem is, I'm not totally against war or anything like that. I've always been sort of military-minded. It's not like Vietnam. I thought that was a useless war." And although he said he didn't mind when a local radio talk show host introduced him as "the wife of Molly Rush," it must have rankled. "I'm not a sexist," he said, but he didn't like some of the "feministical" counsel her friends gave her.

"I get angry and irritated," he said. "I think I see it clearer than Molly sometimes. They might have locked arms around the bomb without smashing it." He too imagined warheads as enormous structures. "The destruction bothered me at first. Not now. They see it as an idol. I see it as a piece of machinery."

"Bill's letters," Molly wrote me from jail, "go from love and support to perplexity and sometimes anger, but he really amazes me with his willingness to persevere and to fight on my behalf."

Bill insisted on knowing from prison authorities everything that was happening to his wife. He became as obsessive about her case as he was about softball, for years his consuming passion. He collected every word published, every document connected to Molly, her time in prison and in court. He put clippings in scrapbooks that fattened rapidly, made photocopies of articles and gave them to reporters and friends. He arranged for radio and, when she was out of jail, TV ap pearances. He tape-recorded or videotaped every speech she made. He took pride in being her self-appointed press agent, convinced that her message ought not to go unheeded. Perhaps he also felt that being on top of all this information would, somehow, give him what he needed to keep her out of any more trouble than she was already in. The dining table of their Dormont house, with its soft, faded Indian cotton cloth, almost disappeared under his clippings, his telephone with its multiple lines, his tape recorder. His scrapbooks piled up on top of the files Molly kept on the old sideboard beside the upright piano, with its clutter of family pictures, dried flower arrangements, and spools of thread in a plastic case.

Bill expected to be fired from his job as a draftsman drawing pipe systems for an engineering firm. "I haven't been doing my work. They've been very good to me," he said, in spite of his preoccupation with Molly in various prisons, his visits to her, "but they're starting to knuckle down." Because Molly was gone, there was also additional work to be done at home, starting with Molly's car. "The engine needed replaced; the repair records are missing; it cost twelve hundred dollars," he said, harried and irritable. New responsibilities and tasks fell to his lot.

Some of the men at work, said Bill, "a lot of rednecks and hunters, if they don't agree, they haven't said nothing. They're supportive toward me, though hostile to her action. 'If that was *my* wife, I'd . . . ' I used to get that all the time."

What seemed to bother him most was his discovery that he had no control over his wife, nor even much influence. "In prison—she's gone," he said helplessly. Bill knew that something crucial had changed. "For years," said Molly, "we were almost leading parallel lives. Bill was never a part of family life." Though Molly had been away a good deal in recent years as the children grew to independence and needed her less, whatever illusions of a normal family life Bill had cherished were gone along with Molly. "With me, family comes first and issues second," he said. "With her it's just the opposite." Molly snorted when she heard that. In her view, he had never done much around the house. She felt that she had given birth to and raised their children with minimal help from him. Once Molly was in jail, their father stayed home more. The children liked that.

Bill had capitulated shortly before September 9, but his torment did not lessen. "What affects her affects me, and what affects me affects the kids." His eyes reddened at the rims, as if from weeping. "The attorneys and the other defendants say she's old enough to make her own decisions. I know that. But I'm not free. Neither is she." He struggled to explain how badly used he felt. "See, the people she's involved with are very religious, and she's religious too. Phil [Berrigan] and Liz [McAllister, his wife] have this attitude that it's right for him to do this. We never had that attitude." Molly knew that her decisions, the response of her conscience to the emergency she perceived, had consequences for others, she could not do otherwise.

Bill wasn't sure how much love there was left between them. "I'm here. It's up to her. She won't answer my questions: does she love me? does she need me? does she want me?" Perhaps he would not marry her if he had it to do over again. "We have nothing in common," he said softly. But later, he worked to find mutual ground in a struggle that tired and exasperated them both. "I've come a long way toward her," he said. "I wouldn't do it if it wasn't worth it."

He acknowledged that Molly was a rare leader. But he wanted some of the credit too. He was proud of his stature among softball players. "I've always had groups following me." He felt confident that she should emphasize her family ties rather than her religious motivation when she spoke. "Nobody's going to listen to you when you start talking religion. That's what I've been preaching to her." He noted that when she talked about her family, "that's the only way she gets her point across."

It was true, Molly admitted. Bill had excellent critical sense. Listening to her speeches, he could often tell what got through to people better than she could. And yet nothing he heard her say got through to *him,* convinced *him* of the unprecedented urgency she felt. His capitulation shortly before the Plowshares Eight acted did not mean he was reconciled to her decision. He saw Molly's act as through a camera lens, one moment in, the next out of focus. "He says, 'I'm with you all the way,'" said Molly, "and then he says, 'You're brainwashed.'"

Bill said, "Molly can't understand people who don't agree or don't see. She's explained it so many times. She gets upset when I question her. She has a real Irish temper." Bill remembered that one time, years before, she had thrown a knife at him during an argument. "The argument was about how I wouldn't argue. I'd just turn my back." But he was prepared to argue now, and over and over again, as the trial and then the appeal dragged along, and then as the question of new civil disobedience arose, he said that she didn't understand him.

"I have a deep understanding of her," he said. "She can hide something, but I can always find it." One of her friends had worried that the key to her safe deposit box was in the purse that police had confiscated in King of Prussia, but "I found it right away," said Bill.

Once she was gone, he said, "I searched everywhere to find out about her. I found she was going to do it from ten years back." There were her books, her writings, her acts, even her mail.

It deeply offended Molly that never, throughout the years of their marriage, had Bill felt any compunction about opening her mail. Because she came from a large, close family, privacy was important to her. "I've never been able to keep a diary," she said, because of Bill's inquisitiveness. Some time before her decisive act, her sisters and some of her friends had seen more clearly than Bill that something was brewing. They had sensed her growing impatience with lobbying and demonstrating, and she had committed several minor trespasses to draw attention to the nuclear arms race, for example, carrying a poster depicting a child burned in Hiroshima by the atomic bomb into the Washington, D.C., arms bazaar, where weapons contractors hawk their wares.

Molly's action awakened Bill's interest in the causes she had embraced. "I looked in the newspapers," said Bill, "and seen what she was talking about. When I used to read the paper, I used to look at the front page, the TV section, the shows. Now I go through the whole thing. I tear things out that may help Molly."

Like James, Bill wrote a letter to the editor of the *Pittsburgh Post-Gazette,* explaining his new awareness. "I now see what my wife has been saying for years and no one has listened, including me. My wife is a good religious woman who stands on true conviction of her faith and I have not met anyone as brave to do what she has done in order to save her children from what we are facing in future years. She is not a criminal or a nut, but a mother who is trying to save her fmily and yours from an earlier death. To do that, all she has to offer is herself."

Bill meant it. He had seen "how deep it went" with Molly, experienced something like her own sense of crisis when he thought he had lost her for good. He took to wearing a yellow T-shirt that said, IF YOU'VE SEEN ONE NUCLEAR WAR, YOU'VE SEEN THEM ALL. "I just felt we should do everything to help her. Now we're closer," he said.

But "I'm still trying to get her to come back home," he said, oddly, after her release; but he knew she would never be as she was when he'd first married her, when the children were little. "I feel that if she put this above the kids or something, I'd get fairly upset again."

"He's never quite understood me," Molly mused. But she was

Bill and Molly before her trial.

surprised that after the action, Bill talked to his father, "the first time since his mother died, seventeen years ago. He's never done more than sit and play cards, never had a real conversation in all these years. He's always distanced himself from his father. In the process, I think he built up a wall against everybody. To see him tear it down is an extraordinary experience, a profound part of the experience." One of Molly's talents was for seeing the odd changes that do not happen in a linear fashion, that come about sideways and catty-wampus when a system changes even slightly. The disorder in Bill's life, brought about by Molly's action, left him open in new ways.

Bill did not argue that she was wrong. "But going to jail—*that* was insane. *That* was the sticking point." She thought it came down to the question of control. He wanted it: she had yielded it.

After Molly's return, she and Bill had to rethink their relationship. "We talk and talk," Molly sighed. She had dark hollows under her eyes. "It's exhausting." Their discussions were often bitter as well as tiring. "I'm asking him to accept the impossible," she said. "He says he wants to try, but he means I should capitulate. We're at an impasse."

"She understands more how I feel," said Bill, but in the next breath, "It's like talking to a stone. You can't reason with her. It's up and down," he said, moving his hand like a sheet of paper caught on a draught.

For Molly, nonviolence and resistance were not like opinions that one could change or be reasonable about. Nonviolent resistance to the end of the world had become her center. "I can't go back on that," she said, any more than her sons, growing tall, could reverse their newly gained height. Nor could she leave acting on conviction to others, while she did safer, tidier work. She knew very well that there were no others better fitted or more willing to resist without violence.

As for Bill, the certitude that Molly should stay out of jail had become his obsession. His solicitude frightened her. If he felt as strongly as she did, Molly speculated, "he'd be a terrorist." At that point in their relationship, she did not know to what lengths he might go to keep her in line. "He'd rather just have a wife, a normal wife," said Dan, whose pretty girlfriend spent much of her time around the Rush household, as did many others of the children's friends. "I don't think," said Dan, that "he goes for all this extracurricular activity. I don't think *I* could put up with it—too much worrying for me."

Bill had thought he was getting an ordinary wife when he married nineteen-year-old Molly. She needed him then. They had met at the streetcar stop on Mount Washington, where they lived across the street from one another. She was on her way to Perry High School, he to Connelley Vocational School, where he was concentrating on plumbing, though, he said, "I was moving into drafting, because I drew all over my papers."

Molly distinguished herself in high school. "I took a test, came in third in the city." Duquesne University, on the bluffs just across the river, offered her a complete four-year scholarship. But she still needed money for other expenses. "I went as far as going to the university and asking them about a job. My family was on welfare. I didn't see how I could do it. I wouldn't have had clothes to wear, transportation." She decided not to go.

Bill remembered differently. "I talked Molly out of college. If we were married," he said, "there was no need to go to school. Now," gesturing at the books that were stacked everywhere in their house, "I feel bad about it." Molly was like her father. She had an inquiring and retentive mind. She read everything she could get her hands on,

Bill Rush at about eighteen.   Bill and Molly, 1953.

absorbing and mastering what she read, integrating it with what she believed.

Her brother David thought "she was goofy not to take [the scholarship]," having seen her oblivious to family chaos when she was absorbed in a book. "I think that uppermost in her mind was trying to get out of that crazy house we lived in at the time."

They were married in 1953. "We were very, very close—extremely close—for the first five years," Molly said. One reason Bill appealed to her was that he drank no liquor—still does not. He would be, she thought, the sort of steady, reliable husband and father she had never had. Like her mother before her, Molly started having babies right away.

"We babysat," said Mary Catherine. "We were at their house all the time." The Rush household was a refuge for her sisters and brothers, when they needed to get away from their own house. "Any time we went there, Molly made you feel extremely welcome and comfortable."

Joann concurred. "Molly didn't know how to say no. I could call in the middle of the night, me, anybody." She associated this generous shortcoming with the power of the Berrigans and John Schuchardt over Molly's life: in her view Molly could not say no to them, either. "She

Molly and Bill ready for Molly's senior prom, 1953.

Molly in her wedding dress, 1954.

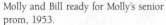

wasn't always committed to social action. She did all this." She swept her arm around her own well-kept kitchen with its yellow tablecloth and tasteful arrangements. "Taking care of the house, taking care of the kids, making dinner. She should have gone to college, but she got married." It had been, thought Joann, the wrong thing to do, "especially for someone as intelligent as Molly." It was Joann who had diagnosed her father's alcoholism as owing to frustrated intellectual needs.

"She always had her nose in a book," said Mary Catherine. And Molly's daughter Linda, pregnant with her first child, recounted, "She could always concentrate. I remember when we were little, she'd read, and we'd jump on her and demand attention and she'd just block us out."

All those years, even after she'd begun to work part-time at the Thomas Merton Center, Molly said, "I'd be home for lunch. I'd be racing, try to be home for dinner and weekends. But not Bill." Bill had "various obsessions that have separated him from taking part in family life." Foremost among them was softball. He played softball, organized

Molly holding Linda, Bill holding Gary, 1957.

softball teams and leagues, umpired softball games, found and sched-
uled umpires for all the games he didn't umpire himself. "It would have
been easier for me if he had had a lover instead of softball," said Molly.

"Bill is a good person," Joann said. "But he's obsessive, like Molly.
It's a good thing he drinks Pepsi and not beer. He just drinks Pepsi and
eats hamburgers."

"Molly was mad when I had a softball game when she was having a
baby," Bill told me matter-of-factly. Sometimes he thought she was
simply getting back at him. "I been hell to her, I know that."

"He has a personality problem. I've never quite understood it. It
goes very deep," Molly said. "Even when he *has* been home, he's been
on the phone or watching TV. So there's been an absence even in his
presence. For twenty years we took no real vacation because of softball,
because of his absolute fanaticism." Family life "is something he's
missed. I've been sorry. I've always enjoyed the kids." Further, she said
with an edge to her voice, "he never checked *his* activities out with *me*."

Their younger daughter, Janine, thought that probably "when they first married, they had the same ideals." But, she said, "I can see my Mom is growing and changing because she got more involved. One issue leads to another. My Dad's been a draftsman for over twenty years. Mom's looking at the broad aspect. He's looking at life a different way."

Parallel lives, Molly said, for over twenty years, two separate lines that didn't come together. Now Bill insisted that Molly must put the family first and do it in the way he understood. "She felt I put softball before everything. Now I feel she puts this before everything," Bill said.

"Twenty years can't be forgotten," Molly thought. When Bill was away, preoccupied with softball, she had worked out her own freedom, developed in her own way, made her own friends, some of whom were almost as possessive of her as Bill. In jail, despite evidence of some new openness in Bill, she worried, "I don't know how I'm going to deal with it after I get out, after years of a different kind of relationship." It would take almost more energy than she had to give, as would the demands of some of her women friends.

One friend, Cary Lund, watched with concern and noted "how she's literally drawn the thread out of her inner being, how she tried to make them [the family] understand. And I think she'll keep on trying, and I'm afraid it's going to wear her out. I don't know," she mused. "If I were in Bill's position, I'd resent it too. But then I think, goddammit! Did John Brown have to bring a note from his mother to go to Harper's Ferry?"

Her brother Eddie was the only one of her siblings to pooh-pooh the notion that Molly had hurt her children. "Maybe her family's to the point where they can take care of themselves," he said. "It takes a lot of time to raise six kids," he added. Molly thought she had raised them well, though Janine gave her father credit for encouraging the children's athletic inclinations.

Well before she left Pittsburgh, Molly spent some time with each child, explaining what she was planning—not the details, but that she might be in jail as a consequence—and why she felt so urgently called to action. Gary, twenty-five, a part-time bartender who lived at home, asked her "penetrating questions," recalled Molly, "and then he said, 'Mother, you have to follow your conscience.'" She went through "a real thing with Linda," who at twenty-three was a housekeeper at a county hospital. She and her husband lived in a smaller version of her parents' house not far from the Rush household. "I didn't try to persuade her," said Linda. "You can't talk my mother out of *anything*."

The Moore family in 1956. Back row: James, David, Molly, Joann, Mary Catherine. Front row:
Tom, Barbara, Molly's mother holding Molly's son, Gary, Molly's father, Ed.

Molly had told Janine, a senior at Indiana University of Pennsylvania, when they were swimming in the municipal pool. "We both got to
the same side of the pool and she told me," said Janine, a born-again
Christian, who saw her mother as "following through on her beliefs."
Bill noted later that, though Molly found Janine's born-again enthusiasm somewhat hard to accept, "Molly's just like her."

Dan, a nineteen-year-old printer, "asked the hardest questions for
me," said Molly. "He said, 'Mother, I don't know what I'd have done
without you if I were Bob and Greg's age.'" His adolescence had been
turbulent and troubled, and his mother had been a bulwark of steadi-
ness and love. Bobby was fourteen. "She kind of told us that she was
going soon and asked if we understood her," he said softly. "She said
she might be going to jail. I thought she was right, but wished someone
else could do it." Greg, twelve, chimed in, "I don't like the idea of
blowing up the world."

When I interviewed her in jail, Molly's voice grew husky as she talked about her youngest sons. "I worry a lot about Bob and Greg, naturally. But I'd talked to them over a period of months as to what was going on in my head, trying to help them to understand." She wanted them to know that being a mother, in this instance, at this time in history, required leaving them and doing what she could to render the implements of death harmless. Both motherly instinct and the culture in which she lived compelled her action, though very few who shared her culture saw it that way. She thought it was futile to see to it that her children were fed, clothed, educated, well brought up, schooled in religion, if the only future that lay before them was extinction.

The children were all torn between admiration for her intervention, which they understood to have been on their behalf, and their wish that their mother could continue as she had been, working, cooking, spending time with them. "I just miss her so much," said Linda, her eyes filling. "It was so nice when I first got married. That house was so noisy. I'd talk to her by phone, do my laundry there." All the children were close to their mother. "We could always sit down and talk, if something was bothering me," said Linda. "You can talk to her about anything." For Linda, "When she believes in something, she really believes in it," though she thought it curious that "she believes in women's lib so much, but it was me and Janine who always did the work. She couldn't get the boys to do it."

As Molly saw it, however, she had raised her children to be self-sufficient, and now that she was away from home, Gary and Dan and the younger boys could take responsibility. "I think it did good for all of us," offered Dan.

Linda, pregnant, found her mother's example both moving and troubling. "I think there *will* be a nuclear war," she fretted. "I think more people should stand up against it. I don't think it's up to the people who run the country. They act like it's their decision. It's not."

Janine, accustomed to "leaving [her] life up to the Lord," said, "Your beliefs are the most important thing about you. She's following through on her beliefs." When she was young, Janine said, her mother had given her the "love and attention that you need from a mother, and also she can look at the world that we have to go out and live in and can show us it's not just the world of the kitchen, that whatever you do counts."

Dan took a pessimistic view. "Man's going to destroy himself, because man makes too many mistakes." But he was impressed at how well he and his siblings had taken over running the house. "We all knew we had to do something, or the house was going to fall to shambles." He had dreaded seeing her in prison because "the low-life of the earth is supposed to be in prison. But she would come out with such a smile, I just couldn't believe it."

Bob continued to help with housework even after Molly came home. His reaction to seeing his mother in prison was to try "to think of ways to break her out [of jail]. People disagree with her," said Bob. "They think if we stop making nuclear warheads and that, then we're an open target. I think that it's true a little bit."

"She thinks," said Greg, always crisp and to-the-point, "we should just stop." He had tried his hand at cooking while Molly was in jail, and while Gary and I talked, Greg helped his mother make an apple crisp. And Bobby cleaned up part of the cellar unasked, a job, Molly said, "he knows I can't stand."

Molly had understood, as few of her contemporaries did, that the continuity of her life—the life of her family and even her species—depended on a kind of discontinuity. She knew and felt clearly that, so long as life went on as usual, the threat of extinction would hang over and corrupt all she held dear. In a small way, in the painful rearrangement of the relations immediately around her, among those nearest and dearest to her, she was able to see the remarkable impact of an action taken by one person.

6

"We may come more close to the point"

"GARY BEGAN to do the shopping when I was in jail," said Molly. "He brought the groceries home the other day, and I started to help him put them away, and he said, 'I have my own system, Mother. You can fold the bags.'" She laughed. "That says to me, the revolution's already begun."

The revolution Molly had in mind did not occur at the barricades. Its power did not grow out of the barrel of a gun. It was a revolution of recovery, of mending.

Mending has always been thought a woman's business—repairing the splits in seams, the holes in stockings, the hurts incurred at play, at work, or in battle. Some of the divisions are very deep, attributed to human nature—between men's business and women's concerns, between public and private affairs, between the great and the homely, between enemies and friends, between working outside and inside the home, between action and belief. By keeping faith, as Molly put it, she recovered a sense of wholeness. Some of the fractures in the reality she shared with her contemporaries began to heal.

Molly had not urged anybody to do anything. What had to be done she simply did. In consequence, much around her changed, including her husband's and her sons' notions of what men might do to keep the household functioning. Molly conceived of her household as a larger place of human habitation. Its preservation and ordering she saw as a matter of prudent housekeeping. Her housewifery she saw as extending to matters of national military policy. She saw herself as husbanding life

105

and what sustained it. Though she worked outside her home as well as in it, she felt her life as one effort rather than several.

She thought it especially important that two women had been participants in the Plowshares Eight action. In her view there was too much separation between nurture and national policy. Her career, however, instead of working against the well-being of home and children, made the care of children its centerpiece. The gender division was apparent in the notion of the "giving *mother,* who gives her *sons* to the nation." Molly's feminism was not a rejection of her traditional role but an expansion of it—an expansion that challenged the core of the tradition that males should dominate in public affairs. "The best way that women can be women," she said, "can be their confrontiveness with the war system—acting outside the traditional idea of what women are." She mused aloud, thinking through what she wanted to say to a female gathering. "There's a tradition of wanting women to stay in the home, of wanting to push women out of the mainstream. It's part of rising militarism," she said. "The drive to dominate reinforces the military system and the military system reinforces the drive to dominate. Women have to break into that cycle. We have special strength in situations where we're supposed to be irrelevant and thereby we become changers and movers."

She had begun by understanding her immediate and personal vulnerability to nuclear weapons. If her children were the "soft targets," her siblings and community the potential "collateral damage" in a nuclear strike—first strike, retaliation, or accident didn't much matter—then what could possibly be safeguarded, secured, or won by such weapons? Her understanding of family and community enlarged. Her nation could not threaten the lives of children, families, and communities in another nation without putting the lives of her own children in jeopardy. If any children anywhere in the world were vulnerable, so were her own children.

She read about and saw pictures of the bombing of Hiroshima with empathy. "Suddenly I wondered what had happened to my mother and sister," wrote one of the survivors, long after the first atomic bomb had fallen on her city, through which seven rivers ran. "I was standing amid the ruins of my house. I discovered my mother in a water tank. She had fainted." Long afterwards, the survivor remembered her terror. "Crying out, 'Mama, Mama,' I shook her to bring her back to her senses. After coming to, my mother began to shout madly for my sister, 'Eiko, Eiko!'"

Another Hiroshima survivor remembered "a charred body of a woman standing frozen in a running posture with one leg lifted and her baby tightly clutched in her arms. Who on earth could she be?" In pictures and accompanying stories, collected in *Unforgettable Fire,* survivors of the first atomic bombing told of that traumatic event.

To Molly, who also lived in a river city, the voices, though they spoke across thirty-five years and in a diferent tongue, were as clear and imperative as the voices of her own children, sisters, and brothers. The mother who had fainted in the water tank might have been Molly herself, awakened by Bobby's cries, and she might have gone searching in an utterly changed neighborhood landscape for Greg. It might have been her own daughters, Linda and Janine, who stood among the ruins of their Dormont house, looking for their mother. Or it might have been Linda clutching her baby, a charred madonna and child.

To Molly, for whom the holocaust in Europe had been formative, it seemed perfectly clear that she was justified in doing what she could to avert the catastrophe that men, separated from the concerns of household and family, were planning and building. She knew that perfectly decent men, good husbands and fathers, neighbors and citizens, somehow divorced themselves from what they loved at home, to make murderous policies and murderous implements to carry those policies out. It wasn't clear to her precisely how, but in some way these men deceived themselves and one another, spellbound by self-importance, secrecy, and faulty reasoning. She felt, therefore, that what she did at King of Prussia was not only justified, but also a plain, common-sense task waiting to be done.

"What does it mean to trust a parent?" Molly wondered. "How does one love one's children?" She pondered aloud the example of her grandmother, Mollie Austin, three of whose six children had died of common childhood diseases. "My mother," Molly said, "had a big vaccination [scar] on her arm. As soon as it was possible to get her children vaccinated, [my grandmother] did." Mollie Austin had not been able to prevent the deaths of three of her children, but the moment there were preventive measures, she took them. Such action, Molly thought, was the way her grandmother had loved her children: it was the fulfillment of their trust in her.

"I may not be able to prevent nuclear war," said Molly, "but it is possible not to violate that trust. When someone accepts nuclear war, she breaks a trust, because it is accepting passively a death that can be prevented—accepting death for oneself and also for those one loves."

She thought such a breakdown had to do with "what's happening between parents and children these days. There are studies," she said, "that show that children whose parents are working for peace have a more hopeful attitude. Those parents—and they're not necessarily effective—are affirming their love and their children's trust. There's a breakdown of trust and love where nothing is done."

Molly's hero, Thomas Merton, had accepted the Pax Medal in 1963 for his writings on peace. In his acceptance speech, part of a collection called *The Nonviolent Alternative,* he said, "This puts me in the rather awkward position of receiving a prize for doing what is only the plain and obvious duty of a reasonable human being who also happens to be a Christian. It is like getting a medal for going to work in the morning, or stopping at traffic lights, or paying one's bills." None of these acts of daily survival would cause comment. But people exclaimed about Molly, "I wouldn't have the courage myself, but I admire you for doing it."

"People think," said Molly, "that if you do something like this, you must be some kind of heroine. I'm no heroine. I don't think I'm so special. Lots of people make sacrifices for their kids."

She had, after all, stayed up through the night with sick or frightened children, mopped up when they vomited or spilled. She had spent a total of four and a half years of her life pregnant, had given birth six times. She had done thousands of loads of dirty laundry, taken children to doctors, made and cleaned up after meals, checked homework, listened to and laughed at old jokes, sewed on buttons, searched for boots, mittens, and shoelaces, and puzzled over the perpetual mystery of socks that disappeared in the wash. Her life had involved unglamorous, boring, difficult, daily tasks.

She didn't want to be understood as nothing *but* a mother. "That's not *all* I am. But it's certainly part of it." She saw the significance of her participation in the King of Prussia disarmament action as "different if it was undertaken by men and women together." She insisted, "If I was to be described as 'mother of six,' then Phil should be described as 'father of two' and John as 'father of three.' Also, my work as director of the Thomas Merton Center should be stressed." She disliked arbitrary divisions of women from women, women from men. As far as she was concerned, there was nothing remarkable about her, nothing that set her apart. "It's really hard," she said, "to see myself in any other light than an ordinary person thrust into an extraordinary situation."

The situation was, indeed, unprecedented. Although civilizations had perished in the past, never before in history had the human race faced the realistic prospect of its possible extinction, not from an act of God, but from the sophistication and refinement of its own knowledge and its application. Analysts of the consequences of various nuclear war scenarios differ about the level of devastation. The more optimistic estimates present nuclear war as involving millions of deaths, but leaving social structures more or less intact. The more pessimistic, which take into account multiple and overlapping consequences— blast, fire, radiation, destruction of the ozone layer, nuclear winter, reduced immune deficiency, destruction of food supplies and insect populations which pollinate crops—make it possible to predict the destruction of the human species.

Admirers and critics alike marveled that Molly Rush had "put her life on the line" for what she believed. David Moore, her banker brother, said, "I've had people say to me, 'I wish there was something in this life that I believed in enough to go to jail for.' I had a guy say that to me yesterday: 'I enjoy your sister, because whether she's right or wrong, she believes strongly enough to put her ass on the line.'"

As far as Molly was concerned, the jeopardy she had incurred for herself wasn't the point. "I didn't especially *want* to put my life on the line," she said. She hadn't been looking for adventure, excitement or heroic reputation. "Our lives are already *on* the line. My choice was to set some terms on that. People say, 'I have my own concerns, other issues,' and I think, 'And *I'm* the one who's crazy?'"

Six months before she went to King of Prussia, Molly spoke to college students at Indiana University of Pennsylvania, among them her daughter Janine. Most experts were "pessimistic about the likelihood of nuclear war before the end of the century," she told them. "I'm the mother of six children, and I find myself almost in despair when I see how people just turn it off and don't want to listen and don't want to hear about it. Because I want my kids to live. I want to have grand-children, and I want *those* children to live." She spoke, as was her way, in a low voice, which was nevertheless passionate.

"Yet I find people either not paying attention, or people will say to me, 'Well, if we're all going to die, we're all going to die.'" She told about her recent arrest in Washington, D.C., where she had gone to the Arms Bazaar—an advertising fair at which arms manufacturers peddle their wares to governments—carrying with her a picture of a child badly burned at Hiroshima. "I've had that ['if we're going to die, we're going to die'] said to me by a policeman as I was being arrested and carted off in a van. I've heard it from people I just happen to meet and talk to on the street. My brother said it to me. I said, 'What's wrong with you? You have four kids. How can you talk like that?'"

She spoke to the students, she said, by way of explanation to her daughter, why her mother would risk a year in jail. "And it's probably not the last action I'm going to take." Molly was, at this point, considering participation in the Plowshares Eight action, and it tugged at her from many directions. "Right now," she told the students, who were getting the education that she had not, "I'm thinking about my eleven- and thirteen-year-old sons and the fact that I really don't want to be separated from them." Her low voice on the tape I heard of this speech rose a little and quavered. "I don't *want* to go to jail. But I don't know how to make people take it seriously enough to do something about it."

The question, she thought, was much better turned around. Not where did *her* special courage come from, but, "how do *you* find the courage to accept nuclear holocaust for yourself, for your children, *without* resisting?"

From jail she wrote, "Who is doing anything to prevent such a disaster?" There were plenty of people busy making plans and hardware for nuclear war, being paid handsome salaries for their efforts, but there was no one, certainly no official or government agency, charged with preventing nuclear war, despite a rhetoric of peace. "The buildup of weapons is speeding up; the time to stop the madness is frighteningly short. Yet we sleepwalk toward the abyss of nuclear destruction, pretending it doesn't exist in the 'real world,' but only in the increasingly unreal fantasies of arms specialists, those who plan and will execute, in the face of our silence, the deaths of our children, of life on this planet."

Why, she wondered, did people seem so indifferent? "Most people just feel helpless," she thought.

The sense of impotence in the face of nuclear weapons was nothing new. Robert Jungk, telling the story of the scientists who invented the atomic bomb, speaks of a "new feeling of helplessness in the face of natural forces which man himself had the power to liberate." It was a feeling "accompanied by a renunciation of civic responsibility. 'I'm not worrying about it,' said one of the average citizens interviewed in August 1946. 'The government is sure to be taking precautions. Why should my heart be heavy over something I can't possibly control?'" Jungk wrote in the fifties. In the eighties, essayist and scientist Lewis Thomas wrote, in his extraordinary essay, "Late Night Thoughts on

Listening to Mahler's Ninth Symphony," of growing up in a world menaced by the prospect of nuclear war: "What I cannot imagine, what I cannot put up with, the thought that keeps grinding its way into my mind, making the Mahler into a hideous noise close to killing me, is what it would be like to be young. How do the young stand it? How can they keep their sanity? If I were very young, sixteen or seventeen years old, I think I would begin, perhaps very slowly and imperceptibly, to go crazy."

Molly encountered what she thought were heavy hearts under the pretense that nothing was wrong, and this pretense, she thought, was crazy. Not a member of her family did *not* feel dread, as if the kinship with the child who had found her mother stunned in the water tank, with the mother searching for her child, with the burned mother and child in the road, hovered just below the surface of awareness. Nor was there any evidence that the government was taking precautions. Her family charged Molly with the duty to stay home, to raise her children, to recapitulate the generations of their own upbringing. Like the larger culture around them, they clung to familiar patterns, familiar dramas, fending off a future that held either annihilation or a change in structure so profound that war would cease to prescribe roles for women and men, would cease to define national advantage, courage, or honor. Either way, in nuclear holocaust or its prevention, there would be great alteration and loss, at least of the familiar world. It was easier, it seemed, to avoid the future altogether by not thinking about it.

For the members of her family, Molly disturbed the delicate, misleading equilibrium that put off the knowledge that a choice was necessary. Yet the attitudes of members of her family belied their own assurances that everything would be all right if only Molly would stay at home where she belonged.

"For us, it doesn't matter," said Molly's aunt Catherine Whitcomb, rubbing the hand with her loose wedding ring over the wrinkled silken skin of the other hand. "I'm not afraid of death. We've done all we wanted to, all we were able to do." A nuclear war, she admitted, would be "horrible. I pray that it won't happen." Nevertheless, she wished her niece "wouldn't jeopardize herself. If it would help any . . . " Her voice trailed away. "But it's not going to. I don't think anything will help." When she spoke of Pittsburgh, she vibrated with love for the place whose past was her own. She spoke of the unpaved roads, where the boys in her neighborhood had played baseball, where she had watched, a nickel in her pocket, ready to run to the store for a new ball if one were lost. There was the old Schenley Hotel, whose snowy linens she and her hotel-manager husband had once washed and ironed during an employees' strike. Pittsburgh was her place, and it troubled her to be resigned to the death of it on behalf of some vague notion of national security. She wondered aloud whether anybody holding public office was honest. She yearned for the old days, when for her neither her country's strength nor its virtue could be challenged. But the nostalgic pride was threaded through with doubt that nuclear weapons could uphold either, and could mean the loss of both.

Momie Ruth, the beloved maternal aunt who had stood so staunchly by her sister and her sister's family in their poverty, also rubbed her gnarled hands as she spoke. "Everybody's against nuclear war. My son-in-law spent thirty years in the navy and he's positively against it. But he says, 'What can we do? We have to protect our country.' The other countries are having it, so we have to be ready for them. What do you think?" she asked me. She seemed to find her own picture of a beleaguered country defending its shores against hostile hordes unconvincing. But she repeated to herself, "We have to protect our country. That's what my navy son-in-law says."

David Moore recounted the argument he and his brothers had used to try to persuade Molly to be sensible and stay out of trouble. "I said, 'I don't know what you hope to accomplish by this. I can't imagine that any action you're going to take is going to change the government one iota.' She said, 'I know what you're saying, and I know where you're coming from, but I believe that if I don't do something, this world is going to be destroyed. And that's why I have to go ahead and do this.' And I said, 'It's crazy. It doesn't make any sense.'

"I was really torn," David went on, choosing his words carefully. "I believe that something has to happen. It just can't go on this way, the nuclear buildups. It's scary. At some point in time, through accident or craziness, something's going to break loose. It's going to be the start of a very mind-blowing, killing experience." He paused. "My question is: what do you do about it? I can't really come up with any really good solutions. Probably the best you can hope for is that you get the right people in the government, who'll represent you and try to protect the country and your viewpoint." Recent history didn't encourage him, however, and he shook his head, stymied. "I cannot believe that we can put a whole hell of a lot of faith in the Russians. There's no good reason to put faith in *them*. They're not going to throw down their arms. And *we're* not going to throw down our arms, and where the hell does that leave us?"

Sad-eyed James, the jokester and clown, thought deeply in spite of his habit of self-mockery. "I don't really understand everything Molly's doing or talking about, you know, because I've never been involved in anything like that. I've always done my own thing, went to work and all that. Let everyone go about doing what they want to do as long as they don't bug me." It seemed to him that "citizens don't have much of a chance against the government. It takes a *lot* of people."

The Vietnam War had been a signal event for James, as it had been for Molly. "I got out of the service just as it started. I was still gung-ho, U.S.A. all the way. It's very hard to get your own mind changed, but between Molly, what she was talking about, and reading the Pentagon Papers—I didn't read 'em all the way through—I read enough to say Ho Chi Minh had one hell of a gripe," said James. "Most people think the Viet Cong were North Vietnamese troops. They weren't. They were South Vietnamese citizens. They weren't being sent down out of China. It wasn't the case."

James had been anything but a pliant soldier. He got in trouble in the army, he said, because of his mouth. "I got busted repeatedly. They offered me my corporal stripes back to re-enlist. I said, 'Stick it in your ear, or give it to someone else.' I was *for* Vietnam. Molly changed my mind. I never let her know she changed my mind, because, you know, 'Jimmy just can't be serious.' But *she'd* talk. And she said, 'Well, if you don't believe me, read the Pentagon Papers.'"

James had tried to brush off these reports of government decision making recorded in the Pentagon Papers, thinking at first that Daniel Ellsberg was their author and their contents fiction. But, he said, "I figured it out that he wasn't really a commie, wasn't really antigovernment, anti-United States, that he was one of [the government's] main people. Just because he didn't believe in what the government was doing any more. So from there it became very difficult to believe in the Vietnam War. Of course, I didn't actively protest it. I'd tell people why I was against it. I didn't march or anything like that. That was for my pinko sister."

Molly and the others who went with her to King of Prussia, observed James wistfully, were "so dedicated to what they believe. Whether they're right or wrong, I'm not positive. If they're right, it's frightening, and if they're wrong, only time can tell. But if they're right, this whole world is in a state where only total annihilation can come about, at the rate we're going. I don't think they're going to change it. They're reaching a lot of people, but they're reaching their own believers," he said, though they had reached him. "They're not getting to the everyday person on the street."

"Even if she's right," said James's son, who was listening restlessly, "no one's going to be around to thank her." He mumbled, self-conscious and gloomy.

"Some people," James continued, "are going to go about their lives and try to do the best they can, work within the system. Some people have got to be like Molly, rebellious, because their inner self is that way. You can work within the system on many things, but sometimes the system needs a good swift kick in the pants." Overall, he said, he was pessimistic, thinking "the system won't allow much." Several notions of how change occurs or doesn't occur seemed to overlap in his mind. "People will be out in the streets," he said, "not just blacks. It's going to be middle America. I'm afraid it will end up to be revolution. I don't think the government can cure itself."

James was quite sure that nuclear weapons were not built and stockpiled out of fear of communism, as the government insisted. "The economy is afraid to stop, because it's built into the system. The system has to say 'more.' Our way of life is projected on growth. And how far can growth take you?"

The problem of bringing about social change adequate to preventing nuclear war put a parent in a quandary, he thought. "You try to raise [your children] so that they can accept the system and survive it," and knowing that these were contradictory goals, he shook his head. "I cannot see an easy way to stop any of it without destroying all of it. You're going to have to tear the whole system down, from the bottom all the way up to the top, and if we do that, you got a revolution. A lot of people are going to get hurt, a lot of people are going to die before anything good could come of it."

I was impressed, listening to David and James, by the sophistication with which they saw the same problem Molly did. The widespread notion of an ignorant and uninformed citizenry seemed to me contradicted by the way these men, who did not pretend to expertise, looked at the world.

For Molly's sisters, the threat of nuclear war and Molly's response to it was seen in the framework of family demands. Joann spoke against the background noise of "Misterogers' Neighborhood" on the TV in the next room, where her youngest daughter watched the kindly Fred Rogers reassure her that she wouldn't go down the drain. "I totally agree with most of the things Molly works on," Joann said, "but it's not fair. She's never home. And neither's Bill." Joann admitted, "We all have a certain sense of self-preservation. It's the people that stopped the war in Vietnam. But I'm going morning, noon, and night," just to keep home and family in order. Joann believed that Molly was a "family person in her heart. She said she'd rearranged her priorities. This is top to her. She has to save her family. Well," she said shaking her head decisively, "I'm not questioning Molly. I'm questioning her act. I can't change the world. I have to prepare my family to accept the world as it is. She wants to change the world." Like most people, Joann compared herself and her choices to Molly and Molly's choices: something about Molly's decision confronted others uneasily with their own.

Joann had a comfortable, down-to-earth way about her. "It's not that people aren't scared," she said. "They are. But our shock level is so high." Joann said that her husband gave Molly credit. "I think he's proud of her."

Mary Catherine, sorting and folding laundry as she spoke with me, called herself a "middle-of-the-roader, right down the middle." Molly, she said, "is the kind of person who deals with great issues. I think my role is at home." Her husband, said Mary Catherine, "feels that Molly's naive. He doesn't like her action." Mary Catherine's friends, on the other hand, were mostly supportive. "Some feel sad. Some have great admiration. Some think she's on the wrong track. Most say, 'How could she leave her family?' I've been surprised." She laughed. "I told Molly, a lot of people say, 'What about Russia?' Molly said, 'If I were in Russia, I'd work on peace there. I'm talking about world peace, not American peace.' Of course," said Mary Catherine, "I'm personally supportive of her. It's hard to define all the rest of it."

Barbara's family—her five children, their friends, a cousin or two— moved easily in and out of the kitchen where we talked. Barbara's small house was on the side of Mount Washington, not far from where young George Washington had surveyed the junction of rivers below. It meant nothing for the Marshalls, Barbara and Dan and their children, to live so near strategic history, where superpowers once struggled for a continent, but it was a big event for an interview to take place. One child played reporter, her pocketbook importantly over her arm, her notebook ready. "May I have a few words, please?" she inquired, and ran away, giggling. Two handsome, bare-chested teenage sons, still

damp from late summer sleep and showers, ate their noontime breakfast within earshot. Barbara's husband Dan, a chef on vacation, came in
with milk from the grocery store. He wandered in and out of the neat,
pretty kitchen with its bulletin board covered with family pictures.

"The mother's the heart of the family," said Barbara. "She holds the
family together." Barbara said she had felt "horrible" when she knew
Molly was going to put herself in danger.

One son piped up from his cereal. "I thought she was going to blow
up a plant or something. I thought she was nuts. I like her, but I think
she's nuts."

The thought of nuclear war "bothers" her, said Barbara. "But I worry
about things closer to home."

The other teenager brushed past abruptly. "If it's gonna happen,
then it's gonna happen. There's nothing we can do about it." His voice
was harsh and angry.

"You be quiet!" Barbara scolded. "I don't feel we have any control
over that," she said softly. "What's important to me is to teach my
children right from wrong—the important things as they're growing
up. I'm not an informed person. I don't read the paper unless Molly's in
it. I don't know if the others [her siblings] worry. We don't get onto this
subject."

Her husband Dan, a compact, steady-looking man, said, "It took a
lot of guts. I don't condemn her, because I don't think there are too
many people who would do anything like that. I think it takes a lot of
guts, a lot of nerve." Nuclear war, he said, *was* on his mind. It worried
him "a lot."

Barbara rushed in to say, "But I don't think we have any control."

Molly's brother Eddie alone proclaimed, "I was proud of her. I *am*
proud of her. My wife's concerned about this," he said. And it was
Molly's action that "brought this up for my wife. But like a lot of us, like
Molly says, we're just trying to forget about it. I don't stay up nights
worrying about holocaust, but it is a fact. I sure as hell don't believe the
government. Or trust 'em. I don't think anybody has much faith in 'em.
I don't know what the solution is. I don't know."

Tom, the youngest Moore brother, said he didn't think about it. "I
don't sit around and worry about it. Eventually, there probably will be a
war—a hothead or something." His wife thought "the wrong button's
going to be pushed." Their little boy had hives and, in the hot, sticky
weather, was miserable. Both parents were attentive to his restless
discomfort. Said Tom, "It's going to come to the point where they're

going to have to stand, and something's going to happen. I'm definitely against [nuclear weapons]. It scares me to think about it." "There's no way out," said Tom's wife, stroking her son's damp hair back from his forehead. "Like Molly said," added Tom, "they're idols. You gotta have 'em. If you don't have 'em, you're scared. You'd have to be scared if you're the United States and you don't have any. As goofy as people are, you don't know. You just don't know."

But Tom and his wife were very clear about the consequences of a nuclear war. The daily newspaper had run a letter to the editor from a pediatrician who had explained some of the things that might happen if a nuclear bomb were dropped squarely on the University of Pittsburgh, across the river from where Tom and his family lived. "We'd be gone too," said Tom's wife.

I decided, by the end of my interviews with Molly's family, that they represented a good cross-section of the public. Though most of them denied it, they were quite well informed about nuclear weapons. They were disaffected with their government. They believed they were powerless, as citizens, to take effective action. They wanted change and were afraid of change. Molly's family provided her immediate context, but it was also the larger context of public opinion at the time. People knew perfectly well of their peril, Molly thought. They were afraid. They felt grief, a sort of preliminary mourning, for the possible—she believed probable—ends of their lives, the end of all life. Usually, grief calls on community to acknowledge loss and to celebrate continuation. But all around her, Molly saw people isolated, in despair, feeling their trust betrayed and their connection with others attenuated. She saw people holding off their despair, exhausting themselves in the effort to live as if nothing were the matter.

"The greater the fear, the greater the paralysis," Molly wrote. She had faced her own fear and in doing so, found the energy to act. She had recognized what she feared as real and, like her grand-mother Mollie, she took the most realistic preventive measures she could think of.

Therefore, she said, she acted out of hope. "Hope is a refusal to despair," she said. She wasn't optimistic. "It's very late in the day." She was too much of a realist to be deluded into thinking that her own action would change everything, but she concluded, "I refuse to despair, to give in."

Molly had pondered the phenomenon of psychic denial and numb-ing. She spoke of the "unconscious fear" of nuclear war. People "avoid thinking about it. They deny or dissociate themselves from it. They look to infallible leaders to deal with this threat which has imperiled humankind."

Molly read constantly, as avidly as any scholar. For her, not going to college had meant only that she would have to educate herself. (She did, when her children were young, take some college courses, but did not complete a degree.) Her reading was more than simple recreation. It was the way she fed her ravenous mind. But maybe partly because she had not learned the purely bookish habits encouraged in colleges, she also educated herself through action. "I've taken personally [what I read] and I've wondered why other people don't." A physician named Rita Rogers had written an article about the responses to the possibility of nuclear war. "It was almost as though human contact becomes not only diminished but nonexistent when one addressed the subject of nuclear danger," she noted. "Interviewers and interviewees seemed constrained from becoming involved with the subject and with each other. The people interviewed shrugged their shoulders, continued their activities, remained uninvolved, and the dialogue ceased. There was no anger, displacement or resentment about being asked: there was only nothingness and uninvolvement."

Rogers, struck by how vividly most people responded to acts of more specific terrorism, noted that the extension of "our *we* feelings" to a community of parents, ancestors and children produces "increased feelings of security and certainty." But "nuclear issues decrease our perceptions of life, the world and our boundaries. Linkages to ancestors and progeny are nonexistent. Our lives possibly become more 'now' oriented, more hedonistic, frantic in action, and almost more diminished in feeling."

Jonathan Schell put it more lyrically. "Indifferent to the future of our kind, we grow indifferent to one another. We drift apart. We grow cold."

Molly saw similarities between the sense of resignation, helplessness, and apparent apathy in the nuclear age and the behavior of victims of the Nazi extermination camps.

Moral philosopher Philip Hallie wrote of the systematic cruelty to which the "maiming of a person's dignity, the crushing of a person's self-respect" is central. "When our lives are so maimed we become things, slaves, instruments." A "disparity of power" conditions the victims to accept their victimizers' assessment of themselves as having little value or strength."

Molly found the parallel both shocking and apt. "We willingly climb into the boxcars that will carry us to the nuclear death camps," she wrote. "We marvel at the courage of those who refuse to climb aboard because they've kept in mind the destination. We accept the death of our minds to reality and the numbing of our spirits to life by refusing to keep in mind the inevitable outcome of our acquiescence: nuclear war. We're already imprisoned in death camps, because we accept it blindly." It haunted her to know that everything the Nazis did was perfectly legal, that to challenge the outcome of Hitler's racial policies or his aggressive wars was *illegal*.

Molly knew and respected Robert Jay Lifton, a psychiatrist who had studied the phenomenon he called "psychic numbing," the "diminished capacity or inclination to feel," in connection with the Nazi doctors and the survivors of the atomic bombing of Hiroshima. "It's painful to think about mass annihilation," Lifton said, "about ourselves being killed and our children and the people we love. We don't like to think about it. Most of the time, we don't.

"There is a second dimension to psychic numbing, and that has to do with the lack of imaginative capacity to really feel what would happen. We have never been through a nuclear war, or anything on that scale. We have had painful experiences, but nothing like nuclear war. How can we imagine what a nuclear war is like? It's a very difficult thing to imagine.

"So psychic numbing pervades our culture. It's a natural human reaction, but, unfortunately, it's encouraged by leaders throughout the world who are invested and committed to the making of nuclear weapons."

Though numbing was commonplace, though it afflicted the majority and was, therefore, in a sense "normal," Lifton thought it "abnormal" in that it flew in the face of the survival instinct. It was a "distorted" psychological reaction, however common, "depending upon the weapons to save us, embracing the weapons. Security is a deeply-sought psychological and physical desire." Therefore, he said, "we embrace the weapons psychologically as the source of making us secure, keeping the world going when, in actuality, as everybody knows when they study the problem with any seriousness, the weapons threaten to annihilate us, do us all in."

Molly had read a book by Philip Hallie about the French village of Le Chambon-sur-Lignon. There, during the Nazi-French collaboration, the villagers gave refuge to and arranged the escape of about six thousand people, mostly Jewish children. Hallie found that the simple, matter-of-fact hospitality of the Chambonnais—which involved great risk, violating the law as it did—broke through the despair that a reign of cruelty inflicted on them—villagers, refugees, and officials. It was the women of the village, mainly, who offered hospitality. Hallie wrote, "The people of the village did not think of themselves as 'successful,' let alone as 'good.' From their point of view, they did not do anything that required elaborate explanation. When I asked them why they helped these dangerous guests, they invariably answered, 'What do you mean, "Why?" Where else could they go? How could you turn them away? What is so special about being ready to help?' They saw no alternative to their actions and therefore they saw what they did as necessary, not something to be picked out for praise. Helping these guests was for them as natural as breathing or eating—one does not think of alternatives to sheltering people who were endangering not only the lives of their hosts but the lives of all the people of the village."

According to the standards set by the people of Le Chambon, Molly acted normally. Psychiatrist Lifton, who later testified in court on behalf of Molly and her companions, thought she did. Nearly everyone else—her family and community, the General Electric employees, right up through top management and the board of directors, the police, and the courts—indeed, the majority, behaved abnormally. The explanation to be sought, Molly thought, was not why did *she,* a perfectly ordinary woman, act as she did, taking perfectly reasonable precautions, but why did everyone else *not* do the same?

"We all live in a nuclear-dominated environment," said Lifton. "We all try to get through our days, to do our work, to raise our families. We all live what I call a double life, because we know, somewhere in our mind, that in a moment everything could be destroyed by these nuclear weapons, but we go about business-as-usual as though no such danger existed."

For Molly, the decision to dismantle two Mark 12A nuclear warhead components was not only a normal and necessary act, but an act of spiritual repair. It knitted together the strands of her past, present, and future. "By accepting the proposition, as most of us have done, that it is necessary to build weapons that threaten the lives of millions of innocent human beings, that threaten the entire fabric of life on the planet, we have caused real spiritual and emotional harm to ourselves," she wrote. "We have had, in order to remain intact, to block from our consciousness the reality of what we, as a nation, are doing. Once she had pounded on the warheads, a stream of letters and articles in which she explored and explained her action poured from her pen, typewriter and—eventually—word processor. They were published in everything from newsletters to books.

Molly wrote, "Going to G.E. and to jail was, for me, an act of freedom, a refusal to climb aboard [the boxcars en route to death camps], a decision to live. Making that decision was a real struggle, a painful one. But once [the decision was] made, the grace flowed in. I found strength I didn't know was there. I found peace that overflows and heals and quiets my fears, a peace that is not simply mine, but comes from God and is meant to be shared." Among other things, she discovered reservoirs of energy, for "it takes a tremendous amount of psychic energy to keep that threat of holocaust beneath the surface of our consciousness."

Molly's act brought submerged anxiety to the surface for others, however. She crystallized the issue that most preferred not to address. Once the reality of the threat was acknowledged, once the imagination entertained the concrete and specific possibility of the end of everything, action was necessary as the alternative to despair. Molly simply nullified the idea that ordinary people couldn't know or act. She was living proof that they could.

Some of her close friends reacted angrily, feeling left behind. One was resentful both of Molly's leaving the life she had been living and of the recognition that came her way, albeit unsought. "You know, it's like having all your teeth removed at once," said her friend Cary Lund. Cary understood, as Bill did, that Molly had gone beyond the possibility of return to the old ways. "As long as someone else does it," said Bill, "it seems all right. Then it hits *your* home, like cancer or a catastrophic accident."

"There's a certain freedom in knowing you have got by on very little," Molly said, when I interviewed her in jail. "Having that sense of freedom, I think I'm less likely to be paralyzed by what I stand to lose in jail or in disgrace with the law. I find—and it's taken me years—that belongings and a need for comfort can be traps. You keep needing more, the latest, the chic-est. These things become necessities, tying us to the status quo more firmly than ever. To cut loose and to deal with an overwhelming enormity like the bomb also means letting go of this entrapment."

Her observation confirmed that grown-ups lived split, divided lives, torn between despair and the conviction that everything was just fine and could go on as it was. Children, tense under the common death sentence their parents did not attempt to commute, had to try to grow up, to make plans, to figure out the world, to get ready for adulthood, knowing they might be dead men and women if they made it that far. Molly's act accentuated awareness of the peril. Therefore, her family and community wished devoutly that she had stayed at home and out of trouble.

"I don't have any tremendous memory of Hiroshima and Nagasaki," said Molly in another interview, once she was out of jail. It seemed odd. She remembered clearly hearing about atomic tests in the Pacific, and her father saying, "'Oh my God!' This tremendous power!'" Her clearest memories of that time, when she was ten years old, were of the Nazi atrocities in Europe as they came to light in the aftermath of World War II. "[There were] pictures of bodies stacked up and the skeleton bodies of survivors, and I remember reading The Diary of Anne Frank when I was fairly young. But I had no criticism of the war per se."

Like his contemporaries, Molly's father had followed the Allies' every move on the radio during the war. Many young men from Molly's high school graduating class went into military service. "I wasn't politically conscious then," she said. The great events of the world were merely background to her more immediate needs to survive the embarrassment of poverty without being disloyal, to decide between college and marriage. "My Dad was a great admirer of [Senator Joseph] McCarthy," said his daughter, who was honored by the Pittsburgh chapter of the American Civil Liberties Union with its Civil Libertarian of the Year award in 1987. "He hated Eleanor Roosevelt and FDR."

When her brother James was a paratrooper, she said, "I was concerned about him, but had no criticism of the military." Her church raised no questions in her mind about the moral legitimacy of warfare.

It was Eddie's going to Vietnam as a cook "that really clicked" with her. "Here was *my* brother and he was over in this war and I had voted for LBJ because I was so worried about Goldwater escalating the war." It amazed her to think back to what seemed a long time before. Eddie had made the war real to her. "In his first week, he was guarding an ammunition dump near where he was cooking. That's when I started marching against the war. And I wrote to him and said, 'Eddie, I want you to know what I'm doing and I want you to know why. It's because I care about you.' He wrote back and said, 'It's O.K. to demonstrate.'"

Molly was, by that time, already taking the events of the larger world personally.

Eddie Moore summed up his reaction to his war succinctly. "The whole thing was wrong." The evidence had been easy to see, and convincing. "You'd see things on the black market—things that were supposed to be *given* to the people. The South Vietnamese government didn't represent the people. They represented themselves. It was just a bad thing."

"Having Eddie in Vietnam turned it into a personal thing," said Molly. "This isn't out there. This is right here! And then Eddie came back, looking like a skeleton. [Eddie] talked about it very little. All I had to do was look at him, this kid who'd gone there as a *cook* and he looked like a *skeleton!* And I thought, my God!" Maybe deep down, Molly put her picture of skeletal ex-GI Eddie together with the skeletal survivors of Hitler's holocaust. She had a keen capacity to link information and experience together.

Although Molly was marching against the Vietnam War, her main ties were with the civil rights movement, which was where her activism had begun. She worried, in fact, that the antiwar effort was "seeping off so much support from civil rights. I was feeling so much the need to keep working in civil rights, where most of my energy was focused." In 1963, working with Pittsburgh's Catholic Interracial Council, Molly leafleted her own parish, Saint Bernard's. As a member of the Christian Mothers' group at Saint Bernard's, she heard a black priest speak. Until then, she'd learned what she knew about the civil rights struggle from television. "I remember being deeply inspired by the moral strength shown during the lunch-counter sit-ins, as demonstrators sat in dignity while louts poured ketchup on their heads." Once she had heard the black priest, she said, "I was ashamed that, busy as I was with four young children, I was doing nothing to help in the struggle. So I sent in my five-dollar dues and became a member of CIC." To this day, writing that five-dollar check stands as a momentous opening to Molly. It was her entrance into activism.

Before long, she was out leafleting with the CIC, learning as she went along. "When we first leafleted," she laughed, "I'd wear those funny little hats and stockings." That was at a time in her life when, each year, she'd wanted "a whole new Easter outfit, from the skin out," so she was well outfitted for respectability.

"Everything that she is, she is all the way through," said Cary Lund. Therefore Molly's work with the Catholic Interracial Council expanded.

In an account of her development written from jail, she said, "Soon I was marching in protests and helping with the study of Catholic grade school texts. I'd been stunned to read in my fourth grader Gary's text that 'the Jews are the world's saddest people because they turned away from Christ.' This, nearly twenty years after Hitler's gas ovens! Despite church teachings against racism, children were being taught with textbooks that were studded with stereotypes." She and her CIC colleagues prepared a report on textbook stereotyping that, when published, hit the *New York Times*. With all the pressure from many sources, publishers around the country began to revise school textbooks. Black stories and black faces began to appear. "I saw that change was possible," Molly said. "I also learned that it was usually just a few determined people who brought about changes."

Her reading enlarged and diversified. "I grew up with the *Saturday Evening Post* and *Reader's Digest*. And I used to read all the articles in there—even as a little kid." She discovered *Commonweal* magazine, columnists Walter Lippmann, James Reston—new worlds of ideas and thought. "They were all critical of the Vietnam War, and I thought, 'they're right.' I was learning so much in civil rights about nonviolence, and it was starting to slop over."

"Molly will read everything that's printed on a subject," said Cary, who had noticed in the early sixties that "her magazine subscriptions had begun changing."

Molly was already feeling a little defensive, long before she went to King of Prussia, either because her sisters chided her or because she had absorbed the same lessons they had about the proper role for a mother. Cary remembered Molly's saying, " 'People wonder why, with all these children I have, I do these things.' And I said, 'I'm sure you do them *because* of your children,' and she said, 'That's exactly why I do them.' "

In those days of civil rights activity, she said, "I learned to face criticism, something I'd earlier feared," Molly said, and it was a good thing, because she got plenty of criticism later on in her life.

She was excited, galvanized by what she was finding out, by the stimulating company of the people she was meeting. Bill, by this time, had in effect left her for softball. Molly and Cary, who had three young children, traded baby-sitting so that each could take part in civil rights and then in antiwar activity. The two young women were part of a much larger phenomenon. All over the country, young mothers seeing Vietnamese babies dead in their mothers' arms on TV saw their own babies in their own arms differently. All over the country, young women who had thought they would spend their days trying out recipes from *McCall's* and the *Ladies' Home Journal,* and seeing to it that their children turned out right, encountered criticism as they joined in protests against a war that killed babies.

But Molly encountered her first public opposition outside her church. "We had permission to sit with postcards, urging people to support the fair housing bill. We got very put down by some people who were walking in to mass. They were worse than rude." She shuddered, remembering. "I was horrified by that." She had to remind herself, "This is my parish, too! Some people would stop and sign cards. Most would walk in, pretending we weren't even there—even with the priest standing beside me!"

Not long after this first insult, a "tiny band" of people from Clergy and Laity Concerned leafleted St. Bernard's, protesting the war in Vietnam. "We went up with one poster," said Molly, still outraged after years, "and the parish called the cops."

As she recalled those years of learning and growth—as the result of which she became known as Pittsburgh's preeminent "peace activist"— we sat in her living room, both curled up on the worn brown couch, drinking the superb, strong coffee she made. The children had gone off to work and school and she was still in her flannel "granny" nightgown, without her glasses. Her hair was tousled, bushier than usual. She looked young and vulnerable for a forty-five-year-old grandmother who had recently spent three months in county jails and would soon be trying to bring the laws of the Commonwealth of Pennsylvania into practical conformity with the tenets of international law. This was the woman, I thought to myself, always called by the newspapers "activist Molly Rush," as if to remind readers that for a citizen to be an activist was not normal.

She shook her head ruefully, remembering the shock she had felt. "I was really taken aback. Here was the church, calling the cops on religious people that were trying to say something about the war. I think I'd have gone to jail then. I was really upset about it."

The "tiny band" had come "down to [her] house, had coffee and sweet rolls" that shocking morning, and wondered aloud, "where is the church on this, that my own parish can call the cops on *me*!" Once again, it was a personal matter. She mulled it over. "So maybe *that* was a turning point in wanting to confront the church. That put me over the line."

On the other hand, there was no one distinct line to step over.

There were dozens of lines, each connected to all the others, and they all needed to be breached. "The whole Vietnam experience was a growth process for me, growth and learning," she mused. "I was learning to make connections that I'd never made before."

Regarding civil rights, she'd thought, "Gee, I'm late in coming on the scene." But she had never doubted that, once racial discrimination was brought to official attention as undesirable, "it would be fixed up."

Her words came faster as she recalled the inner commotion caused by outer turbulence. "King was shot. [Robert] Kennedy. The Demo-cratic Convention. I wanted to be in Chicago at that time, but Gregory was two months old. It was like a sea change. Every bit of my thinking was just going through this tremendous change! LBJ! It was incredible! How could he *say* these things? The idea of having a president that *lied!* Everything was being shaken. This trust that the government was good and was concerned about our welfare! The whole thing! The *whole vision* of what this country was about was completely shaken.

"I really did grow up in this patriotic era and really did believe that what the government did was good for us. I really didn't understand the McCarthy era. It was clear in the Stalin era. We didn't want *that* in *our* country. And then, all of a sudden, step by step"—and indeed, it seems to have been both suddenly and gradually that Molly's perceptions and convictions changed—"it becomes not just a criticism of this war, that all we have to do is let our policy makers know that there've been some mistakes made, but the beginning of a whole economic criticism, of what the multinationals were doing, of why militarism, the whole thing."

It wasn't just her own private change of heart she described, but a much larger event. "[There was] a sea change in a whole lot of people's thinking, and it was part of just revising my whole view of patriotism and militarism. I wasn't putting it in the light of the Gospel at that time. At that time, I was believing what Martin Luther King was saying. And I was really getting closer to the idea of nonviolence. But I wasn't doing it consciously. I mean, what I was doing was looking at government policy and saying, 'This is wrongheaded and mistaken for all these reasons.' But it wasn't from a Gospel basis." At that point in her life, profound and sweeping change "was just pure pragmatism." The policies that governed public life were "just obviously so dumb and crazy."

The decade of civil rights work led to antiwar work, until the two were inextricable: both had to do with the costly devaluation of inconvenient or negligible people. Molly attended her first national peace conference in Ann Arbor with some of her friends. Though she had spent four years and some summers in New Jersey, Ocean City having become a sort of family annex to Pittsburgh, "It was the first time I'd been away overnight, except to have a baby in the hospital. It was a mind-blower! The Vietnam Veterans Against the War were there. Between meetings, I talked to them." They told her "how they'd carried Vietnamese ears on their belts, the whole experience they'd been through.

"*Everybody* was there. Everyone, of every stripe, was there. It was my first brush with the peace movement. There were all these big battles, and I didn't have any notion what was going on." At the Ann Arbor conference, she heard about the Harrisburg trial of the Berrigan brothers, priests who had destroyed draft records with homemade napalm. "It was a real opening for me."

When the Pittsburgh contingent to the Ann Arbor meeting returned, they had dinner together. One of them, Larry Kessler said, "Well, what we need is a full-time justice and peace center. We need a budget of $20,000 a year. We should just *do* this.'" Another, Father Jack [O'Malley] said, "'Yeah, I think we could get the priests to support it.' We got at least thirty priests who said they'd give ten dollars a month to start a full-time peace and justice center. We went to all our friends, everybody that we knew. Larry quit his job and went on welfare and just took this chance. By March, we'd opened our doors.

"So we got the Thomas Merton Center started. Larry had fantastic organizing skills. I never would have been able to put it all together." But she watched him and learned. A year later, when Kessler moved out of town, Molly became director. The salary of workers was a hundred and fifty dollars a month. Religious communities "more or less donated the services of sisters," who worked as staff alongside Molly.

"I thought, well, it will last a year. Our main goal at the time was ending the Vietnam War. So I didn't really think of it as a long-term commitment. I thought, I'll just do my best."

Sixteen years later there are many peace and justice groups in Pittsburgh, but the Thomas Merton Center is widely regarded as the premiere peace organization, supporting and connecting all the others. Staff are now paid minimum wage. Molly is no longer director, but a member of a staff that has no director.

"The year I started," Molly reminisced, "was the year of the Sahel drought, so we began to work on that." One man, who donated his time, "was very interested in the hunger issue. So that became one of the things we got involved with."

When she had helped to found the Thomas Merton Center, Molly knew very little of its namesake. "I hadn't read any Catholic writing for years. I thought of it as a lot of piety, not very interesting, not very good intellectually. *Commonweal,* at least, had a little meat to it." But the Trappist monk's work, his extensive meditations on injustice and war, nonviolence, and Christian faith, moved her deeply. She grew to love and rely on Merton.

Once, she told me, when the Thomas Merton Center was in financial trouble, she had just "laid it down. I said, 'All right, Tom. This thing is going to die. It's up to you. I just can't do one more thing.'" She laughed at the picture of herself, talking to Thomas Merton, deceased. "I shouted at the sky saying, 'All right! You're part of this!'"

She remembered, blushing, her "famous crying speech," made when the Thomas Merton Center had become fairly well established. But "several people were leaving. We owed money. We didn't know if we'd make it through the summer. I showed [the Sisters of Mercy] 'The Last Slide Show.' It really affects me. And I was so full up with seeing the slide show, with my own sense of the arms race, where it was going, how dangerous things were, and the fact that nobody was doing any-thing about it, I started talking and I broke down into tears. [It was] the only time in my life that I've ever cried in public. And I was so embarrassed. And they were so moved by the slide show, and so moved at my crying and saying the Merton Center wasn't going to continue, that they voted to give us two thousand dollars. I still haven't recovered from the embarrassment." The Thomas Merton Center recovered to face repeated financial crises.

"I've gotten to the point where I just say quietly before a talk, 'Tom, what am I going to say?'" She had for years, she said, tried to make careful outlines for talks. "I just do it so badly. If I have it all together in my mind ahead of time, it doesn't go very well." At that time in her life, public speaking terrified her. "I still don't consider myself a public speaker. but I'm less frightened now. You're always taking a chance." In truth, she was not mistress of rhetoric, stagecraft or other oratorical arts. When she spoke, she explored, worked through ideas, reached for clarity. She did this no matter how big or august the audience. It was her way of honoring an audience, to share her thinking as it developed. She listened seriously, even to questions she had answered hundreds of times, formulating her answers thoughtfully.

"I always knew I was opposed to nuclear war, but I hadn't focused on the probability of nuclear war and the arms race as leading towards it," she said of another important intellectual transition. It too grew out of a conference, a weekend affair in Washington, D.C., that sharpened her focus. "It was shortly after the counterforce thing had been publicly put forth for the first time. And I hadn't heard about counterforce. All this stuff was laid on me at one time."

Counterforce means the targeting of weapons or other military installations. Its opposite is countervalue, the targeting of populations. The notion of deterrence is based on the idea that governments will not attempt nuclear strikes for fear of losing large numbers of their people.

Counterforce, wrote aeronautical engineer Robert Aldridge in *The Counterforce Syndrome,* "has offensive connotations. By definition, it means that nuclear missiles are aimed at strategic military targets in the Soviet Union such as missile silos, nuclear stockpiles, and command and communication centers. Since these targets are 'hard'—deeply entrenched and coated with thick concrete—a high explosive force is desirable and precision is mandatory. These are the targets of a disabling nuclear strike."

Aldridge had once put his talents and training to work for Lockheed, designing Polaris, Poseidon, and the early stages of Trident submarine ballistic missiles. He had resigned from his job when he "discovered the Pentagon's interest in acquiring a precise 'counterforce' weapon capable of destroying 'hardened' military emplacements such as missile silos. This was a profound shift from a policy of retaliating only when fired upon, because it does not make sense to attack empty silos, which is all that would be left following an enemy first-strike on the United States. It took a strong shock to pry me from that engineering career and financial security, but the sinister behavior I witnessed was enough to create the needed jolt." Like Molly, Aldridge took personally what he discovered. He wrote, "It is our personal action, or lack of action, that sustains the nuclear arms race and provides the weapons which inflame hostilities."

Of the conference at which she first learned about counterforce, Molly said, "It was devastating. I walked away saying, 'Oh my God!' I'd been very concerned before, but this counterforce thing! People had sort of got the feeling that, you know, deterrence worked. It's taken me some time to see that the move from deterrence to counterforce, a very dangerous step, is a logical progression." Once you think through counterforce, Molly said, you "have to go back and ask about deterrence."

Deterrence was the doctrine almost everyone believed in. It sounded sensible, to prevent an hostile power from doing something bad. But "it hasn't worked," said Molly. "It hasn't worked at all. It's been the basis for convincing people that they were going to be safe. And so it's been the basis for the continuing arms race."

Aldridge's explanation was that once there were more than about four hundred warheads in the United States' arsenal—enough to do what the Department of Defense considered "unacceptable damage" to the Soviet Union—another doctrine was operative. He thought that emerging technologies drove policy. New capabilities, precision, the miniaturization of great destructive force, were more highly profitable to manufacturers than they made military sense. But the public heard only the familiar language of deterrence, which aroused the supposed lessons of Munich and Pearl Harbor, shared public myths that required no logic. Aldridge thought it both scandalous and criminal that policy makers had kept the American public from knowing about first-strike strategy, understanding of which led him to resign his job as a well-paid engineer and to make his technical expertise available to the peace movement and the public.

Molly had heard the evidence of this shift of policy. With her quick imagination, she clearly understood that, for all its enormous and sophisticated arsenal of weapons, her country could not defend her, her children, or any of its citizens against a nuclear attack, that the latest in weapons technology had nothing to do with defense. She recognized at a visceral level that, while her country was capable of inflicting great damage on others, everyone, from the top officials in the Pentagon to the neighbor children who played with her children on the streets of Dormont, was as vulnerable as the mothers and children of Hiroshima had been.

She had also begun to recognize, at the same level, that none of what she had learned about "just wars" as a Catholic made any sense, certainly not in a nuclear age, possibly not ever. There wasn't any way that a first strike could be considered defensive, the rules of war be observed, innocents, civilian structures, or the environment be spared.

"At that point," she said, "you start to put it together in a Gospel perspective. Because what you hear is a voice speaking from two thousand years ago about the need to love your enemies."

That voice, like the voices of the mothers and children in Hiroshima and Nagasaki, suddenly took on compelling urgency and power. It spoke to Molly not just in the pages of old books or in church liturgies. It was the voice of a person who seemed in most ways quite ordinary, a carpenter who taught the people who lived in his neighborhood, telling them homely stories about commonplace things—mustard seeds, lilies, sparrows, wheat, lamps, and coins. He wasn't an intellectual or a theorist, not a great orator. Even as translated in the time of King James, his words in English lacked the splendor of the king's contemporary, William Shakespeare.

The man who spoke to Molly across two thousand years had no specialized training or talent. But people listened to him, sometimes enthusiastically, sometimes dismissively. He had a temper and created disruptions in people's daily lives. He consorted with undervalued women and with men others considered riff-raff. He cared for weak people, the hungry, the despised, the sick, more than he cared for the high and mighty and the laws they made to preserve their interests. His genius was that as he instructed his followers to love their enemies and to refuse violence toward them, he practiced what he preached.

That voice, said Molly, "has been ignored by practically the whole Christian church since the third century, when Constantine's mentality took over" and the state became Christian, subordinating pacifism to the state's military needs. "For seventeen hundred years," she went on, "we've had this idea that wars can be fought justly. And all of a sudden, I think what we're face-up against is the logical conclusion of all those centuries. And all of a sudden, what Jesus said—which seemed through all of those centuries could be weasel-worded and could be seen as unrealistic—all of a sudden, it's the only way we're going to get out of this. It's the only realistic answer. "So then you go to the Gospels and begin to take them very much more literally. Because, having grown up with this tradition of just war, very well laid out—self-defense, that you don't cause unnecessary damage to civilians—the whole thing is blown away. I just get infuriated now, when *Commonweal*, which taught me so much about Vietnam, is still talking the just-war thing and still talking pragmatic realism and that there are some weapons systems that are O.K."

When the American Catholic bishops met to examine the church's position on nuclear weapons, prior to issuing their pastoral letter in 1983, Molly was one of the four women—the only lay peace worker—to testify. It distressed her that the bishops contradicted themselves, both rejecting nuclear weapons and accepting their deterrent value. She thought they were either not thinking clearly or had bowed to political pressure.

She had once taken a course at the University of Pittsburgh in the administration of justice program. She admired the teacher, found him able and stimulating. But she took "great offense" at his position, which "was against natural law. He was saying there's absolutely nothing that is morally reprehensible. I tried to pin him down. What about the Nazi burning of the Jews in the gas ovens? And he would not budge. Nuclear destruction of civilization? There could be no absolutes. I found myself resisting the whole course. It's difficult to argue with a professor. You're always at their mercy. But to argue that there is absolutely nothing that is absolute! I just found it repelling."

As far as Molly was concerned, there was an absolute. It was life. And the precondition for life was an "alternative vision, that war as an institution, has to go. *Has to go!* When the choice is so clear that it's between life and death, people will choose life." She wrote of this vision as a break "with our warfaring history, when we are able to imagine a world free of weapons and of war and then live as if such a dream were possible."

The thing that made Molly different from most of her contemporaries was that she did not wait for the vision to materialize full-blown before she acted on it. She acted as a way of bringing her vision to life, saying, in effect: these are the last days; it's time to start beating swords into plowshares; I am the "they" of whom the prophets spoke; I am already bound by Pennsylvania law (which lays on citizens the obligation to act to prevent a catastrophe), by international law (which lays on citizens the obligation to act so as to prevent war crimes and crimes against peace and crimes against humanity), and bound also by the commands of Jesus (which lay on believers the obligation not to kill and to love their enemies). Molly was quite sure that so long as the weapons were being built, so long as security was perceived as relying on massive and indiscriminate firepower, alternative visions and habits would not develop. The way to "live as if such a dream were possible," she thought, was to stop waiting for permission and the right time (always some other time), and to demolish the weapons.

It seemed to her that the time had arrived to do something more than she had been doing in her work at the Thomas Merton Center, with Amnesty International, with the American Civil Liberties Union, with the Hunger Action Coalition. She might well have rested on laurels far more abundant than crowned most Pittsburgh women. She had been given the John La Farge Award for her civil rights work in 1979. She had been Pennsylvania's delegate to the first National Women's Conference in Texas. She sat on the boards of directors of the Catholic Interracial Council, the American Civil Liberties Union, and the Hunger Action Coalition. Pittsburgh Unitarians had named her Humanitarian of the Year in 1980. Locally, she was someone to reckon with.

But, she said, "I'd been feeling over the years that something much more serious needs to be done. I was looking for something that went beyond symbolic action." For a time, some of the symbolic actions—like pouring blood and scattering ashes in the secretary of state's outer office—had bothered her. "I've spent my life cleaning *up* after people and the thought of making a mess was really too much for me. But now, I think of the mess they're contemplating—the mess the secretary of state's making in El Salvador. I think of people dragged out of their homes and shot in the street. Why shouldn't he have to walk through ashes and blood to get out of his office?"

Molly met the Berrigans, first Philip, whose influence she resisted at the beginning, "feeling he was too judgmental. My stance has always been to encourage any sign of hope, of activity on behalf of justice. He seemed to be saying these were all worthless, that we were called to risk even our lives if we were to be faithful to God's judgment. I was pragmatic, not certain his methods were bringing any more results than mine." She felt the man's power. "But what could I do? I had a family. I couldn't be traipsing down to the Pentagon, getting arrested. What about my children?

"But as time went on, the question became, indeed what *about* my children? Would they live to grow up? Or would these weapons with their push-button death management go off first?"

She described what it was like to speak to people about her thoughts. They "would lean forward, in frightened fascination as I described the threats posed by the arms race. Then they would fold their arms, hugging themselves in a gesture of self-protection." It was "as though a curtain had come down. I would see that they were shutting it out, the implications—too frightening." She was seeing psychic numbing in action. "I admire what you're doing," she would hear, "but I'm really too busy."

"I began to be more ready to hear the Berrigan message," she said.

She and Daniel Berrigan were asked to be resource persons at a retreat in Cleveland. "That retreat changed my life," she wrote. She had been asked to lead the reading and reflecting on words of the apostle James: "Only be sure that you act on the message and do not merely listen."

"No word about results. Those were in God's hands," Molly wrote. "At last, I was ready to take a step, to act on my beliefs."

She committed civil disobedience several times during the next year and discovered what a "freeing experience" it was. "As I let go of my trust in myself and began to trust more in God, fears that earlier immobilized me faded away. I was more and more living and acting at one with my conscience. So, when the idea of the witness at G.E. was presented to me, I knew I had to consider it seriously."

That idea for an act of direct disarmament and international law enforcement in King of Prussia "came from the observation that it was a really sloppy place," a judgment made by the Brandywine Peace Community, a local group that had mounted protest demonstrations outside Building Number 9 for many months. As far as anyone could tell, the place where the Mark 12A was constructed—"the ultimate male toy," Molly called it—was not under particularly tight security.

It took several months to find the people who wanted to go in. Molly especially wanted the Berrigans to be part of the group, since their presence would signal religiously based civil disobedience, quelling accusations of terrorism that might well be made. The group laid the groundwork carefully. "We knew that the guards that were visible were not armed," Molly said. "That's one reason we knew it was a good choice of places. We were very conscious, all the way through, that we were going to be very, very careful in our demeanor, so as not to arouse fear or bring on a reaction from security people. That was very, very deeply part of the planning. We wanted it to be nonviolent in every aspect, including our attitude toward the people we encountered."

There were some who took exception to the notion of nonviolent damage to property. Molly, however, felt that such property as she and her companions damaged, was fair game. It was, for one thing, paid for from the public purse. For another, it had no use except the destruction of people and their environment. Nonviolence, as Molly construed it, was not to be confused with passivity. It required vigorous action to dismantle the nuclear arms race. As folksinger Charlie King put it in a song later written for the Plowshares Eight, "For swords into plowshares / The hammer has to fall."

The Plowshares Eight were well aware they might be ineffectual, that they might not reach or influence the public. "What we were really trying to do was witness the truth of military weaponry, that it needed to be confronted and resisted," she said. "We were aware that we could do this in total obscurity, that it might be quickly forgotten. But we were focusing on fidelity to the truth in a Gospel way.

"We went in with a great deal more hope than information," Molly said. The eight had a map of the inside of the plant, an enlargement of General Electric's own telephone directory floor plan. And they had studied the outside carefully, trying to integrate the two pictures of the place. "But we didn't know much else. We didn't know if the map was out of date. We didn't know what was there," Molly explained.

"When we were trying to decide if we had enough information to go ahead, we talked about how we might get someone inside that plant. Somebody suggested sending a floral delivery truck with flowers to somebody inside." The idea tickled Molly, who laughed with pleasure at the picture of a Trojan horse made of flowers. There were plans for several contingencies: if they didn't get inside the first door; if they didn't get beyond the second door; if they didn't find the weapons; and if all went as, in their wildest dreams, they hoped. At the least, they thought, they could pour the blood they carried, kneel, and pray.

"But then Phil said, 'I think we'll get in. And I think we'll find the nuclear warheads. And I think we'll damage them.'" And with that hope, they slept on Monday night and rose before dawn Tuesday morning. "The stars were out," said Molly. "I remember one of the men looking up and saying, 'I haven't seen the Pleiades for years.'"

They drove through light traffic to the parking lot of the Howard Johnson's Motor Lodge, just a few hundred feet from the old King of Prussia Inn, and they waited there until they knew that the security guard—Robert Cox—would be finishing his night rounds and unlocking the back door at Building Number 9.

"Who are my judges?"

"NUCLEAR WAR is not on trial here," said Judge
Samuel W. Salus II, in some exasperation.
"You're not being tried for civil disobedience,
but for criminal charges."

The trial, which lasted two weeks, began
on February 23, 1981. The twentieth-century
Judge Samuel Salus bore some similarities to
the seventeenth-century Judge Samuel Starling.
Like the lord mayor of London and judge at the Old Bailey, Samuel
Salus, recently elected judge of the court of common pleas in Norristown, the Montgomery county seat, saw himself as a bulwark against
disorder. Like his counterpart three hundred years earlier, he was
sworn to uphold the law, which he saw as unvarying.

The eight defendants, brought before Judge Salus in the court of
common pleas in Norristown, Pennsylvania, were to him what William
Penn was to Judge Starling: Penn's "whole business," wrote Starling, "is
to asperse our Religion, Laws, and all men that are not of their cursed
Principles." Starling wrote of "Penn's impudency carrying him still
further, to endeavor in a popular way to subject the fundamental Laws
of the Land." Like Starling, Salus knew ahead of time that the defendants were up to no good. "The entire production in my courtroom,"
wrote Salus soon after the trial, "was a flashback in performance that
the Berrigans have tried at least five times before. Their actions were
improper in method and meaning." Even though Salus sat behind
an enormous slab of marble in a large and heavily cushioned black
leather chair, it was clear from the first that he felt his authority to be
both fragile and impermanent. Like Judge Starling, Judge Salus mis-

understood the nature of power. Determined to exercise power, each sabotaged his own authority.

Also like Judge Starling, Judge Salus possessed a wig, though unlike Starling he did not wear it. It was a pretty thing, soft, gray-white, finely curled, shoulder length. It sat on an egg-shaped hairdresser's block made of well-rubbed wood on a pedestal just at the height of the judge's head on a shelf behind the desk in his nicely appointed office. Whereas Starling's wig testified to his enthusiasm for the winning party of political upheaval, Salus's wig had been given him as a joke by the Montgomery County Bar Association in 1980, after his elevation to the bench. Similar wigs had been given to two other judges as well, Salus thought, "because we all have a lack of hair on our heads."

I found Judge Salus in his office in the new wing of the old courthouse. It was Friday, February 27, the end of the trial's first week. Salus was flustered to be found reading a story about himself, with his picture, on page ten of the *New York Times*. "I don't even have the kind of ego that I bother to read the papers," he explained. He said he didn't watch TV coverage of the trial, that he preferred to spend time with his family, a wife and two young sons.

Salus was forty-eight, a neat, dapper man, nattily dressed, his well-cut suits in evidence only between his office and his chambers, where he put on his black robe. The son of a judge and grandson of a state senator, he had graduated from Cornell University, had spent two years in the navy, had earned his law degree at the University of Pennsylvania, and had been straightaway admitted to the bar. Twenty years later, he had been elected to the bench.

The trial, he told me, was taking its toll. It was an enervating affair for him. "I feel I wouldn't want five of these cases," he commented.

Before his election to the bench, the Montgomery County Bar Association's Judiciary Committee declared Salus "unqualified." He was too "quick-tempered" and lacked "judicial demeanor," said the Judiciary Committee. "The political background didn't have anything to do with my competence," said Salus, quoted by Leonard Karp in a series on the county courts in the local paper, *Today's Post* (December 22, 1980). "The bar vote was an attempt to blacken me. Their criticism was bar politics. It had nothing to do with my qualifications."

There was no question that the courts were highly political, as they were in Sir Samuel Starling's time. Karp reported that Salus was a member of the Republican party's executive committee, which voted on judicial nominations, including his own. According to Karp, Salus had raised $19,800 for the party and had donated at least $5,000 himself. Karp quoted another local judge, Vincent A. Cirillo: "Show me a judge who is a good politician and I'll show you a good judge. A judge with a political background will give the public what it wants. The public doesn't want a theoretician. There's muggers on the street. The public wants law and order." And so, commented Karp, "The party gave the people Judge Samuel W. Salus."

Salus wanted the law, which he called "the bottom line," to be as fixed and indubitable as the granite courthouse with its massive pillars outside and its marble, brass, and mahogany fittings inside. Salus explained to me that he was "not insensitive to how the defendants feel nor to their obvious candor." He said, "At various times people feel different things are threats to society. The leaders have to set policy in accord with the consensus as well as they can." The courthouse was the more solid structure, proclaiming by the gravity of its architecture that justice was firmly grounded and would be dispensed therein. It was an "imposing" building, Molly thought, which she had first encountered through the basement holding cells, waiting for various hearings after her arrest. The neighborhood surrounding the courthouse was run-down and grimy and the jailhouse stood nearby.

The eight defendants had considered making no defense at all, Molly said. They thought the destruction of the warheads might be statement enough. "Our expectation was pretty limited," Molly explained. "We felt that it might be very difficult, that a judge could very easily tighten down the hatches." But as they searched for unity, through a series of "incremental decisions," she added, they came to the conclusion that they would "do everything we could to talk about the issue, to focus on G.E., put G.E. on trial." Every strategic decision was made with the view to determining "how best to address the truth in court."

Assistant District Attorney Bruce Eckel, the young prosecutor, intended to make the same kind of simple case that Starling and Howel had wanted to make against Penn and Mead. General Electric's prem-ises and products were private property, and that's all they were. By entering, hammering, and spilling their blood, the eight had broken the laws of Pennsylvania, which allowed companies like General Electric to do business.

Like William Penn and William Mead, the defendants intended to raise more complex issues. As they saw it, their government was engaged in breaking the law: the Plowshares Eight were engaged in law *enforcement*. Unlike Penn and Mead, who had been able directly to

challenge the law they objected to, the Plowshares Eight were confronted by the widespread assumption that nuclear weapons were, if
not a good thing, at least necessary and inevitable. The law, by treating
these instruments as ordinary property, "blessed" the weapons, explained Molly. The Plowshares Eight planned to argue that the objects
they had damaged, though regarded as "property" and protected by the
law, did not qualify as ordinary property, and in fact they *violated* the
more fundamental law.

"Property," argued Daniel Berrigan later, "is familiar to all of us. We
touch it, handle it. We own it. We rent it. We need it. We are clothed in
it. We have this understanding that property is what is proper to
human beings." And therefore, he went on, "to apply the word 'property' to nuclear warheads is to degrade and cloud the issue of what is
proper to us. It is to declare ourselves people of vengeance, people of
enmities, people who are willing to go to any length, including our own
destruction, to make some crazy point."

The defendants were prepared to admit—in legal language, to
stipulate—that they had entered General Electric's Building Number 9
for the same reason they had decided to make their case in the Court of
Common Pleas. They wanted to plead for what they had in common
with other human beings. To make this plea, they had indeed gone into
a place that declared them unauthorized to enter (though they had not
"broken in," as was often said, both in the courtroom and in the news).
They had indeed damaged some of the objects manufactured in that
building. They did not contest the factual allegations made against
them any more than Penn had contested the charge that he had spoken
in Gracechurch Street.

But the Plowshares Eight were prepared to argue that they had
acted in order to prevent the commission of crimes. They were justified
in their action by Pennsylvania statute, by international law, and by
fundamental or natural law.

Title 18 of the Pennsylvania Consolidated Statutes justifies conduct
"which the actor believes to be necessary to avoid a harm or evil to
himself or another," where "the harm or evil sought to be avoided is
greater than that sought to be prevented by the law defining the offense
charged"; or "conduct required or authorized by the judgment or order
of a competent Court or Tribunal"; or "conduct involving the appropri-
ation, seizure or destruction of, damage to, intrusion on or interference
with property under circumstances which would establish defense of
privilege in a civil action based thereon."

Justification is not an unusual defense. A person charged with murder might argue that he or she killed someone in self-defense. The Plowshares Eight thought of themselves as knocking away and damaging in the process a gun held to the head of a hostage. The life of the hostage was more important than the gun, though the gun qualified as property. In the litany of natural rights, life came before property. They also thought that General Electric's property put into jeopardy all other property. The warheads did not yet officially belong to the government, though the taxpayer had already shelled out handsomely for the work that General Electric did.

Grotius had formulated international law on the premise that "things which are manifestly iniquitous are not to be done." Grotius admitted, "There is no lack of men who view this branch of law with contempt as having no reality outside of an empty name." But, he said, "The maintenance of the social order, which is consonant with human intelligence, is the source of law." Therefore, "The state which transgresses the law of nature and of nations cuts away also the bulwarks which safeguard its own future peace."

When William Penn made his case in Sir Samuel Starling's court, harping on "fundamental law," he referred to the idea that there are some laws that may not be broken even by governments. Fundamental or natural laws have been held superior to the enactments of parliaments, presidents, kings, and courts since ancient Greek and Roman times. Penn made specific reference to the Magna Carta, which spelled out—for the first time in England—limits on a king's power, reserving to individuals certain inviolable rights. They could not be robbed or ruined at the ruler's whim.

John Locke, older than Penn and younger than Grotius, said that individuals arrived squalling into the world naturally endowed with certain rights, which were as much part of them as their noses and lungs. They were naturally entitled to worship as they were led to, naturally entitled to have a voice in the way they were governed, naturally entitled to hold property, which the king could not seize nor invade at his pleasure. The concept of private property, with which the Commonwealth of Pennsylvania intended to defend General Electric's right to manufacture nuclear weapons, was defended by Locke as a means to limit the power of the government to pursue policies injurious to people. But when large corporate interests can define as private property immense taxpayer-supported enterprises, collaborating with government to make products able to destroy all citizen rights, the notion of property has a different aspect.

William Penn had tested one of these natural rights propounded by Locke during the breakup of church monopoly, when king and parliament, fearing anarchy, sought to restrict religious doctrines so as to control their political implications. Penn and the juryman, Edward Bushel, tested another natural right when they contested that it was manifestly iniquitous for a judge to threaten and punish a jury so as to coerce its decision. The Magna Carta had said that a person could not be deprived of life, liberty, or property without the judgment of peers, and if the judge could bend those peers to his will, it was no judgment at all, but rather fiat. Penn, with his radical, challenging, legal mind, had influenced the shape not only of several American state constitutions, but also of the founding documents of the United States.

The Declaration of Independence based its list of grievances and its reasoning that the colonies should renounce their allegiance to the crown on the proposition that natural and inalienable rights—to life, liberty, and the pursuit of happiness—had been and were being violated by the king. God or Nature had given these gifts equally to all people (although *people* were then defined as white and male). Government was designed to ensure justice, domestic tranquility, the common defense, the general welfare, and liberty for those the Declaration's authors called "ourselves and our posterity." Future generations were not to be endangered, for they too held title from God or Nature to fundamental rights.

Judge Salus reflected on the idea that we can have a perfect society. "Our forefathers knew it was impossible. We'd constantly attempt to reach the ideal." Therefore, he told me, "We have to work within that. Leaders have to set policy in accord with the consensus as well as they can. I don't pretend to know what's right and wrong." For Salus, the consensus was all-important.

For a few men, operating largely in secret—Molly and her companions contended—to have the power to rob or ruin them and the people they loved, was iniquitous. But at the time, as had also been true earlier, to change the consensus required that someone make that familiar iniquity manifest.

The legal community has largely kept silent on the matter of nuclear weapons, wrote Richard Falk, Elliott L. Meyrowitz, and Jack Sanderson in the same year that Molly went to King of Prussia, hammer in hand. Nevertheless, they wrote, "The legal developments at Nuremberg in 1949 reaffirmed the applicability of traditional rules of war to modern warfare [and], in fact, strengthened them by making governmental leaders individually responsible for the policies they formulated and executed." International law, they wrote, "has been at all stages an outgrowth of moral convictions that rested on some sense of underlying reality; a foundation for international law often associated in the West with 'natural law.' " There is evidence of "the illegality of current dispositions by powerful governments toward the use of nuclear weapons," and therefore, "*citizens with reason to believe that such illegality exists have the right and duty to act in such a way as to cause such violations to end.*"

The defendants took the manufacture of nuclear warheads to be manifestly iniquitous, and therefore their manufacture was not to be done. The iniquity of these weapons lay partly in their destructive power: each warhead was capable of blowing up hundreds of thousands of innocents—babies, mothers, invalids, prisoners—and of destroying civilian necessities and amenities—crops, water supplies, bridges, roads, cemeteries, museums, libraries, schools, and symphony orchestras. Nuclear warheads, however precise, were incapable of *not* blowing such things up. Their destructiveness violated nearly all of the precepts laid down over time in international law to restrict the bestiality of war. (The defendants also objected to the vast outlays of tax monies required to manufacture, support, and deploy such weaponry. However profitable to G.E. and other military manufacturers, Molly and her companions felt that military expenditures bilked the public of the funds needed to meet human needs.)

The Plowshares Eight were prepared to show that the laws on the books of the Commonwealth of Pennsylvania, as well as the precedents of international law, particularly those established by the Nuremberg Tribunals, obliged them not to countenance such manmade catastrophes, which in time of war would amount to war crimes. As individuals, they felt conscientiously obliged to refrain from killing. But they also thought their individual duty, their response to conscience, should accord perfectly with their duty as members of the international community. And Molly, as a Pennsylvanian, had the additional responsibility to uphold the laws of her state. Therefore, they planned to argue, they had observed the law, not broken it.

Because they did not expect Judge Salus to be receptive to their plea, they planned as well to acquaint members of the jury with their right to use their own judgment, even if that judgment were not in accord with the instructions they received from the judge. They would urge "jury nullification," the right that Edward Bushel had won for them in the seventeenth century.

The defendants were right about Judge Salus. He did not want the issues of responsibility under international law nor justification under Pennsylvania statute raised in his courtroom. Nor did he see conscience as a commanding concept. He certainly would not be inclined to tell the jury that it could ignore his instructions. Salus might have enjoyed comparing notes with Judge Starling and complaining about his difficult ordeal in the company of the notables whom Starling invited to feasts held during court recesses. Salus would, no doubt, have felt that in Starling he had found someone who could understand him. He would almost surely have concurred with Starling, that were people like Penn to prevail, "justices will be but Cyphers, and sit there only to be derided and vilified by every saucy and impertinent fellow."

The trial brought a great many people to Norristown. Molly's family were there, staying with friends. Family members and friends of the other defendants came for a day or two or for the full two weeks. Reporters from the TV networks, large daily newspapers, wire services, and small magazines and papers were there. I found a young couple hospitable to my need for a bed for what was, at the beginning, an indeterminate time. We had all been patted down for weapons before we were allowed into Courtroom B, an austere and formal room with an ornately decorated ceiling. The room was designed to direct all attention toward the outsize raised marble bench, behind which rose a triptych of gloomy murals.

"Oyez! Oyez!" proclaimed the court crier.

Judge Samuel Salus, diminished by the great marble bench, warned those assembled that he required "correct demeanor." There will be "no outbursts, no unruliness, no unbridled colloquies in the presence of the jury," he said. "I hope there will be no occasion for contempt rulings, gaggings, or removals from the court." Clearly he expected the worst. He might have been Sir Samuel Starling berating Penn for the supposed sins of his father.

The defendants were all shabbily dressed in the kinds of clothes that suited their pocketbooks. All had forfeited good income to do the work they had chosen. But there was also an element of fashion in their choice of apparel, which was like Penn's refusal of "hat honor," a sign of resistance to the court's authority. I suspected that to the judge their

The Plowshares Eight during the trial. Back: Father Carl Kabat, Elmer Maas, Philip Berrigan, Father Daniel Berrigan, John Schuchardt. Front: Molly Rush, Anne Montgomery, Dean Hammer.

fashion statements were an indication of unruliness. Further, they had chosen to defend themselves. They were advised but not defended by three attorneys, Charles Glackin of Philadelphia, Michael Shields of Norristown, and Ramsey Clark of New York.

Glackin, aristocratic and elegant in a silver-gray suit that perfectly matched his wavy hair, told Judge Salus that Molly had not come into the courtroom with the other defendants. She was waiting outside with her children, Bobby and Greg. The guards—"I was overwhelmed with how many there were," she said later—had not been willing to admit her boys, and she was unwilling to enter the courtroom until they were allowed in. "It was one point on which Bill and I were in strong agreement," Molly said. "The boys had started to walk in and they were stopped. The judge had said 'no children.' I was outside, very angry and upset. I said, 'Well, if they can't go in, I won't go in.'"

Salus was instantly imperious. "Molly Rush will *be* here," he said. "Children of tender years are not allowed in except as they're involved."

"They've come all the way from Pittsburgh, your Honor," said Glackin.

"Well, they're unnecessary in the courtroom. I've ruled against," shot back Salus. "Call Mrs. Rush."

There was a flurry of activity at the door, guarded by Richard Giangiullio, the tipstaff, and armed policemen. Molly was escorted in. She looked tired, her eyes outlined by dark circles. It was a hard time for her, surrounded by much of her anxious family, frightened and bored away from home. She wanted them to be part of this event, for not only had she acted on their particular behalf, they represented the posterity out of regard for whom things manifestly iniquitous were not to be done. Eventually, Molly and Bill, appealing to the Superior Court, were able to override Salus in this matter. Salus was, however, a thin-skinned man, who bridled as much at opposition as Starling had centuries earlier.

When she finally entered Courtroom B, Molly said she had the same reaction as in her childhood at Latin mass. "The priest up at the altar. One didn't talk in church. You sat still. And you genuflected when you went in. It was," she sighed, "an overwhelming experience to walk into that courtroom." To Molly, "the whole procedure was very foreign and very pompous." Before any evidence could be heard, the jury had to be selected. Before the jury could be selected, there were various legal issues to settle. Sparks flew from the first.

John Schuchardt had been trained as a criminal lawyer. He explained that the defendants had only just received the state's bill of particulars. They needed time to study the grievances alleged against them so as to prepare questions to ask potential jurors. "We want to put [our defense] in the context of another trial concerning war and peace," said Schuchardt.

Eckel objected and Salus agreed. "That's not relevant."

Schuchardt's rejoinder alluded to international law, "which is relevant to Montgomery County." Article VI, Clause 2 of the Constitution of the United States specifies that international law, embodied in treaties, "shall be the supreme law of the land; and the judges in every state shall be bound thereby, any thing in the Constitution or laws of any state to the contrary notwithstanding."

Salus said no. "The states have the responsibility for the criminal codes. I'm not interested in international law." Further, he said, "this [case] doesn't involve national power or national interests."

"You should excuse yourself if you can make that statement," said Schuchardt hotly. Salus tried to interrupt him, but Schuchardt continued, his voice rising, "Nuremberg said that Pennsylvania criminal law *ought* to be breached if war crimes are being perpetrated."

"You'll have to show me that war crimes *were* involved," retorted Salus.

"I have the right to speak," Schuchardt insisted, intending from the start to lay out the basis of the defendants' argument.

"You'll have the right to speak, like any other criminal," said Salus. Several reporters sitting near me gasped at that.

Schuchardt said, "We have the time here to think about war crimes."

"They're not being charged here," said Salus.

"No," said Schuchardt, "that's just the point."

Schuchardt infuriated Salus from the moment he opened his mouth. Schuchardt wore an aureole of anger, which "mounts when he goes into a courtroom," explained Molly. "John's anger comes out of his experience of jail, of spending days, weeks, months with the victims of that system." She knew from her own experience that "the time you spend in jail makes it clear that people are crushed by that system." A tall man who had come to court in blue jeans and a work shirt, Schuchardt felt his legal training was a source of betrayal to him. He felt that the law served the rich and powerful, who used it unjustly to injure the poor and the weak. He seemed, by and large, a gentle man. His radiant fury was directed at the law, which sustained the violence of a world convinced that warfare was permissible, that comfort was more important than justice. Like his colleague, Philip Berrigan, forceful, demanding, as handsome as a movie star, Schuchardt had been a military man in his early years. Both men held themselves commandingly and spoke in the imperative.

It wasn't until the second day, when the preliminaries had been concluded, that voir dire began. *Voir dire* literally means "to see to speak," but in legal usage the term means "to make true answer to such questions as the court shall demand." A pool of possible jurors, drawn from the vicinity in which the crime took place, is supposed to represent the interests of the community, but not the interests of the parties to the dispute. The voir dire process seeks to establish an individual juror's ability to represent the interests of that larger community. Normally, the examination of potential jurors is conducted with considerable latitude, since the object is to discover conflicts of interest. The defendants thought it would be hard to find an unbiased jury, given General Electric's prominence in the area, but also given the widespread acceptance of nuclear weapons. So they planned to use the voir dire as they would the rest of the trial, to prompt questioning of the legitimacy of the weapons themselves. Each side in this adversarial undertaking saw political possibilities: whereas the judge saw better order in the status quo and intended to reinforce it, the defendants saw the ultimate disorder in the status quo and meant to subvert its notion of necessity.

The jury trial, first guaranteed to English-speaking people by the Magna Carta, has evolved through history like other aspects of law. It developed as an alternative to the clumsier judgment of disputes by combat or ordeal. Usually a jury is regarded as the finder of fact. Out of the welter of information provided by witnesses and exhibits, the jury tries to determine what happened. The judge is usually regarded as the provider of law. The judge tells the jury what the law says. The jury then combines what happened with what the law requires to determine guilt or innocence. In this case, however, the facts of the case—what happened—were acknowledged by both prosecution and defense. The defense wanted the jury to think in a new way about both the facts of the case and the law. Therefore, the defense wanted the voir dire to introduce to the jury ideas of justification under Pennsylvania law and international law, as well as the jury's right to disregard the judge's instructions. There was bound to be a struggle.

To be able to seat the first jury panel of forty in the spectator seats, Salus ordered the public and press to vacate the courtroom. The judge explained his order as a matter of courtroom space. He queried the assembled jury candidates as to whether they felt they could not hear the evidence impartially, in response to which several raised their hands. The defendants asked for their dismissal.

Salus regarded this request as an "outburst" and said he didn't want "any more outbursts." He expressed his irritation. "That's what happens when you represent yourself."

"Our decision to go with advisory counsel was to give us the opportunity to do what a lawyer frequently can't do," explained Molly later. "In a courtroom, [a lawyer] is an officer of the court. We weren't expected to have that legal understanding." Their advisory counsel were willing to advise, but "they took it in good part when their advice was rejected," she said.

Salus took it as an insult for nonlawyers to attempt to represent themselves, evidence of the kind of larger malaise that people like the Plowshares Eight represented. When, writing to Salus later, I offered an observation on one of the legal briefs submitted during the trial, Salus rejoined, "I didn't know you were a lawyer or qualified to analyze the entire spectrum of legal authority."

While Salus objected to unusual behavior in the courtroom, Molly was—as always—pursuing her education. "The whole courtroom scene was fairly new to me," she said later. "[This was] the first full-scale courtroom I've been involved with. I had no clear understanding of what we could and couldn't do. So I spent a lot of time trying to take notes about the jurors. Ramsey [Clark] took better notes. He knew what to look for."

Salus, perhaps realizing how unwieldy it was going to be to question forty prospective jurors at once, changed the voir dire procedure, having four prospects brought in for questioning at a time, and permitting some of the press back into the courtroom. He allowed mainstream journalists—from the networks, news services, and large daily newspapers—to be readmitted. Those of us who were freelance journalists or who wrote for small newspapers or magazines he refused to readmit. "You'll have to do it our way," said the courtroom guard, when I protested that we all had the right to cover the case. I called Donald McDonald, editor of the *Center Magazine* of the Robert Maynard Hutchins Center for the Study of Democratic Institutions, and asked him to wire the judge, certifying that I was a legitimate reporter. On McDonald's say-so, I was let back in. In an exchange of letters with the judge following the trial, Salus noted, "Incidentally, I was well aware that you were consorting with, and sympathizing with, the fringe press during the entire trial and after our interview." I responded that not only the mainstream press, but all of the press was constitutionally protected. Little by little, over the course of the long trial, the public returned to the courtroom "in dribbles," as Ramsey Clark later put it. He speculated that in response to the appeal of the defendants and their advisory counsel, Salus had been instructed by the Superior Court to readmit the public. The exclusion of the public and the press later became one of the grounds for appeal.

At the beginning, the defendants, representing themselves, asked the questions, while Salus and the prosecutor objected to any attempt to introduce concepts of war, nuclear weapons, international law, or the freedom of the jury.

"We're not going to have a circus in here," said Salus, when some questions about nuclear weapons were raised. Such questions, he said, were not germane. The proper question to prospective jurors, he instructed the defendants, was "whether they'll be fair and impartial."

The defendants wanted more detailed questioning. "Judge," inquired Philip Berrigan, "why do you assume that, by some kind of psychic magic, the mere fact of *saying* they're impartial, they will be?"

Ramsey Clark reinforced Berrigan's objection. "You won't permit probing about military experience and contracts," he said. Therefore, to find out potential jurors' attitudes was "an impossibility." Clark, a tall, ginger-colored man, spoke quietly with a gentle and precise southern voice.

"Your objection is noted," said Salus. While addressing the defendants, he often tipped back his enormous black leather chair as far as it would go, gazing at a point well above their heads. Salus had as obviously chosen an adversary's role, as Judge Starling and his cohorts in the Old Bailey had. Arraigned before Salus were eight people who were articulate and sure of themselves. At one point, he complained under his breath, "[They] attacked me personally verbally, and I don't know that it won't come to more than that." At another point he said, "I'm sure you love the odds, Reverend [Daniel] Berrigan, of eight against one."

The voir dire process was repetitive and disjointed and took six of the trial's ten days. The jury panels seemed to find it bewildering. They were nervous and edgy, not sure what to expect, having no protocol for the occasion. They fiddled with their collars and felt for their cuff buttons, bit their lips and touched their strings of beads, acting as if they felt *they* were on trial.

"Are you aware of your power to ignore evidence or the courtroom charge?" Philip Berrigan inquired of one jury panel.

"Yes," said Salus, "you may overlook evidence in total or in part."

"*And* the instructions from the bench," Berrigan added.

"No," said Salus, instantly alert to his prerogative. "They will follow the law as I define it in this county."

Molly asked one panel about the blood, sure to be shown in photographs of the wreckage in Building Number 9. Would it cause them to feel squeamish?

Prosecutor Eckel objected. In murder cases, he pointed out, blood was not mentioned in the voir dire.

"But this is a different case," said Molly. "We are trying to show we're people of *nonviolence.*"

"If you were nonviolent," said Salus, "you wouldn't have destroyed government property."

"Have *you* considered what the government is doing with this property?" Philip Berrigan inquired of Salus.

His brother, Daniel, followed up in his fluty voice. "Would you believe it was all right to destroy gas chambers in Nazi Germany?" His manner of speaking combined solemnity with playfulness.

"I'm not on trial," protested Salus.

The term *nonviolence,* often mentioned but never defined during the trial, likely mystified those who imagined that it referred to a sort of benign and ineffectual passivity. The defendants saw themselves in a tradition of aggressive nonviolence laid down by people like Gandhi and Martin Luther King, Jr., who challenged social arrangements with revolutionary seriousness but without resorting to violence. The Plow-shares Eight were perfectly willing to damage warheads and to shock by spilling their own blood for its symbolic value. They were not will-ing to engage in shedding blood, however, and therefore allusions to murder were misleading.

One prospective juror was not at all sure he could be impartial. "I'm Catholic, and I find it hard to understand a priest who's done anything wrong." It would be hard, he said, for him to judge a priest. "My conscience might bother me."

But what, Salus prodded, "if the judge instructed you to leave out all extraneous influences—religion, culture?"

"I want to say yes, your honor, but my conscience might not let me." He apologized. "Conscience has been drilled into me since I was six years old—that a priest could do no wrong. I don't know." His voice trailed away in perplexity.

Elmer Maas, a musician, balding, cheerful, a man with an indis-tinct, shapeless look, like a comfortable old shoe, put a long and rambling question to the conscientious man, who asked the judge, "Does he mean do I think it was wrong or right to bomb Hiroshima and Nagasaki?"

"Hiroshima and Nagasaki are irrelevant here," said Salus.

The defendants chorused, "It *is* relevant!"

Salus blew up. "Stop this intransigence!" he ordered. "There will be no more outbursts or I'll do the voir dire. I've ruled time and again and I'm tired of it."

Outside on the courthouse steps, supporters of the Plowshares Eight held banners, chanted, sang movement songs, chatted, and joked. They were heavily dressed against the cold. They were met with some hostility. "Why is the city kissing their rump?" groused one passerby. Courthouse officials found the demonstration a breach of decorum. "It makes me want to change my religion," said the woman who presided over the Hunting Licenses and Dog Tags office. "I'm ashamed to be a Catholic. I think we should be the strongest country in the world."

One prospective juror was pleased with the sympathetic demonstration on the courthouse steps. "I enjoyed it. A good show. They were singing good songs and playing the accordion. I liked it." But another was distressed by the demonstration. "I was very much upset when I saw what went on in front of the courthouse. I just couldn't understand that anybody would be out there and having such a tremendous carrying on, just for my benefit. I just felt I couldn't possibly be a part of anything like that. Singing and yelling and performing. It just unnerved me. I just couldn't imagine people just doing things like that."

The next morning, the courthouse steps were cordoned off with sawhorses, ropes, and signs that read POLICE LINES: DO NOT CROSS. The steps had become a kind of theater. The defendants' supporters attempted to show that they were more than eight strong. The city attempted to show the defendants and their supporters as a danger to public safety. Inside, Daniel Berrigan was outraged. "Prospective jurors and others have to pass through police lines, vans, and armed guards and so forth. It creates an atmosphere of deliberate violence," he said to Salus. Berrigan said he had spoken to a police sergeant, who said Salus "had the power of cooling it out there."

I didn't create it," said Salus, "and I don't have the power to cool it. I didn't order it specifically, and I'm not going to order it to be stopped. I'm here to conduct this trial. I'm not responsible for the security around this building."

The prosecutor suggested that the demonstrators might "move to maybe another location."

"They belong *here,*" said Berrigan. "This is the outside scene of the inside trial. They are nonviolent people. There has been no incident and there *will* be no incident."

Both the defendants and the judge, representing the commonwealth, had an acute awareness of the political dramaturgy of the trial. Both tried to set the stage, inside the courtroom and outside, so as to make their case most persuasively. If Hiroshima and Nagasaki were part of the defendants' setting, Montgomery County politics were part of the judge's setting.

"Well," said Salus, "I didn't order [the police] there."

"Well, how about ordering them out of there?" asked Daniel Berrigan.

Molly, the author, Bill in front of the Montgomery County Courthouse, Norristown, Pennsylvania, during the trial, 1981.

Salus refused and tried to return to the business at hand. He explained that voir dire was going too slowly. Therefore, he announced, *he* would ask the questions. Defendants could submit in writing any questions they wanted him to ask, though he would decide which were appropriate and would leave out others.

But Carl Kabat was still worried about the police outside the courthouse. The mild, blond priest proposed that the defendants ask the president judge to remove the police lines. As the defendants left the courtroom to seek the hearing of the president judge, Salus grumbled, "If they can't get a delay one way, they'll do it any way they can." He saw evidence of orchestration. "They've done it for years. They're pros at it."

The president judge arranged for police to stay in the background so long as the demonstrators left sidewalks and front steps clear. The defendants returned to Courtroom B.

Molly rose to make formal objections to the new voir dire procedure that Judge Salus had just announced, trying her hand at representing herself and her colleagues. Although the defendants had at first been permitted simply to ask questions, the judge tried to limit their scope by insisting that the questions be written ahead of time and asked from an approved script. Schuchardt amplified her objections. "This is the third radically different jury selection procedure," he said. "We objected the first day to being given fifteen minutes to reduce questions to writing. The second day, we brought in a panel of forty and about half of them nodded and raised hands indicating that they had formed an opinion about this case. That shows the extent of the media coverage."

"You," broke in Salus, "are the ones who are granting interviews to the press after each session, not I."

The third day, Schuchardt went on, there were panels of four. "We developed an understanding as to the kind of questions that we could ask. We work on the experience of the preceding day."

"The obvious reasons for why I have taken over," said Salus, "are clear to everybody who was here yesterday. I'm not going to have redundant objections. These are just delaying tactics, and you have already put on the record what you have to say. I'm not going to have any more outbursts from you, and I'm telling you right now, if I do—and I have warned you before—the necessary consequences will take place."

To the jury panel, he asked, "Where did you hear about this case, and what if anything did you hear in this regard?" The defendants produced a blizzard of slips of paper with their questions. The jury panel responded: each had heard about the case in the newspapers and on television.

"Can they answer the second part of the question?" asked Schuchardt. "You asked *what* they had heard."

"They said the newspapers and television," answered Salus.

"You asked *what* they had heard," Schuchardt repeated.

Salus went on, ignoring Schuchardt. "Would the fact that you have this knowledge from the news media affect your ability to determine the facts from the testimony and the witness stand?" he asked.

"No," said two of the four. "No, sir," said the other two.

Salus was ingratiating with potential jurors, showing his impatience with the defendants, for the most part, when the jury panels—and later, when its members had been selected, the jury—were out of the room. The defendants, he explained, "have the mantle of innocence about them, even though they are charged. A charge is no evidence of their guilt or innocence. The only way they would be found guilty is if the commonwealth proves to your satisfaction and to eleven others', if you are chosen as jurors, that the defendants are guilty beyond a reasonable doubt, from the testimony which comes from the witness stand, and not anything that you have read or heard at this time. Do you understand that?"

"I'm not sure," said one man.

One woman said, "I work in a hospital. We do discuss things. There has been talk that—well—they broke the law, and the law is the law. No matter who they are or what they are, they should be tried on that basis. That's really, basically, what most of it was."

"I do work for General Electric," said another, "and there *is* talk about it. The only things I know are from the newspapers and television. As far as anybody talking about it, where I work, they don't say too much about it. I do not work at King of Prussia or Thirty-second Street. I work at Sixty-ninth and Elmwood Avenue, which is a General Electric plant also." The issue of the impartiality of G.E. employees was later to be an important point of contention.

One woman said, "I told my employer where I was going and he said, 'You might be on a jury for this here case which is coming up now.' No one said anything about guilt or innocence or anything like that."

The defendants tried to raise follow-up questions.

"Your Honor," reminded the prosecutor, "You're conducting the voir dire." He wore neat dark suits and white shirts and offered his objections with an air of irritated weariness, which seemed at odds with his fresh-faced youth.

Salus scolded the defendants. "I'm conducting this voir dire. I am going to tell the defendants once and for all that there is not to be this interruption while I'm conducting the voir dire. If there is, you will suffer the necessary consequences of a consideration of direct contempt from this court. I'm telling you that right now."

One woman reported that her husband had told her, "You might be picked for jury duty for this trial," when they saw the story on the news. "I said, 'Oh gosh, I hope not.'"

"Why?" asked Daniel Berrigan.

"Because I'm nervous," said the woman.

"Relax," advised Carl Kabat mildly. He wore his clerical collar in court.

"Reverend," admonished Salus, "I'm not going to have this interjection. I'm not going to warn you again," but he did, over and over.

Schuchardt inquired about one woman who said she had formed

an opinion. "How can she set aside the opinion that she has already formed?"

"She has indicated that she would," answered Salus, "so I'm not going to ask her how."

"Well, you're standing up and lecturing her," Schuchardt pointed out.

"As a matter of fact," said Salus, arms akimbo, "I'm much further away from her than you are." But during the next round of questions, he explained a little apologetically, "These brass lamps implanted here [in the marble bench] block my view. So that's why I stand up."

"Would the fact that the defendants have a particular philosophy with respect to nuclear weapons in any way affect your fairness and impartiality?" Salus inquired.

"No," answered each panel member.

"Your Honor," objected Daniel Berrigan, "it's not a philosophy. It's a religious conviction."

Salus must have felt that the defendants were always upping the ante, finding new issues. To him, the distinction Berrigan made was unimportant. "Well, whatever you want to call it. It's just a matter of verbiage," said Salus.

"Verbiage!" exclaimed Berrigan. "It's a matter of life and death to us. We don't have a philosophy. We have a faith."

"The Reverend is cautioned," said Salus, "that whatever the verbiage is, or whatever your faith is, they said they would not have any prejudice against it."

In fact, this distinction went very deep. As far as Salus was concerned, views about nuclear weapons were like views about whether to plant petunias or daisies, a matter of personal crotchet. To the defendants, views about nuclear weapons sprang from divine and natural law. Later, when Berrigan raised the issue again, Salus tried to clarify. "The philosophy that you are trying—or the calling or faith that you have—is a matter of substantive evidence, once this trial gets under way. At that point, you will then be able to introduce whatever you want in terms of your faith and your substance." Like Samuel Starling, Samuel Salus—to quiet the defendants on one occasion—promised them that they would be heard on another occasion.

There was a similar contest about the idea of conscience. Salus told one panel that "an individual juror is not to agree to a verdict if it does violence to his conscience." Conscience, he explained, was the ability "to hold out" on a decision deriving "from the facts that you hear from the witness stand and the charge of the court as to the law as I give it to you."

Schuchardt objected, "Conscience is not related to the instructions you give or to the facts. [The jurors] are free to follow their consciences regardless of the law."

No, said Salus, "The matter of individual conscience arises from the facts and the testimony and the law."

No, countered Schuchardt, "It's implanted in every individual. It doesn't ·come from the law. That's as to right and wrong, ultimate, fundamental right and wrong."

Father Kabat inquired, "So if their conscience—before God—says that I'm guilty or not guilty, they should wipe that off and do as you say?"

"This is not," Salus explained, "an ecclesiastic or clerical conscience that's involved here. It is a conscience with respect to a juror based on the facts of the case." He seemed to have a picture of conscience as something like a wardrobe, different suits for different occasions.

When the defendants had written down the questions they wanted him to use for the voir dire, he paged through them rapidly and ruled out all but a few, explaining that the questions suggested were meant "to slow up the jury process," though Daniel Berrigan pointed out that "dispatch [had] not been promoted" under the judge's questioning.

Salus asked one panel, "Has anything that has happened here prejudiced you?"

Schuchardt interjected, "How likely do you think it is if you ask a juror whether they are biased or prejudiced, that they will say yes?"

"The question as I read it," said Salus, "was 'Has anything occurred this morning to create prejudice in your minds?'" His patience was elaborate. "Now anything is anything under the clear blue sun—and red blood." Interestingly, the trial transcript here differs from my notes. The transcript reads "anything under the clear blue sky." I noted Salus's odd metaphor and underlined it in my notes.

The defendants subsided as jury panels responded "yes" or "no" to questions asked in quick succession. After a while, Anne Montgomery stood to say, in clear tones, "We would like it on record that our silence in seeming acceptance of the questioning process was just because we felt that it was fruitless to intervene. We do not feel," she said, addressing a jury panel, "that we had a chance to know you or you to know us, or that we had an adequate ability to probe your real opinions on any of these subjects we feel are crucial." She was thin, intent, and scholarly-looking with a fresh-scrubbed complexion and a cap of gray hair.

Molly also rose to object to the explanation the judge had given of the justification defense. He had kept to abstractions: justification, he had said, meant "an excuse, or no responsibility." The behavior of the defendants, said Molly, was neither to be excused nor considered irresponsible. She wanted Salus to give examples.

Salus suggested someone receiving a vase as a gift, not knowing it had been stolen.

Elmer Maas suggested that a better example would be bursting into a burning house to warn or rescue its occupants.

But that, Salus objected, "is really absurd. If there is no crime in going in to save human life, there is no crime at all."

"Exactly, Judge," said Molly. "Thank you."

It seemed, for a moment, as if recognition broke through. Salus used the example of the burning house thereafter, though it undermined his insistence on the simplicity of the issue before him. To explain justification as he did seemed to the defendants to be a promise that their justification defense would be heard.

Salus explained the presumption of innocence to a woman who wasn't sure she understood. "Every criminal defendant is presumed innocent. That means that they are innocent at this time, even though there are charges against them."

"It's a question you have to think over a long time," she said with a soft laugh. "It's not easy to do this," but yes, she could presume innocence.

Philip Berrigan asked, "Do you believe that we *broke* in?"

"Excuse me?" asked Salus.

"There's a huge difference," said Daniel Berrigan, "between breaking in and walking in."

"You do not incur upon their province to be the exclusive judges of the facts," said Salus. "I am not going to invade the province of the jury to find the facts in this case," and he was correct that whether the eight had broken in or simply walked in was for the jury to determine. But the press almost always used the term "broke in."

Prosecutor Eckel reminded Salus, "Your Honor ruled that you were going to do the voir dire and there have been three questions that have been asked by the defendants."

"You know how to raise any questions that you want," Salus admonished. "I told you that you have the perfect right to write any questions that you want."

"The problem is," said Elmer Maas, "that we *have* raised the questions and they haven't been asked."

Out of the jury panel's hearing, Salus and the defendants discussed whether working for General Electric, in any capacity, at any plant, ought to disqualify a person for jury duty in this case.

Schuchardt argued, "[Since] General Electric is the complaining party, they shouldn't be allowed to sit on the jury."

"I think a person who is working for G.E. certainly is not going to feel the same," said Molly.

Salus interrupted her. "If he is selling G.E. air conditioners, he has nothing to do with G.E.'s nuclear warheads or anything. General Electric is a very big, big company." This was one of the few times during the trial that Salus used the term "warhead," which he tried as much as possible to keep out of the courtroom.

"G.E. employees receive their paychecks from G.E. They are biased in favor of where their bread comes from," said Daniel Berrigan.

Salus thought not. "That employee of G.E. works in the city. He doesn't know anything about this plant out here."

Schuchardt doubted that idea. "One of our friends," who "has a brother-in-law who works for General Electric in Virginia, three hundred miles away, and they are all talking about the case down there. They have all formed an opinion."

"So has everybody around here," said Salus, "because they read about it in the newspapers."

"I'm glad you acknowledge that," said Schuchardt. It was his contention that, in such a high-publicity case, a more careful voir dire was needed.

"And you give them interviews," retorted Salus. He added, "If I feel they should be removed for cause, they will be." Salus was sore on the subject of news media coverage. "You know, Mr. Schuchardt, I didn't give individual interviews. I didn't give various statements to the press. We all want freedom of the press and freedom of speech. Now that you're exercising it, and it is being published, you are objecting to it."

"We are not required to suspend our Sixth Amendment rights to an impartial trial because we have exercised our First Amendment rights," protested Schuchardt.

Salus maintained, "There is a balancing test between the right of a free press under the First Amendment and the right to a fair and impartial trial under the Sixth Amendment." The lines, he said, "have been tediously and carefully drawn, case by case by case."

"I know of no such case that says you surrender your right to an impartial jury or an effective voir dire," argued Schuchardt, "because you have exercised your First Amendment rights."

Sounding like Sir Samuel Starling, confronted by knowledge of the law other than his own, Salus grew imperious. "Well, that is a conclusion and an assertion that you are making, sir, which really is without foundations, which we, in a logical and judicious manner, try to decide."

Salus asked two General Electric employees, "Due to the fact that you are employed with General Electric, would that in any way affect your impartiality inasmuch as being part of the company?" Neither thought it would.

One woman sat by herself in the jury box. The other three of her panel, the two who worked for General Electric and the one who had been so distressed by the demonstrators on the front steps, had been excused. The remaining woman told of the stress the prospective jurors were under.

"Don't feel intimidated," Salus urged her. "You are a star, now."

The woman had small white hands. She kneaded the clenched fingers of one hand with the thumb of the other. Back in the jury room, she told the judge, "There is a group of people sitting in a room whom I have never seen before. We are sitting there. Maybe four or five are playing cards or reading a book. We are not allowed newspapers. There are no telephone calls. After you run through 'What do you do?' and 'How many children do you have?' and 'Why are they taking so long?' and 'It must be a pretty important case,' of course you wonder. I go home and my husband says 'Oh no, you have to go back again tomorrow?' I have been sitting next to this Joe, who I never met before. I already know about his baby and his job. It's strictly. . . . "

"Small talk?" offered Salus.

"We are passing the time talking, because you are sitting there—and I'm a very busy person. I'm not used to sitting. It's very difficult to be in a room with people you do not know." She worried, she said. "What would you do if you got stuck on a trial that goes on for four or five weeks? I would probably end up in a divorce court."

· The defendants wanted to know what she had heard about the case. She was almost in tears. "Like I said, I have two young children and I'm a housewife. I do volunteer work. I didn't even read the articles in the newspaper. I don't know enough about the situation to form an opinion."

Salus, perhaps out of sympathy, warned the defendants. "I am going to tell you that anybody who asks a further question [to a jury candidate], that's it." He had earlier charged Schuchardt with contempt.

Somewhat later in the proceedings, Schuchardt said, "We all want to thank you for the last voir dire," in which Salus, despite his warnings, had permitted some questioning by the defendants along with his own.

One woman fretted about imposing her four- and six-year-old children on neighbors. "My husband can't take off from work. I have no family that lives in this area."

One man said, "I don't know anything about G.E.'s operations. First, when this so-called thing happened—maybe I should say alleged happening—that's the first I knew we even had such—supposedly— missiles in the area. They are cones or something. I didn't even know what they were for, or anything like that."

A peppery old man with one leg complained. "First of all, I been sick for two days with a headache, and I got a head cold. I been trying to get off for two days, and I can't get off. I wanted to go to the doctor and get something. I have a trip planned for Tuesday to go to Arizona. I paid for this trip already. I got high blood pressure. I know my blood pressure is up today, sitting around here doing nothing. You should have brought me in here first thing in the morning."

If the prospective jurors grew tired as the first week wore on, so did everyone else. Each courtroom day seemed more exhausting than the last. I wondered what the judge and prosecutor did to unwind. Each night, the defendants, who stayed in the large house volunteered by a local peace activist, had to prepare for the next day's work. "It was an incredibly intense process," said Molly later, "not only in court, but meeting over lunch in Michael Shields's office, then meeting at night." It was "very demanding of us all emotionally. And Bill was extremely anxious and upset, anxious to be part of the discussion and having a difficult time understanding why he wasn't in on the meetings, which were already incredibly difficult with the defendants and the lawyers." Bill and the children were housed by another local activist. Bill was unhappy to be apart from Molly. "I understood that he was frustrated and felt left out, and there wasn't anything I could do about it. I had to just focus on the trial."

That intensity, she said, "was broken up by having, sometimes after our meetings, a little wine or scotch—Dan's favorite drink—and Dan would prevail on Elmer to play the piano. I remember a scene where he got Elmer to play 'The Rosary,' and he sang it." Molly imitated Dan, exaggerating a vibrato and laughing. "And then a couple of times after we'd finished our business, we'd talk with Ramsey. For me it was almost like participating in a seminar about world affairs, when he'd start talking about his Iran visit and his trips to South Africa and South America. And one night, Richard Falk [a Princeton professor of international law] and Robert Jay Lifton [the psychiatrist whose work on psychic numbing that Molly had found so illuminating] came over and that was almost like an informal seminar." In addition, Molly and her co-defendants took part in the nightly Evenings of Hope held by activists at a nearby college. Speakers, musicians, poets, and dancers presented their gifts, each evening a different and substantial program. Since Salus had barred the public from the courtroom, it was the only chance for supporters of the Plowshares Eight to get the courtroom news, summarized each night by one or two defendants. Each night there was music. One night, a man with a gray suit and matching hair, a red bow tie and steel-rimmed glasses, sang heartily, "This land is your land, this land is my land." A thin black man wearing a purple shirt and a yellow sunflower behind his ear jigged in the aisle. Children joined the musicians on the stage, bobbing and hopping in rhythm. An elderly couple hooked elbows and danced stiffly in another aisle, "This land was made for you and me."

The next morning, having interviewed Ramsey Clark before court convened, I rode down in the elevator in the lawyers' office building with Molly, Bill, Bobby, and Greg. Molly looked drained and tired. Shyly, Greg gave his mother the starry russet burr from a horse chestnut tree. Molly's eyes lighted. She kissed him. "I'll keep it on the table in front of me and think about you whenever I look at it," she promised. It was a quiet moment, barely noticeable.

Back in Courtroom B, Molly moved—as the defendants had repeatedly moved—that the courtroom be opened to the spectators whom Salus had excluded when he brought in the first jury panel of forty. She added, "Also, I would like you again to reconsider our request for my children to be in the courtroom. It's unfortunate that children have to hear about nuclear weapons, Your Honor, but I think that nuclear weapons are the reality that confronts them, and the possibility that they won't live to grow up is very much a part of why I am here. I have tried to resist this. This is why I want them to hear and understand, Your Honor," said Molly.

"Well," said Salus, "I'm sure that you have discussed these things with them and my ruling still stands." Aside from the fact that, once he had made a decision, Salus seemed loath to reverse it, it was never clear why he refused to let Molly's children into the courtroom. His own children, along with his wife, were present for the sentencing.

A lively discussion ensued about whether several jurors should be dismissed for cause. Salus was exercised. "There was a gentleman here from G.E. and you were screaming and yelling about the fact that he was from G.E. and he was obviously from King of Prussia, and he couldn't possibly not have heard about it, and it turned out that he was down in Philadelphia in another division of G.E. that had nothing to do with defense contracts, nothing to do with nuclear weapons, nothing to do with what was relevant one way or the other, and yet you asserted to me at sidebar that the guy was going to be prejudiced and that he knew all about it. These are the kinds of spurious arguments you are making." And so, he said, "I, in an abundance of caution, dismissed him purely because he gets his paycheck from G.E." He discharged another prospect in "an abundance of kindness."

Again the question of conscience arose. Salus insisted that "a matter of individual conscience arises from the evidence, from the facts that they hear and determine, and from the law as it is given. It does not arise out of the clear air like a dandelion seed and waft through the air on the whims of the wind."

"I don't think that conscience arises from the law," said Anne Montgomery quietly, "but from a person. The person applies it to the law."

Daniel Berrigan added, "Conscience for the defendants arises from religious tradition, from prior training, from the reading of the Gospels, from their understanding."

"You are not on trial for them," interrupted Salus. "You are on trial for the violation of the Criminal Code of Pennsylvania. Any justification or matter of conscience will arise from the law that pertains thereto."

Furthermore, said Salus, "I am the person who is in charge. It is my responsibility to carry out this trial in accordance with the law and in accordance with the procedures in the Commonealth of Pennsylvania, and I intend to do so."

Salus thought a woman who held shares in General Electric should not be dismissed. "Her shareholdings in G.E. are not relevant." A little later, having denied several motions to dismiss jurors with military predilections, he asked, puzzled, "You're not against *all* military forces, are you?"

"Certainly," responded Philip Berrigan.

Salus was incredulous. "What do you expect us to do? Just sit there and let everybody . . . ?"

The prosecutor spoke up, earnestly, "Your Honor, some people might have G.E. toaster ovens and color television sets, and if G.E. went out of business, they wouldn't have their warranty service."

"I would say *that's* a brilliant application to what we are discussing here," said Philip Berrigan tartly.

"They bring good things to life," commented his brother Daniel, quoting General Electric's advertising slogan.

Schuchardt complained that it had been impossible to ask follow-up questions. "Something that reveals to all of us that follow-up is necessary is when a juror mumbles, body language, hesitancy in answering, or a qualification such as 'maybe' or 'I think so.'"

Salus was livid. "I didn't know, Mr. Schuchardt, that you knew the immutable truth of what that body language means, and that you had some seance and irrevocable standard by which you and you alone know the immutable truth!"

Out on the street at noon, tempers were as high as inside. According to a priest, the police had "hassled passersby all morning." When people did not move along quickly enough, several were arrested. The elderly woman who had danced arm-in-arm with her husband in the aisle the night before to the chorus of "This Land Is Your Land" had sat on the pavement in front of a police car when the first two or three persons to be arrested were put inside. "A lot of police cars were here very quickly," said the priest, the first to have been arrested. A young photographer was grabbed as he took pictures and shoved into the police car, his camera seized and tossed in after him.

"What happened?" I asked a man from the sheriff's office, jotting the name he wore on his uniform in my notebook. All I can see now are the 'S' that began his name and the 'o' that ended it; he reached out with a ball-point pen and gouged out what I had written. He grabbed at my notebook—the page is torn halfway out—but I pulled it away, put it behind me, and backed against the granite wall of the courthouse, protecting nearly a week's worth of notes.

Sheriff Frederick B. Hill, a genial, rosy-faced man, said that demonstrators had blocked the sidewalk, that a policeman had asked them to move, that they hadn't, and that two had been arrested. "Others tried to grab and jump on the police officers," he said. Still others "lay down in front of the car and were arrested. The majority of these people are decent people. It only takes one or two." The theory operative in Norristown during the trial, inside the courtroom and outside, was that only a few objected to the government's and industry's business-as-usual, and that those few were inordinately dangerous.

A woman, overhearing Hill, queried, "How come I wasn't allowed to stand and watch?" and frowning, her brows drawn inward, "It's a police state!"

I asked why, if some people had jumped on the police, it was those who lay down who had been arrested. That was all he could tell me, said Sheriff Hill, a little less genial.

Inside the courtroom, Daniel Berrigan protested. "[We object] to the extremely disturbing incident [outside], which we believe is directly related to this trial and its conduct. We would like some thoughtful response from you. We are quite determined to do our best to have our people observe the rules of nonviolence and sensible access for others in the middle of it all. We were wondering if in some way or other you couldn't speak."

Salus wasn't sure. "I don't control the Norristown police. I can't enjoin them from being hasty or something of that sort, because it all boils down to a factual basis of whatever reasons they felt they had to act." But there was concern in his voice. "I am disturbed by this, and I feel that it's an unfortunate incident either way. You know, I feel that in a spirit of peacefulness, that if you are appropriately asked to move along, that you should do so in an appropriate manner, just as I would do, or you would do. It's unfortunate." He said, "I will try to get hold of the mayor of Norristown and see if I can't talk to him, and maybe even the chief of police. I can't wipe out what's already occurred, but maybe I can prevent it in the future."

"Maybe," suggested defense attorney Michael Shields, "you would talk to the captain, just to try to cool things down before they heat up again."

"I will call him at the same time," Salus offered.

It was as if the tension in the courtroom, manifested outside, frightened the judge. "I am only human," he wrote to me later, "and perhaps that is the chink in my armor as in everyone else."

In a letter to me, Salus wrote that he feared "anarchy in lack of rules or structure. A capitulation of 'inner conscience' over the conscience of the community would allow for no rules and regulations. What would result would be a complete lack of order." Yet efforts to quell "inner conscience," both in the courtroom and on the public steps and sidewalk, *resulted* in minor anarchy. Interestingly, Salus associated being human with being exposed; he feared "inner conscience" as he would an army; and he saw humanity and conscience—expressed as metaphors of military weakness and military force—as resulting in the breakdown of social order. The defendants also feared breakdown and anarchy. They foresaw these results in the armoring of humanity and the indifference to conscience.

Judge Salus spoke with various city officials and assured the defendants that, so long as stairways and streets were not blocked (as they had not previously been), demonstrators would be left alone. But, he said, "when there is a threat of breakage of that particular order, they necessarily will have the necessary equipment to take care of anything that might transpire." He added, "Participation [in demonstrations] out here, outside this courtroom, is not in any way aiding anybody one way or another. This is a court of law, and the issues of law will be determined by what occurs in this courtroom."

Molly rose to object to the voir dire of jurors who had been in military service in 1945, when Hiroshima and Nagasaki were bombed. "I think their attitude in the dropping of the bomb will have great bearing on their attitudes that they bring to court with them when we are talking about the morality of nuclear weapons."

Salus said, his voice rising, "We're not trying Hiroshima. We are not trying Nuremberg. We are not trying whether or not nuclear weapons are or are not appropriate."

"Our defense certainly does bear on these questions," said Molly.

"You certainly will be allowed to put whatever defense you deem appropriate," answered Salus. Molly thought Salus had made another promise to permit their justification defense.

"What we are trying to get at," said Molly, "is the attitude of the gentleman [being questioned] toward nuclear weapons."

"The attitude is irrelevant," said Salus.

"Then," said Molly, in a burst of temper, "this court is irrelevant."

"You're losing your coo-ool, Mrs. Rush," taunted Salus, making the last word into a little song.

Molly, recognizing her hot temper, took a few moments to collect herself. "I'm sorry," she said. "I apologize to the court."

"That *could* be a matter of contempt," said Salus, "but I will consider it just a rare slip on your part."

To Molly it was important to communicate with Salus the passion with which she and her colleagues had approached the nuclear problem. "We're trying to defend lives on this planet," she explained. "If you can't understand the heart and soul of our defense and the heart and soul of our action."

"That," interrupted Salus, "will be exhibited before the jury in full force. You will be allowed to do so."

Salus thus once again promised that the defense would be heard, and Molly, distressed by the defendants' apparent inability to "get a jury [that would] understand what we're talking about," took heart from it.

"The judge clearly said, 'You'll present your justification defense when the time comes,'" Molly recounted later. "I remember going to the Festival [of Hope] and quoting the judge and saying, 'This is a very positive thing.'"

It had been a hard day, Salus said, shortly after his exchange with Molly. "I'm going to close the questioning at four-thirty tonight— give everyone a chance to cool down a little. And I have a Cub Scout meeting."

But the next morning, it was as if he had found no respite with the Cub Scouts. Salus seemed tired and irritable. It was the day the *New York Times* had published an article with his picture and an interview. The *Times* quoted Salus as saying, "'It's a different kind of case. In any case of civil disobedience, the prosecutor, the judge, and the jury are put on trial. That's their strategy.'" Further, he was quoted as saying, "'I don't see that there are any international treaties that involve themselves with this.'"

Schuchardt insisted that these statements expressed bias. The defense had not yet presented evidence or legal argument about the bearing of international law, "which of course applies," said Schuchardt. "The United States does not enter into treaties to be told that they are of no effect in Montgomery County because you are the presiding judge."

Salus returned, "The statements [in the *Times*] that were made by Mr. [William] Robbins in that article were taken because Mr. Robbins was sitting in the body of the courtroom yesterday, and he obviously had seen the proceedings here and he knows what has gone on."

But, said Schuchardt, Robbins referred to a private interview and his article quoted statements not made in court.

"I am not under cross-examination, Mr. Schuchardt," said Salus. "This man came into my chambers and introduced himself to me. He

asked me how I felt, and I told him how I felt, in terms of my health, in terms of whether or not I was getting tired, and. . . . "

"And opinions about the case, apparently, Your Honor," interjected Charles Glackin.

"No," said Salus, "there were no opinions." And he cautioned Glackin, "You better not make these snide remarks or conclusions. That is your emotional overlay and not mine."

Glackin protested, "It's an observation of fact." Salus had granted an interview, complete with opinions about the case.

"It's not an observation of fact at all," Salus snapped.

Salus had also granted me an interview, welcoming me to his office because, he told me, he had a sister named Liane. He was open in discussing the case with me, sharing his view that "unilateral abandonment [of nuclear weapons] wouldn't serve humanity or the world." If the defendants, he said, "can raise the issue in Russia and get them to disarm, then their position is well taken." He found himself, he said, in a "no-win situation."

Sister Anne Montgomery, who wore a habit of stillness, attempted to make something clear to the judge. "I wouldn't like you to think that this is a personal issue, although it may seem so. We have been put in an adversary position to get what we know are our rights. We must stress them as strongly as possible." she said.

Salus leaned forward toward her. "I want to say this. In the number of days that I have been here, the one very strong impression that I have gotten is that *you* are from head to toe a *lady*." He didn't want to be misunderstood. "That is a compliment from me. I think you have intellectual integrity. I can say this—though I did not do so—several of the remarks which were made in this last four jurors bordered on being contemptuous. I did not involve myself with it, and I will not involve myself with it. It is gone and past, but I could have."

Montgomery spoke quietly. "I have learned a great deal of my nonviolence from the people here. We are all nonviolent people. We are all peaceful. I think the very terms that are used—legal, the court, whatever—is putting this in a perspective that we are not used to dealing with. We are used to dealing with human beings. I think that's the way we wanted to approach the jury, as fellow human beings, and you can't do that unless you can talk to them personally."

"I understand your position," said Salus, who seemed genuinely touched by the slight, contained woman before him.

Dean Hammer, young, bearded, and dark, spoke up. "Is there any way," he asked, "we can address the hard feelings created between us at this point?"

Salus leaned back. "I don't have any hard feelings at the present time, Mr. Hammer," he said coldly. Then, inclining again toward Montgomery, "I was thinking about Sister last night. I was thinking to myself how I personally was impressed with her character. Let's put it that way."

Molly thought Salus's remarks to her colleague, Anne Montgomery, reflected the "traditional deference toward nuns," as she commented later. "And she was a little fragile-looking. She was livid about Salus's praise. She hated it. She didn't want to be called 'a lady' in that situation." Molly compared the judge's attitude toward her. "I think he was personally offended that I, a wife and mother, was doing these things. I think perhaps he identified me with his wife. This was offensive, that a wife and mother would do something like this. I had the strong feeling that he did not like me."

Each of the eight, said Molly, had his or her own sense of who the judge liked and didn't like. In her view, "He hated John. He did not like Elmer. He did not like Dean. Didn't seem to have any terrific animosity toward Phil and Carl. Dan and Anne were his favorites."

By Friday afternoon, the voir dire, which had gone on for five days, was still incomplete. Everyone needed the weekend. At the Evening of Hope program, Molly said she was finding it hard to keep her temper. "We've tried to break through in a process that's hard to describe, hard to anticipate." She described the difference between the defendants and the judge. "We believe the law comes from conscience. The judge believes conscience comes from law."

But she remained hopeful. "Today the judge said, 'You will be able to introduce into evidence anything you want concerning your faith and beliefs.'"

Dean Hammer said the week in court had been "like going into a deep sea dive" every day. Daniel Berrigan said it was more like going "into the city morgue."

Ramsey Clark had once been the attorney general of the United States. When I spoke to him a few days earlier, he said he hoped the law might rise above its limitations. "Grace," he said, "is an important element of justice." He believed that Salus "could handle this with far more grace than he has. He conveys the impression that he doesn't really want to hear. He's unable or unwilling to do an innovative thing."

The question for Clark was "whether it's possible under our rule of law to handle these concepts. I think it *is* possible, in fact, necessary and vital," he said. For "the preservation of society is the purpose of law. The court could address this issue in ways that could be illuminating. It can't ignore these questions." In his soft voice, he added, "If it can't consider history, why, what an imperfect creature it is."

8

"The law by which they should measure the truth"

IT TOOK SIX DAYS to choose a jury. They were eight women and four men, a clerk, a utility operator, an accountant, two auto mechanics, a title examiner, two teachers, a church secretary, two housewives, and a woman whose son served on a nuclear submarine. Each had been in the courtroom for a brief and disconcerting voir dire, during which each had a quick and disconnected glimpse of the persons and issues in the case that they were to hear as representatives of the community's conscience.

After Judge Salus explained the gravity of the jury's task, the prosecutor, presenting the commonwealth's position, and three of the defendants, speaking as their own legal representatives, made opening statements to the jury. They were like actors in a play swiftly setting a scene and organizing the audience's attention.

"It's not my function to explain the defendants' motives," said Bruce Eckel, the competent and orderly assistant district attorney, presenting the state's case. "I have to show you evidence that proves the defendants criminal in various offenses. These crimes are set out by the legislature." The law, he said, would be explained by the judge. He outlined the events of September 9, 1980, clearly and succinctly.

Sister Anne Montgomery had been chosen by the defendants to open because of the judge's deference toward her. She said she was happy to speak to "ordinary people like [herself], because the decision as to the morality of [her] intentions and actions is rightfully in the power of members of the community *not* trained in law, but guided by their own common sense and sense of right and wrong." Addressing the jury, she said, "You can judge the facts, but also see beneath them to the truth, the sacredness of life and the real threat to it." The defense, she said, would explain *why* they had done this thing. "We're not here to defend ourselves, but to defend human life on this planet, which is in more danger than ever in history."

The Plowshares action, she said, had been "a real and symbolic act of disarmament, too limited in its scope to terrorize anyone, but very clear in its message. We acted from no hatred, but rather from the love of our neighbors in this country and throughout the world. We acted on conscience, which ultimately can give law its only validity."

Briefly and carefully, she told the jury the story of William Penn's jury, "jailed for refusing to convict him." She quoted John Adams, who had said of the juror, "'It is not only his right but his duty to find the verdict according to his best understanding, judgment, and conscience, though in direct opposition to the directions of the court.'"

Dean Hammer, the young divinity student with black beard and high color, spoke second. "We believe we acted according to the code of this state, with its requirement to act so as to prevent harm. Our testimony will explain the capabilities of the Mark 12A and first-strike strategy." Nuclear weapons, he explained, are "a crime against humanity, because they can't discriminate between civilians and combatants. The property we damaged is different from every other kind of property. Just as we would have damaged the gas chambers of Nazi Germany, we damaged these instruments of genocide."

When Philip Berrigan rose, the third of the defendants to make an opening statement, Salus told him, "You have five minutes, Reverend."

"We are commanded both by the law of God and human law," said Berrigan, his chiseled face intent. "We acted in accordance with the *whole* law." He spoke of money diverted from the service of human needs to build elaborate and costly weapons. He spoke of the imminence of nuclear war, which the defense intended to establish by calling expert witnesses. "Our duty," he said, "is to share the reality of our plight. Experts believe that any use would result in suicide for the species."

"All right, sum up, Reverend," ordered Salus.

Berrigan had a commanding presence and he also had information to lay out, which he did, drawing from legal, medical, and biblical sources with practiced ease. His conclusion, like Penn's, appealed to higher law. "We acted to prevent destruction of God's people, God's earth."

The built-in difficulty for the defendants was that there can be no hyperbole in talking about nuclear war. The probable and imaginable effects stagger the imagination and tax the vocabulary. And yet, hyperbole always carries its own caution: beware exaggeration! Everyone who tries to talk about nuclear war encounters this difficulty. And so, in addition to the judge's determination that nuclear war should not be discussed in his courtroom, and in addition to the natural human reluctance to entertain thoughts of a rupture so stupendous as that a nuclear war would cause, the jury was faced with what good sense told them was no overstatement, but what linguistic reflex nevertheless told them to discount.

District Attorney Bruce Eckel called a parade of witnesses, General Electric employees, local police, and FBI experts, to lay out the story of the events of September 9 in Building Number 9. He also introduced into evidence photographs of the Non-Destructive Test Area, taken after the Plowshares Eight had left. The most dramatic physical evidence he brought into court was the pair of damaged warhead casings. It seemed quite extraordinary to be seated some four or five feet from these inert objects that looked something like cheerleaders' megaphones. Direct examination went crisply. Cross-examination was something else again.

"Did General Electric tell you what they were making in that building?" John Schuchardt asked security guard Leon Simmons.

"Objection," said Eckel.

"Objection sustained," declared Salus.

"Well, I think it is pertinent to his job," said Schuchardt. "And I think we are entitled to know."

"It is not whether they are entitled to know. It is whether it is relevant. And it is not relevant, your Honor," argued Eckel.

Salus agreed. "We're after the relevance of what they did on that day, what his duties were."

"Were you going to permit him to answer?" asked Schuchardt.

"I said if you ask him a relevant question," said Salus.

Schuchardt tried again. "Were you ever given instructions in what nuclear weapons are and what the Mark 12A warhead is?"

"Objection."

"Sustained."

Schuchardt paused and rubbed the back of his head as if it hurt. "They won't let me ask any questions, so thank you very much," he told Simmons.

"I think the record will reflect," said Eckel, as Simmons left the witness box, "he was permitted to ask questions."

The jury was usually sent out of the room when procedural contention arose, though most often such contention concerned the substance of the defendants' case. Out of the jury's hearing, Philip Berrigan explained to the judge the purpose of Schuchardt's questions. "Did General Electric tell people what was being manufactured in this building and what they were protecting or guarding? Or did they not?"

"There is nothing wrong with determining what his duties were as a security guard," said Salus, "what he was told that he should do, whether he was told that he was guarding secure places and whether he understood why they were secure. Those things are all relevant questions to his duties. If Mr. Schuchardt had asked the right questions with regard to security and with regard to what he thought his duties were, and what he was guarding, instead of putting it up front in terms of making a speech, those questions could be asked."

"These aren't questions of philosophy or theory," said Daniel Berrigan. "They're questions of fact. Did they know what they were guarding or didn't they?"

"That question wasn't asked," said Salus.

"It *was* asked," said Berrigan.

"No, it wasn't," insisted Salus.

Philip Berrigan was equally insistent. "Mr. Schuchardt asked if General Electric had ever taken any moves to instruct people like Mr. Cox and Mr. Simmons as to what they were guarding."

Salus said, "That was not the question he asked. He started about nuclear warheads and the G.E. Mark 12A." But the question Schuchardt had asked, read back by the court reporter, did not seem so bad after all. "I will allow that question," Salus decided.

The jury came back and Anne Montgomery asked the witness, "Mr. Simmons, as a security guard, did you know what you were providing security for?"

Simmons spoke carefully. "When I was hired, I was not a security guard. Three years I worked as a janitor. Then I went over to Building 9. And this is when I was hired, still as a G.E. employee. And my job is basically in the front of the building and back of the building, to check people coming in and people going out of the building, see that they are properly badged.

"They have to wear it in plain sight at all times. And we have two doors for people to come in. One is the rear lobby, and one is the main lobby, front of the building.

"Now, when they come in, we are placed at the front of the building, as I have stated, four hours a day. And we have breaks. And you walk around inside of the building for four hours.

"So my job is to check people coming in and make sure that nothing goes out as G.E. property."

Montgomery persisted gently. "In your position, walking around inside of the building, were you required to check anything in particular?"

"No," Simmons answered, "that is not my job."

"At any time have people told you what you were protecting in the security area?" prodded Montgomery.

"Well, we're supposed to protect General Electric property."

"Property? They didn't tell you what the property was?"

"I didn't ask them what the property was. My job is checking people coming in."

Judge Salus complimented Montgomery on her "directness of cross-examination."

Dean Hammer asked one witness about what the witness had called a "scuffle" in Building Number 9's back lobby between Robert Cox and Father Carl Kabat. "So the scuffle seemed to be to get the phone out of his hand?"

Eckel objected. "He can't answer for Father Kabat."

Salus sustained the objection. "Don't cross-examine the witness," he scolded. "Just ask him questions." In the appeal brief, filed later, the defendants pointed out that Salus had protected the witnesses from proper cross-examination. It was as though Salus, knowing how fragile the membrane was that protected *him* from what *he* knew, wanted to safeguard it, to keep it intact, for those who appeared in his court.

When Philip Berrigan asked one witness, "Were you familiar with what General Electric is manufacturing at Plant Number 9?" the witness replied, "Yes I am," but he also said he knew nothing about the Mark 12A. "All I know is we make hardware, OK?"

Schuchardt asked, "Are workers forbidden to refer to nuclear warheads or Mark 12A specifically?"

"I don't know what you mean by nuclear warheads," protested the witness. "I have never seen a nuclear warhead."

"Show him one," said Carl Kabat. Schuchardt asked Eckel, "May I have the exhibit of the photograph of these two warheads, please?"

Eckel responded, "Your Honor, I object to his characterizing any of the evidence."

"You asked me to identify that as a nuclear warhead," said the witness. "I can't do that."

Daniel Berrigan piped, "Do you think it is used in kitchenware?"

"That retortive question will be stricken from the record," ordered Salus.

"He must think this is being used for *something*," insisted Berrigan.

"We're not going to have speeches, Reverend," said Salus. "I am not going to have this kind of disruption."

"Do you ever feel there's a moral issue in working on such products?" inquired Berrigan.

Eckel objected and Salus sustained the objection.

"Do you know where the shells are delivered to?" queried Berrigan.

Eckel objected. Salus sustained him. "It may be a matter of security, national security. It will not be answered."

"It's not a matter of my security," quipped Berrigan, who inquired of Robert Hartmann, Building Number 9's manager, about his security clearance. To counter objections, Berrigan explained, "Maybe his promise to G.E. supersedes this one [to tell the truth]. I think we have to find out which oath takes precedence in this courtroom."

"We are not trying oaths in this courtroom," said Salus. "We are trying acts."

Berrigan persisted, asking whether Hartmann "promised not to tell certain things about certain weapons?"

"I promised nothing," said Hartmann.

Berrigan wasn't satisfied. "We want to know the difference between ignorance declared here and the promise not to tell something."

Hartmann said he didn't understand the question, and Judge Salus clarified. "Those things that you said that you don't know about, did you say on the basis of actual ignorance or not being involved in that aspect of it? Or are you saying that because of your security clearance?"

"I said that because of ignorance," said Hartmann.

Berrigan mused aloud, "It's very difficult to understand how one can be so ignorant of what he's doing."

Salus objected without prompting from Eckel. "We are not going to impugn the witness one way or the other."

A tool maker testified, "I signed a statement, I think maybe not to reveal certain things," but it had been thirteen years ago, and "I really don't remember what." It was recommended by General Electric, he said, that employees not talk to their families about what they did, and to fellow employees "only if it is pertinent to what you are doing with them."

Daniel Berrigan said, "Your Honor, the jury are among the few in the world that will see these weapons before they are used on people. Very few in our whole lives see a nuclear weapon."

Salus sustained Eckel's predictable objection. "We're not making any speeches about these weapons—or whether they are, in fact, weapons."

"Laughter," wrote the court reporter in the transcript, "emanates from the body of the court."

"Is that a joke or what?" inquired Kabat.

"No, it's not a joke," said Salus. "It seems to be a pathetic mistake so far." It wasn't clear what the judge referred to.

"Do you mean building them?" asked Daniel Berrigan.

"No," said Salus.

Berrigan promptly moved that a mistrial be declared. "You referred to the action of September 9 as a 'pathetic mistake' in the presence of the jury."

"No, I did not," said Salus. "I said that, from the testimony so far, it *appears* to be a pathetic mistake. I made no opinion whatsoever about this trial."

Salus had not referred to the action as a pathetic mistake. But, when Berrigan insisted he had, Salus concurred, quarreling with Berrigan only about the absoluteness of his statement. You called our *action* a "pathetic mistake," Berrigan charged. "I said it *appeared* to be and made no judgment about the *trial*," responded Salus. I had thought the object of Salus's comment was the *warheads* the Plowshares Eight had damaged, what they were and how they should be named. It seemed to me that what Salus had called a "pathetic mistake" was calling the weapons "weapons." I came to think that the reluctance to call them weapons was not only a legal maneuver, but a kind of magic, the magic that employees at General Electric used every day to protect themselves from what they didn't want to know. The judge did the same thing. If he could claim that the weapons might be something else, that trying to name them and to know what they were for was a "pathetic mistake," they would not be what they were, might not be anything at all. It was difficult to see how the defendants could be prosecuted for damaging something that hardly existed. One juror's wife later told me that her husband commented, "That nose cone looked like a nose cone, smelled like a nose cone, tasted like a nose cone, but nobody knows it's a nose cone."

John Schuchardt asked Augustine Healy, General Electric's accountant, whether he believed "that a weapon of mass extermination is a thing of value."

Salus said, in objection to the question, "This man is a financial expert as to the cost and pricing of these particular objects, nothing more and nothing less."

Schuchardt wanted to discover if Healy understood what the Mark 12A was. "I am afraid Mr. Healy may confuse this with a wide range of other products that General Electric produces. He keeps referring to it as a 'product.'"

"Mr. Schuchardt," said Salus, "He is testifying as to its value. He's not testifying as to its nomenclature or what it's used for."

At a sidebar conference, out of the jury's hearing, the prosecutor objected to the term *kiloton,* saying, "It's not relevant."

"Why?" asked Daniel Berrigan. "Is it true or isn't it?"

"Whether you know it to be true or not, that's a matter of your proof," said Salus. "The proper person to elicit this from is some engineer."

"Expert testimony, we will get expert testimony," said Berrigan.

The defense plan was to call an array of experts. The judge had said repeatedly that the defendants would be able to present their defense, and the defendants had promised the jury that experts would appear. In order to get at what they called the truth—which was that General Electric daily manufactured aggressive weapons of unacceptable destructive magnitude, they had summoned the following: Robert Aldridge, engineer and former designer of submarine-launched ballistic missiles, to explain why the Mark 12A was a first-strike weapon and why possessing it made nuclear war imminent; Daniel Ellsberg, nuclear strategist, to explain how the United States had threatened repeatedly to use nuclear weapons; Helen Caldicott, physician, to explain what the medical consequences of their use would be; George Wald, Nobel Prize-winning biologist, to explain what would happen to the environment in such circumstances; Robert Jay Lifton, psychiatrist, to explain the psychology of not knowing; and Richard Falk, lawyer, to explain the imperatives of international law. The role of these experts was to establish that there were reasonable grounds for believing that the act of September 9 was justified, even obligatory.

The questioning of G.E. employees went on. It was designed to tell the jury the story of events on the day in question from the prosecution's point of view, that eight intruders had broken into private property and had committed vandalism. The defendants tried, on cross-examination, to instruct the jury that this was no ordinary trespass. Often electric moments of dramatic revelation arose suddenly from a mundane question or answer.

It was on a small matter—how long the defendants had been held in jail before they were allowed to see their attorney—that Charles Glackin, one of the defendants' advisory counsel, wanted clarification.

"You know how it is proper to raise that question," said Salus to the cool, aristocratic-looking but passionate lawyer Glackin. "You are not to interrupt this trial and this orderly process," Salus scolded him.

"Orderly as to what?" inquired Glackin.

"Orderly as to admission of what this person testifies," said Salus of the policeman being cross-examined.

"And I think that should be the truth," asserted Glackin.

Salus exploded. "Well, nobody gave you the right, or the arrogance, or the privilege to have the unexpurgated truth in this matter!"

The effort to tell the truth, unexpurgated, demanded great concentration. It exhausted Molly. In addition to the group planning sessions every evening, despite their "remarkable rapport," she said, in addition to the Evenings of Hope, and in addition to the informal seminars with Ramsey Clark and visiting experts, Molly had an angry, frustrated, fearful husband to deal with.

Bobby and Greg, still banned from the courtroom, had been enlisted by a volunteer attorney, Norman Townsend, to help with research on the appeal of that ban. Townsend took them to the Children's Law Project and had Gregory do some of the research. Molly later recounted, "Gregory found a paragraph somewhere that Norman incorporated into the appeal, so he was delighted." Molly said, "I was more worried about the effect of Bill's emotional upset on *them* than what was happening in the court."

Bill was distraught and angry. "His major concern," said Molly, "was that we were not doing anything to make things better for *us*. Although he did understand our wish to put G.E. on trial, he had a terrible conflict over that if it meant. . . . " She searched for a way to explain. "He was terribly angry when we stopped our defense [later in the proceedings] because he felt that we didn't do everything we could to present our defense. He wanted me to spend more time with him during the trial, which just couldn't happen. He had a very hard time understanding that."

She knew and sympathized with his ordeal. "He was incredibly worried and upset about what was going on, knew what the consequences were going to be, and just couldn't separate himself out enough from what was happening to me and what *my* consequences would be from what we were trying to do in terms of challenging the legal system. And feeling I was being dragged along on this and wasn't making my own decisions, which really wasn't the case."

At the evening decision-making meetings, she said, "He wasn't capable of sitting there and listening." He wanted attention. He wanted Molly. The crisis she had precipitated for Bill by leaving their Dormont home the previous September was by no means over. At one point, she said, when the eight were assembled, "He expressed his frustration, his wish to be part of the decision making. He felt he had every right to be sitting in on these meetings, because everything that affected me affected him. And it was just impossible."

Bill was at his best "when he was either dealing with the media— setting up interviews—or working on the appeal to get the children into court. It gave him a role, something that was his. Otherwise, he was just feeling very left out, and so what he would do, he would get into the car alone with me. All the frustration would come out. He'd start screaming at me, losing control in a way I've never seen him do. He did this the night before I gave my [opening] statement. He would say, 'I won't do this again; I'll be fine,' and then he'd just burst out all over again."

Ramsey Clark "was wonderful to him," said Molly. "He would listen to Bill. He would talk with him. He would accord him a great deal of friendship and sympathy and understanding. Bill came out of it with a great deal of respect and admiration for him. "I was under increasing tension, with the feeling that I had to get away from Bill in order to be able to concentrate on what I was doing in court." For Molly, the formalities of courtroom procedure and the complexities of legal maneuvering were braided together with the demands of her husband. She felt very nearly used up.

Judge Salus had announced that he would hold an evening session to wind up the prosecution's case and begin that of the defense. That meant Molly, already exhausted, would have to make her opening statement, present her part of the defendants' case, at the end of a long and difficult day. She had a headache and borrowed some aspirin. She was, she said, discouraged and tired. While Bill was "driving [her] crazy," the judge was wearing her out. "Judge," she said, "it's been an incredibly grueling session. I wonder if you would reconsider the evening session."

"I have already ruled on that," said Salus.

"The [courtroom] temperature is so hot," said Molly. "I have asked the court employees about lowering it. They said the maintenance people are gone," she pleaded.

Schuchardt pointed out that the prosecution had presented thirteen witnesses as well as sixty-eight exhibits. "I believe we have the right to a fair hearing, where people are not exhausted." Cross-examination, he said, had tired the defendants and, he was sure, the jury.

Salus, having made up his mind, could not be budged. "I am not subjecting anybody to anything that is unduly harsh or improper." So the county fed the jury their dinner and everyone trooped back into court. Molly dreaded having to make her opening statement following the prosecutor's one remaining witness, who testified that the security at General Electric was adequate—though why this was germane was never clear. Having won his point, Salus relented, giving Molly a reprieve, by declaring the court in recess till the next morning.

When the court reconvened the next day, however, Molly was still weary and there were verbal fireworks to irritate the judge before she began.

Dean Hammer rose to object to the "multiple and fabricated charges" against them. He referred to the burglary charge, which overlapped with criminal mischief. Defendants were not supposed to be charged with the same offense in several ways. "That's unconstitutional," chimed in Schuchardt. "And any judge ought to recognize it. For you to put your rubber stamp on it is a disgrace!"

Salus purpled. "That was blasphemous!" he shrilled. ("I think he has a little identity problem," commented Ramsey Clark mildly, during the next recess.)

It wasn't a good prelude to Molly's opening. The night before, once again Bill had given way to one of his screaming episodes with Molly, which terrified her. "I was in pieces," she remembered. "When I stood up to give my opening statement, I could barely get through it, I was in such a state."

She summoned her remaining energy to pay close attention to the jurors. "I wanted to try to communicate directly about what must have seemed complicated and difficult."

She spoke as personally to them as she could. "You are in a position of having to deal with a very special moment in history, because we are raising questions of survival of the human race. So it puts a tremendous burden on all of you, to not only deal with our legal arguments, but with something that gets to the heart of this whole question."

The jurors, she remembered, listened very hard. "You get this feeling of twelve faces concentrating on you."

Her voice was low. "I think what we're asking of you as jurors is an extremely difficult task. The prosecution and perhaps the judge have indicated to you this is a simple criminal act that we are dealing with today. And yet, the reason all of us are here is that we are talking about something that goes beyond the question of the criminal act.

"We have already indicated that we have nonviolently participated in every aspect of the action as described, only questioning the statements that had to do with whether we threatened anyone. We certainly didn't do that.

"What we hope to prove puts you in a position of having to deal with a very special moment in history, because we are raising questions of the survival of the human race. We're raising questions that are not simply criminal questions. And we are going to be presenting a defense that is not simply a normal criminal defense.

"We live in a country in which our Declaration of Independence declares, and our Constitution is supposed to guarantee, the right to life and to liberty and to the pursuit of happiness. And yet we find ourselves in a historical situation where that very foundation is being called irrelevant when we try to deal with the issues of nuclear—"

Eckel objected. "I think Mrs. Rush is getting into the law. I think that is Your Honor's purview."

Salus said, "The law is my prerogative. It is not to be infringed upon by the district attorney or anybody. Outline your defense."

Molly went on. The issue at the heart of the defense, she said, was one that "most people in their ordinary lives tend to shove aside, tend not to think about. The seven or eight years of my life devoted to ministry for peace and justice in Pittsburgh reverberates when I see those nose cones. What I see in those nose cones is potential for twenty-five to thirty Hiroshimas."

"Objection," sang out Eckel.

"This is not the issue," said Salus.

"We have G.E. employees, your Honor, using words to describe these as 'hardware,' 'structures,' 'products', 'shells,' 'shields and shells,' 'nosecones,' none of which communicate the awful terror—"

"Objection," said Eckel. Sometimes Salus upheld Eckel's objections, sometimes he did not respond.

"I was determined I was going to say what I was going to say," she remembered later, but the objections were "very distracting."

She persisted, "In dealing with those legal questions we are asking you as human beings to understand. And we will be presenting evidence with our expert witnesses as to the terrible numbing effect that the reality of nuclear weapons has on all of us."

"Objection."

"Objection sustained."

"I'm talking, your Honor, about a witness that we intend to bring before the court who is an expert—"

"Objection, Your Honor."

"She's outlining her case," interjected Daniel Berrigan, addressing the judge. "What's the problem?"

"Well," said Salus, "she's outlining what she intends to prove." It was just what the prosecutor had done in his opening.

Molly tried to explain to the jury the emotional difficulty of the task before them. She urged them, "Listen to [the] evidence, listen to our expert witnesses with an open ear. It's something no one wants to think about, particularly myself, as I look at my pregnant daughter and think of that potential grandchild. But that is a reality we are dealing with.

"Now, in terms of our legal defense, in terms of questions that need to come before a courtroom. There's the question of intent. If you find that our intention in going into that G.E. plant—"

Eckel objected, but was overridden by Salus. "She can say what she's gearing her defense for."

"Thank you," said Molly. "If you find our intention was not criminal, then you must find us not guilty. We will prove that we consciously, knowingly, willfully acted to protect and save the life of the human family. And so when we went into that G.E. plant, our intent was not a criminal intent.

"Then there is the other question of justification. What justification means is that we only need to prove that we entertained a reasonable belief—"

"Objection," said Eckel. "Once again she's getting into the law."

"Yes," said Salus. "Just indicate what your defense is going to be."

"That's the seventh objection in seven minutes," Schuchardt pointed out.

"But your opening statements are to be an outline of what your defense is, not what the law is," said Salus.

"She's not a legal expert. She's a human being," said Daniel Berrigan.

"Thank you, Daniel," Molly said quietly. She stood her ground gamely, but it wasn't easy.

"She's being forbidden human language," Berrigan added.

"I'm not a lawyer," said Molly.

"Well," said Salus to Eckel, "refrain from interrupting her. The jury is to understand that I am going to give you what the law is."

Molly thanked the judge, took a deep breath, and explained, "The act was necessary to avoid a harm or evil that was greater than the damage and the harm that we did. We will be bringing in expert witnesses to give you information about the kind of harm or evil that we were trying to avoid. We will be presenting expert witnesses who will give you information about the immediacy of the threat of nuclear war and about the effects of nuclear war." There would be, she said, experts speaking about "the Nuremberg standards of international law, presenting testimony from—"

"Objection," said Eckel.

"—from an international law expert at Princeton, which makes clear that the principles of international law are binding in a Pennsylvania courtroom. We're arguing that G.E., King of Prussia, and the people who operate that plant are bound by international law just as the German citizens and the people who conducted the death camp operations in World War II were bound in principle to follow international standards of law that our own government imposed on them after the war."

The jury in this case, she pointed out, "is to be not simply the conscience of this community, but the conscience of the nation. I most seriously charge you, that is your deepest duty and your deepest responsibility, if we are to have life, liberty, and the pursuit of happiness."

"I was glad to get through it," she remembered later. "I think I had a much clearer idea of what I wanted to say than what came out in the courtroom."

Although Eckel found it easy to object and Salus to admonish

Molly, neither interrupted Daniel Berrigan, who made his opening statement next. Ramsey Clark thought maybe it was because of his celebrity, to which both men deferred. Molly thought it was because of his verbal wizardry. "Poetry flows out of the man," she said.

Berrigan wove an enchantment of words, holding the stage with the authority of a seasoned actor. He wanted, he announced very quietly, almost in a whisper, his elfin face solemn and weathered, to reflect on the word *property*

"There was and will be a great effort to talk about these things"—he gestured at the gold-and-black warhead shells that lay just in front of the jury on a table—"in ways that keep them at a distance.

"We have seen people in this courtroom walking away from these things, refusing responsibility for them, talking as though they had nothing to do with them. People close their briefcases and they close their eyes and they close their hearts and they go home.

"God lays on all of us responsibility for our world," he said. You could have heard a pin drop in Courtroom B. "He says, quite simply to the first man and woman, name the world. Call things by their name. Call the shots. Be responsible.

"You have heard talk of hammers and blood," he reminded the jury. "These things," he gestured again toward the warheads, "are the hammers of hell. These things are the hammers of the end of the world. These things are the hammers that will break the earth to bits and all life within." Berrigan didn't raise his breathy voice. "We are trying to call these things by their name, because that command has been laid upon all of us. They confront you as well as us with this necessity of thoughtfulness, of conscience, of responding."

Surprisingly, there were no objections.

"We're here," said Berrigan, "to invite twelve good people to think about these things, to think about the dangers that experts will testify to. There will be experts who will give the earth five years, six years, if this continues.

"Dear friends, we would like you and ourselves to ponder together what befits us. What will make the next generation possible."

As I listened to Berrigan, I was able to imagine that the Plowshares Eight could have had a very different kind of trial, with a different judge, a different prosecutor, an inquiry conducted in a different way. Had the eight committed a crime? Or had they rendered an essential service? What conclusion about the law *would* make future generations secure? I felt regret for an opportunity foregone.

But it was not a different trial. John Schuchardt rose to his lanky height slowly, expecting less deference, which was what he got. He named the experts the defense would call. Robert Aldridge, "fifteen years a Lockheed missile engineer, who will testify that these are nuclear warheads that carry a destructive capacity of twenty-five to thirty times the destructive capacity of Hiroshima."

Eckel objected every few words, with Schuchardt driving right through the prosecutor's efforts to stop him.

"We are going to outline your defense, Mr. Schuchardt," said Salus, "not what your evidence is going to show. We want to know what your defense is."

"What's the difference?" asked Daniel Berrigan.

Salus replied, "The difference is that nuclear warfare is not on trial here, as you well know. The defense of this case is defense to the charges, what your justification is under the law and what you're trying to prove." It was precisely on this point that Eckel had objected, on opposite grounds, to Molly's opening statement.

Salus was satisfied that he was being a stickler on the laws of Pennsylvania, even though the Pennsylvania criminal code provided that "in any prosecution based on conduct which is justifiable under this chapter, justification is a defense."

Schuchardt was trying to explain to the jury what kinds of witnesses would be called to establish the reasonableness of belief that had led the eight to engage in the kind of conduct described and permitted by the statute. The justification defense requires the establishment of reasonable belief that an otherwise prohibited action is necessary to prevent a crime or a catastrophe. The witnesses would make it clear that such warheads as the eight had damaged made nuclear war more imminent, that nuclear war would cause unprecedented and indiscriminate destruction, and that the eight, reasonably believing that such was the case, had the legal obligation to act to prevent this criminal catastrophe.

According to Pennsylvania law, once the defense of justification is introduced, it is up to the prosecution to prove beyond a reasonable doubt that the accused are *not* justified in their conduct, and it is up to the jury to determine whether or not the prosecution has accomplished what the law requires.

But to do this, Bruce Eckel would have had to tackle the substantive matter of the manufacture of nuclear warheads. He would have had to show that they would *not* cause harm nor evil, that they violated *no* laws—at any level, international or state—and that destroying them was *not* a public duty—all this beyond a reasonable doubt. And that would have meant tackling not only his own psychic numbing and that of the community of which he was a part, but also the enormous vested interest of General Electric, with all its political power, as well.

Schuchardt went on. "We will call to the stand Richard Falk, an expert in international and domestic law, in the law applicable to Montgomery County."

"Objection."

"Sustained."

"Our hope is for a full and fair hearing," said Schuchardt. "To be interrupted in this way by judge and prosecutor five times in the matter of two minutes is not a full and fair hearing."

Salus said, "I have shown an abundance of patience with your outbursts and diversions. You are to outline the defense."

"The defense is that it is a crime against humanity, as defined at Nuremberg and as established by the United Nations. Our government initiated the United Nations Charter, and established as ruling and binding in this court the concept of a crime against humanity and a crime against peace and a war crime. And an element of that crime is to prepare, to plan, to attack. Such a plan, such a preparation, is going on at General Electric." Each point he made was interrupted, but he barreled through the objections.

"It is almost absurd," said Schuchardt, "to be arguing that the survival of the human family is illegal. Survival is a precedent to law. Survival is the first issue." It would be, he pointed out, an historic trial, bringing together such expert witnesses, to explain in a court of law what nuclear weapons were, what they would do, and how they were prohibited by centuries of legal development.

Schuchardt looked squarely at the jury. "Of course the law must be brought into conformity with conscience. Conscience is first. And we all have conscience. The law that I am talking about really doesn't need to be argued. It is written in your hearts. We all know that mass extermination is not a fitting undertaking for the human family, and that the destruction of all life on this earth is not an appropriate final chapter to our common life." He had had his say. It had been building in him far too urgently to be stopped by the prosecutor's objections to bringing that larger narrative into this courtroom in which only a short story was to be told.

Catholic Bishop Michael Kenny had come to Norristown from

Alaska, as had another bishop, Antulio Parrilla-Bomilla, from Puerto Rico. Both bishops had offered to speak from the witness stand as character witnesses if that were desired. But the defendants' advisory counsel were concerned that to call character witnesses might change the nature of the defense. Defendants and lawyers alike were determined to argue the justification defense fully, to present both the reasonableness of the belief that had led the defendants to act and their intent in acting. After the defendants were assured by the judge that character witnesses would not compromise the justification defense, the bishops spoke.

Under cross-examination, Eckel asked Bishop Kenny, "In terms of the criminal law or civil law, what is [Daniel Berrigan's] reputation for law-abidingness?"

The bishop replied, "I guess that is for the civil law to judge. I stand here as one representing God's law. I come from a long line of two thousand years, when my most illustrious predecessors on occasion have broken the civil law. And some of them died for it because they preferred to obey God's laws instead of human laws."

Eckel retreated from that line of questioning in a hurry.

Bishop Parilla-Bomilla spoke rapidly and in a thick accent. He was interrupted so often by the prosecutor that Daniel Berrigan interjected. "We didn't bring you here to be humiliated," he said to the bishop. "If at any point you have had enough, please, just step down. We honor you and respect you, and if this court is impossible for you, it's impossible for us."

The frustrated bishop, with pent-up and powerful emotion, began to speak, fast and loud, ignoring objections. He compared the people on trial to biblical prophets. "You will find that sometimes they were not listened to. And they were making signs that were dramatic, so that the people will understand their message. In modern times, in order to preach the Gospel, you have to do that. If you want to show that the Gospel has a message of peace, you have to do great things and dramatic things to be listened to." He knew this from his own experience. "I have been arrested in trying to stop the navy of the United States from bombarding the Island of Vieques [a small island off Puerto Rico, used for U.S. military maneuvers]. We are now playing with toys that can kill whole people, whole countries. I am afraid about the fate of my country, Puerto Rico, because they keep nuclear weapons there." The presence of such weapons in his tiny land, he said, only assured that it would be a target.

At this point, on the second day of the second week of the trial, the moment the defense had tried to prepare for had come. It was time to present the substance of the defense, the expert witnesses whose role was to establish the reasonableness of the defendants' belief that they had had a duty to act as they had acted.

"We would like, at this time, to call as a witness Robert Aldridge," said Anne Montgomery, the defendant least likely to be quelled.

Aldridge, a former employee of the Lockheed Corporation, who had resigned from his job after he realized that he was designing first-strike weapons, had flown from his home in California to testify. He had been in Norristown since the beginning of the trial the week before, and in the courtroom since Eckel had made his opening statement. He was a shy man, tall and rawboned with a lock of gray hair that fell over his face. He looked more like a farmer or a midwestern grocer than an aeronautical engineer who had designed the systems to launch ballistic missiles from submarines.

When he listened to the General Electric employees testify, he was reminded of his corporate life. Although the G.E. employees questioned in court did not design the weapons, he saw in them the same "displacement of responsibility."

He had explained to me several days earlier. "You put it out of your mind," he said. "You rationalize. You're only following orders. They're not going to use them. They're a deterrent. If I quit, someone else will do it." He was a serious man, miserly with words. "You want to leave the *choice* to experts."

Aldridge told me that his work at Lockheed had been exciting, "at the frontiers of technology." However, he said, "I was being exposed to eighty million fatalities as an 'effectiveness measure,'" he said, and "I began to understand the push for more accuracy and power, and it churned me up inside. There was a greater interest in more accuracy than was needed for cities. It was what you'd need to hit silos. That meant first-strike." A book had moved him, he said, *The Respectable Murderers* by Paul Hanley Furfey. Aldridge told me to read it, and I'd understand more about his experience. Furfey, a writer as stingy with words as Aldridge, described a "stress which can be simply overwhelming. If [a person under such stress] follows his conscience, he will perhaps suffer social ostracism, perhaps financial ruin."

Aldridge began to consider resigning from Lockheed, but he had ten children to feed, clothe, and educate. He was afraid to tell anyone about the tension building inside him. "I was afraid of losing my job." However, he realized that, as Furfey put it, "if [one] yields to social pressure, he may pervert the essential purpose of his existence." Aldridge recognized the truth of this, and found the courage to act. As he wrote later, "Fear is the main obstacle to moral action. Prolonging this decision [to quit] was compromising my human integrity."

Finally, with his family's support, Aldridge resigned from his job as a missile maker to spend his time, energy, and expertise explaining what he had come to understand, using his credentials to try to undo the work he had done. For this reason Aldridge had traveled across the continent to provide the first piece of expert testimony that would explain to the jury that the defendants had good reason to think that the Mark 12A was an instrument and harbinger of likely and un-paralleled catastrophe.

The moment Anne Montgomery called Robert Aldridge to the witness stand, Prosecutor Eckel requested a sidebar conference with the judge, the defendants, and their advisory counsel.

"Who is Robert Aldridge?" Salus asked.

Montgomery laid out his credentials. "He's a scientist. He graduated magna cum laude, with honors in aeronautics; worked sixteen years with Lockheed, design specialist, leader of the advanced design engineering group, helped develop five generations of strategic missiles."

"I don't see how it's relevant to the criminal charges brought against these defendants," said Eckel. "He's not a fact witness. As to any expertise he has, it's not relevant, not bearing on anything that's an issue in this case."

Salus made the pivotal ruling of the trial. "He may not testify because it is irrelevant."

It seemed to me that everyone in the courtroom held his or her breath. This was the test. In the tense silence, Montgomery spoke pleasantly and carefully. "During the voir dire, your Honor, I think you said this would be the proper time to present this kind of fact. You questioned the justification and this part of our testimony related to that of our intent. And these are the facts."

"The proper way to prove your intent," said Salus, "is for *you* to testify. A third-party witness is not relevant to indicate any side issues which are herein involved. I told you from the very start this was a trial under the criminal laws of the Commonwealth of Pennsylvania and that whatever justification there was would be pursuant to that."

Philip Berrigan reminded Salus, "During the prosecution case, the

prosecutor constantly stated that this or that General Electric witness
was not an engineer and, therefore, was not qualified to testify about
the destructive capacity of the weapons. Now we advance an engineer,
a man who has not only worked with them, but knows them thor-
oughly and can testify about these Mark 12A's, and it's not allowed."

"The Mark 12A's are not on trial one way or the other," said Salus,
"nor is the fact that they are or aren't nuclear warheads on trial."

Ramsey Clark had spoken little up to this point. He had something
to say. "The intention of the defendants, to introduce into evidence
expert testimony to show both how they formed their personal intention that led them to do what they did and to show justification under
the statutes of the State of Pennsylvania, has been clear to the court
from the beginning." He referred to the voir dire question about the
burning house, "informing all the prospective jurors that this defense of
justification was something that would come before them, and they
should be expecting it." Of the six opening statements, in "at least three
of them, it was stated, and without objection, that evidence of justification would be shown."

Clark spoke quietly. The judge, he said, "has always implied that
he had to hear the evidence first, that until he heard the evidence, he
couldn't rule; that the witness—in this case, an expert witness—would
testify, to determine whether it came within the statutes of Pennsylvania." It would, he argued, "be clearly prejudicial to the rights of these
defendants at this time to deny the jury the chance to hear this
testimony. They're entitled to put their witness on, entitled to have his
qualifications presented, and entitled to have what he will say be said so
it can be determined whether it presents, under the law of the State of
Pennsylvania, justification."

"All right," said Salus dismissively, "I have heard your speech."

Clark said, "You call it a speech because you are terribly prejudiced."

"I'm not terribly prejudiced," said Salus. "I'm telling you un-
equivocally, the defense of justification is properly allowed if the defendants themselves want to get up and indicate what justification they
felt they had." But the witness was irrelevant, because what he had to
say would go "to the horrors of nuclear warfare and, therefore, is not
relevant. Anything they say about justification, they can say as to
themselves."

Clark, a disciplined man, never raised his voice. "You'll remember
Molly Rush. It took her six or seven years to reach the state of mind and

develop the intent that she had on September 9, 1980. The defendants would testify that, in the forming of their intent, they read the writings of Mr. Aldridge."

"They can testify to that," Salus said. "The defendants have any right whatsoever to put themselves on the stand and allude to whatever justification."

Charlie Glackin said, "The point of the experts, is to show the *reasonable* basis for their belief, the *reasonable* basis for their justification defense. Not that of crazy people, as they have been characterized by witnesses here."

Salus interrupted. "Nobody has challenged their right to speak in a free way for what they believe. And nobody has said what they believe is necessarily right or wrong."

"But here are experts," said Glackin, "to show there's a *reasonable* basis for what they believe."

"But that isn't the issue," said Salus.

"Of course it is," said Glackin.

"The issue here," Salus said, "is whether they were justified in breaking the criminal laws of the Commonwealth of Pennsylvania."

Clark pointed out, "These witnesses have testified in similar cases, including similar federal cases. Their names have been mentioned to the jury without objection, because it was clear from the beginning— and the only reason for understanding the defendants—would be they would be able to put these witnesses on in justification."

"And I can show you just as many, Mr. Clark," retorted Salus, "where federal courts and other courts have not." He offered some examples, which Clark recognized as having been cited in Eckel's memorandum on the matter of justification. Clark pointed this out.

"That's what my law clerk dug up," retorted Salus. "Let's have a little truthfulness about what you state."

Now Clark was angry, though his voice stayed even. "What I said was true. Don't call me untruthful and don't imply it."

"Don't call *me* untruthful," snapped Salus.

Clark repeated his observation that the cases in question appeared in the prosecution's memorandum.

"Well, that may be," said Salus.

"Don't say it's untruthful, because you said that about the defendants in the presence of the jury three times," insisted Clark, his dander up.

Salus referred to several cases, but Glackin pointed out that they were all federal cases, none having anything to do with Pennsylvania's justification statute.

Further, Clark said, "you will find in many of those cases, witnesses *have* been permitted to testify."

"I have made my ruling," said Salus. "If I am wrong, a higher court will certainly tell me very rapidly."

Glackin objected that although Salus had seen Eckel's legal memorandum, the defendants had not had the chance to enter similar memoranda.

"On an intellectual basis," said Salus, "I have examined the cases that are pertinent to this particular issue through my law clerk and myself. I have looked them over, and I am convinced that my position is correct. I have not read nor will I read the District Attorney's justification brief, because you have not submitted one yet." He also insisted that he had had no idea, until Aldridge was called, that there were going to be expert witnesses. "I assumed they were going to be their own experts, testifying as to what the justification—"

"How could you assume they're experts?" queried Clark.

"How can anybody testify as to anybody's conscience?" asked Salus.

"He's not," said Glackin. "He's going to talk about the reasonableness of their conclusion, which led to the conduct, which is their justification."

Salus repeated, "That is not the issue."

Clark told Salus that, to be fair, "You would have to hear the evidence, read the statute, determine whether the evidence was legally admissible under the statute to present the defense of justification. That's precisely what you're refusing to do." He gave the judge a short memorandum on the subject, that the defendants had assumed they would submit before instructions were given to the jury. "Because [of] all you had said, we assumed that's when justification would be ruled on," Clark said.

Salus retreated to his chambers.

The memorandum Clark had given Salus to read argued, "Unlike most criminal cases, the major task for the jury here is not to answer the purely factual question: did the defendants commit the acts charged against them? Rather, this jury must confront much more serious and complicated questions. Was the defendants' conduct noncriminal by reason of the defense of necessity [or justification] since it was motivated by their perceptions that the weapons policy pursued by the United States and illustrated by General Electric's manufacture of Mark

12A re-entry vehicles posed a grave and imminent danger to all people? Did the defendants, who believed their acts were compelled by international law, have the *mens rea* [intent] essential to establish criminal liability for the crimes charged? Did they lack criminal intent altogether? Without the expert testimony being proffered here, the jury will be unable to answer these questions and defendants will be deprived of a fair trial."

Molly later described how the eight met and discussed breaking off their defense. When the judge returned and the court was once more in session, he ruled against them. The decision was hard for Molly to believe, even in retrospect, after all that had gone before.

"We won't have any argument at all?" asked Glackin. "You don't need argument? You read all the cases?" The defense memorandum was full of citations of other cases.

Salus responded, "I have read those which I feel are pertinent." He must have read quickly, having spent only about half an hour in his chambers.

"You understand it's the most crucial issue to the defendants in this entire case," urged Glackin.

Michael Shields said, "Your Honor, at sidebar you indicated we would be permitted the opportunity to argue this issue, oral argument, your Honor."

"That's our understanding," said Philip Berrigan.

"Well," said Salus, "I changed my mind. My ruling is that the testimony will not be proffered. It is not relevant."

The dismay in the courtroom was palpable. ("We didn't think he'd simply break his promise," Molly said, later. "We were trying to be realistic, but we'd invited these expert witnesses in. We thought there was some possibility of presenting a defense. Otherwise, we wouldn't have gone to all the trouble to bring witnesses in.")

"This is an important moment for you too," Schuchardt said gently to Salus. "This is a case of genocide, which is homicide a million times over." The justification defense was clearly permissible in a homicide case, as Salus had acknowledged.

"I have agonized over it every night that I have gone home, believe me," said Salus, though he also maintained that, until an hour or so earlier, he had no idea what the defendants planned to introduce into evidence. "The mere assertion of a proposition doesn't make it legal tender. Now I have looked at it from every possible angle. And it is clear to me that the testimony to be proffered is not relevant to the issue at hand."

Schuchardt pleaded again. "These people that we have called are the most qualified, knowledgeable people in the United States."

"The mere assertion that you say they are the most qualified. . . . ." Salus began and paused. "For everyone that you have to testify, there would be somebody on the other hand."

"Let them be heard," said Schuchardt. "If the government wants to call somebody on the other hand, let them."

But Salus had made his ruling and would not retreat from it. He made another promise, though. "The defendants may testify as to why and what they feel was their justification to the fullest extent."

"Judge," said Philip Berrigan, his voice bleak, "you probably will change your mind on that too."

"No, I won't," said Salus.

"We will be interrupted constantly," said Berrigan.

"No," promised Salus, "you won't."

Later on, Molly recalled the crisis. "Phil was ready to drop it. 'Forget it. Let's quit.' Ramsey was very anxious that we testify. That night we decided to get on the stand ourselves—a sense of making every effort. Our whole discussion focused on trying to speak the truth in that courtroom."

The next day, having decided to do what they could without their expert witnesses—some of whom had offered the testimony they had come prepared to present on the front steps of the courthouse, in the keen cold, to whatever reporters would listen—Daniel Berrigan took the witness stand. He seemed to the group to be least likely to be harassed with interruptions.

Anne Montgomery conducted the direct examination, asking simply, "Why did you do what you did?"

Once again, Daniel Berrigan held the courtroom rapt, speaking no louder than a whisper about the formation of conscience. His parents, he said, had taught their six children "that you do what is right because it is right, that your conscience is a matter between you and God, that nobody owns you."

Like each of the jurors, Berrigan said, "each of us eight comes from a community—brothers and sisters with whom we live, with whom we pray, with whom we offer the Eucharist Mass, with whom we share income, the care of children." He wanted them to understand. "Our conscience comes from somewhere. We have not come from outer space or from chaos or from madhouses to do this thing. We come as a community of conscience to meet your community of conscience and to ask you, are our consciences any different about the lives and deaths of children?"

There was a cathedral hush in the courtroom, into which Berrigan's voice wove its breathy spell. "We come from churches. We come from America. We come from neighborhoods. We come from years of work. We come from earning a living." He bent his energy to make the jury understand that the eight were ordinary people, like the jury, like the judge, like the prosecutor. "And we have come to this. And the judgment of our conscience that we would like to present to you is something like this. We could not *not* do this. We were pushed to this by all our lives."

Molly later reflected on his words. "He said so well, for all of us, that we were coming out of a background, a history," she said. "It was the most human moment in the whole trial for me."

Berrigan wanted it to be clear to the jury that the likely consequences of such an act were no pleasure to him. "With every cowardly bone in my body, I wished I hadn't had to do it. That's been true every time I have been arrested. My stomach turns over. I feel sick. I feel afraid. I hate jail. I don't do well there physically.

"But I have read that we must not kill. I have read that children, above all, are threatened by this. I have read that Christ our Lord rather underwent death than inflict it. And I'm supposed to be a disciple. The push of conscience is a terrible thing."

Berrigan was a master at avoiding the terms that lit the judge's and prosecutor's fuses. "We believe, according to the law of this state, that we were justified in saying we cannot live with that," gesturing at the warheads, "saying it publicly, saying it with blood and hammers, because that thing," gesturing again, "being produced in our country every day [is] the greatest evil conceivable to this earth. There is no evil to compare it with. Multiply murder. Multiply desolation. Multiply."

"Tell us please," Montgomery instructed him, "about the work you do."

Berrigan spoke of working in a cancer hospital in New York City and in a college in the South Bronx. Again gesturing at the warhead casings, he said, "Those things make cancer the destiny of humanity." And for each student he encountered in a "culture of poverty, twenty have died on the way or are in prison or are suicides or have given up. I discuss freely in class, Why are we so poor? Where is the money? General Electric costs the poor three million dollars a day."

Eckel tried to object, but Berrigan controlled whatever stage he stood on.

"The only message I have is: we are not allowed to kill innocent people; we are not allowed to be complicit in the killing of innocent people; we are not allowed to be silent while preparations for mass murder are proceeding in our name, with our money, secretly."

No one stirred for several moments. Around me, people dabbed at the corners of their eyes. Molly said later, "It was astonishing that Dan was able to speak without interruption. Dan managed to transcend the whole thing."

Bruce Eckel had the unenviable task of cross-examination. He asked Berrigan where the eight had spent the time before they went to General Electric, where and with whom they had conspired. Berrigan wouldn't tell him. And then Eckel wanted to know how they had arranged themselves so as to get from wherever it was to King of Prussia. Berrigan appeared not to understand.

Salus prompted, "Were [the cars] following each other?"

"Well," said Berrigan solemnly, "they were following each other, or one was leading another."

"Was there any secrecy to what you were doing?" asked Eckel.

"I really don't understand the question," answered Berrigan.

"Oh," said Salus, "I think that you do."

"Well, now," said Berrigan, "you help me."

"Did you have the hammers hidden?" Eckel asked.

"Yes," said Berrigan, "because we didn't want to intimidate."

Eckel pounced on that. "You do admit that hammers are intimidating and threatening?"

"Well, if they are brandished at people," said Berrigan.

"Did you know whose property it was?" asked Eckel of the warheads.

"Well, first of all, we didn't consider it property," Berrigan answered.

Eckel insisted, "Did you know whose they were?"

"They shouldn't be anyone's," Berrigan said. "They shouldn't exist."

"But *knowing*," said Salus, "they *do* exist, whose weapons are they?" Salus had named them: *weapons*.

"Good God!" Berrigan exclaimed. "I don't know. No one at General Electric will take responsibility for them!"

"Don't you think using a hammer upon an object is violent?" queried Eckel.

"Oh," said Berrigan like a wise gnome. "Not such an object. See, if these things contained buttermilk or ping-pong balls, I'd leave them alone."

"You say that some laws you respect and others you don't," said Eckel.

Berrigan answered gently. "You phrase things, I think, a little bit badly. Let me try to put it my way. If a human law is in contradiction to the law of God, we will obey the law of God."

Still barely hopeful that the judge would let them testify "to the fullest extent," as Salus had promised, as to why and what they felt was their justification, Elmer Maas took the stand and Carl Kabat asked, "What was your intention?"

"Well," said Maas, "let me just say, as I begin, that as Dan spoke to you a few minutes ago—"

That was as far as he got before Salus interrupted, saying, "I am going not to interrupt you, but you have a tendency to ramble on." That was true: Maas had, on earlier occasions, rambled, but he had not at the moment had the chance to ramble. "A question was asked of you that you should answer," admonished Salus. "And then, if you want to say something else, that is fine. But answer the question that is addressed to you."

"I wanted to say that I heard part of myself speaking as Dan was speaking," said Maas, even-tempered. He said that he had entered General Electric with "seven of my very close friends. It was my intention to carry out this act—"

Eckel objected. "I think that goes beyond the question."

"I was asked my intention," said Maas. "It was my intention to carry out this act in witness to the all but virtual certainty of global nuclear war within the next fifteen years."

Again he was interrupted. The objection, Salus said, was that he was "giving an opinion beyond even his prescience in terms of what is or what is not in the future. Don't say 'almost certain nuclear war in fifteen years.'"

Maas asked mildly, "I have a short thing that I would like to say. Could I request that I be allowed to say it?"

"What I'm saying is you can't give opinions which are not based on any sound facts," said Salus, as Philip Berrigan had predicted he would.

Dean Hammer said, "We had the experts yesterday. And you wouldn't listen to them."

"For every piece of evidence there is, in terms of opinion, there is another piece of evidence which will deny it," Salus said.

Maas tried again. "My state of mind includes the awareness that there is, in fact, a very probable if not certain prospect of global nuclear war within the next fifteen years, based not upon idle speculation or a lack of information, but upon some very careful consideration of the issue." He tried to explain how he knew that the warheads that lay before the court were for first-strike use.

Eckel objected and Daniel Berrigan asked why.

"The objection," said Salus, "is that it is not sticking to why he did it, and it is going into the very opinion evidence which was not permitted as relevant with regard to yesterday's testimony."

Philip Berrigan was on his feet. "That is a first-strike weapon. And that *was* his motivation in going into King of Prussia."

Eckel objected. Carl Kabat offered Maas another angle.

"Elmer," he asked, "What is that here?" He gestured at the pair of warheads.

"That is the Mark 12A. That is a first-strike, counterforce—"

Eckel objected, but Maas went on. "In my mind, it was necessary to do what we did together on September 9, 1980, within the context of the biblical imperative to beat swords into plowshares, to act in some small way to do what is possible to avert the greater harm of nuclear holocaust, by committing this act in witness to the perils of nuclear annihilation."

How had his view developed? Kabat inquired.

Maas explained in his easy, amiable way. He had taught college courses about the history of civilization. "In teaching the history of this century, it became very difficult to talk about the genocide of the Nazi government, the gas chambers, the horrors and atrocities and the racism without being able to open my eyes to what was in the society around us."

Eckel objected. It was "another issue."

Salus agreed.

Maas offered to rephrase what he had said. Salus scolded, "I'm not going to have you shout out again." Perhaps it was the comparison that had shouted at Salus. Maas had not raised his voice.

Maas was determined to have his say. He had to thread his way through incessant objections, which were sustained, nor was he particularly adroit. The war in Vietnam had aroused his awareness: "We were being called upon to endorse genocide and racism. We could not sit back as many sat back during the Second World War, as many others have sat back at other times, as people might have said, 'I'm just doing my job. I'm just tooling on a machine. I don't even know what I'm producing.'"

And out of this awareness, Maas said, he had developed another. "There was not only this arsenal, there was not only this possibility of a use of these weapons during the period of the Vietnam War, but there was, in fact, a plan for their deployment and use that was, in the words even of the administrators of the government, part of a first-strike or counterforce weapon system."

Objection, objection, caroled Eckel.

Sustained, sustained, chorused Salus.

The Mark 12A, said Maas, would be fitted into the Minuteman III missile system, which "will have such quality and such technological ability that it can destroy that target before any retaliatory forces can be brought into play."

Eckel objected, moved to strike "that last paragraph, or whatever."

Glackin pointed out, "This is the information that he based his action on. This is his state of mind."

"I don't care what his information is," said Salus. "We are not going into his information in detail. He can say he thought it was a first-strike instrument." But Salus wouldn't let him say anything about *what* he knew.

"They are not on trial for opposing nuclear weapons," Eckel said.

But Maas was firm. "The only reason that we are in this courtroom today is, we have carried out an action that is intended to call attention to the perils of the arms race and to do what is possible to bring some focus to the possibility of the destruction of all nuclear weapons as an alternative to the arms race."

"The law and what they are on trial for will come from the court," said Eckel.

"That is correct," said Salus.

Over repeated objections, Maas laid out the evidence of first-strike capability. He began to speak of the Nuremberg principles that "focus responsibility on all citizens." His knowledge of international law, he explained, came from "books written by Richard Falk—"

Salus interrupted. "I am not going to have you gagged. Don't go beyond that. Mr. Falk was not allowed to testify, and so forth. He can say that Mr. Falk's views influenced him, but I am not going to have him go into the philosophy of Mr. Falk, or whatever."

Maas steadfastly named the authors whose work had influenced him: Robert Aldridge, Helen Caldicott, Richard Falk, Daniel Ellsberg,

George Wald, Robert Jay Lifton, "all of whom have been called to witness, and to provide the kind of testimony that would have given, in each case, the background and the factual information that has been objected to," he said.

But Salus saw it otherwise. "You are trying to get in the back door [what] you can't get in the front."

Charlie Glackin tried to help. "We are trying to get in the front door what belongs in the front door, which is the truth about this man's motivation."

Eckel objected to Glackin's addressing the court as advisory counsel.

Glackin rejoined, "As an officer of the court, I am trying to bring clarity to the witness's statements. I think that Elmer Maas needs a little assistance in getting to the point that he is trying to make."

"Yes," said Salus, "he has needed a little assistance all throughout this trial in getting to the point."

"The law in the Commonwealth, Your Honor," said Glackin, "is that a defendant has the right to testify broadly."

"And I indicated to him the parameters," said Salus. "He can say anything about why he did it."

"Well," said Glackin, "the why is part of the background of what he knew. And part of what he knew is what Dr. Falk wrote about. And part of what he wrote about, it was a violation of international law to produce these weapons."

Salus said, "Mr. Maas has any right to discuss why he did it as a result of reading these things, what his justification was in his own mind. Mr. Maas can very easily describe these things because Mr. Maas is an intelligent person. He's been a teacher. And he understands what he reads. And he can explain what he reads. And if he wants to do so, then he should do so."

Carl Kabat asked, "Then he can explain the Mark 12A then?"

"No," said Salus. "He cannot explain the Mark 12A."

"His understanding of the weapon, Your Honor," said Glackin, "is part of his evidence as to why he did what he did. He wants to talk about the weapon, what he knows about it, why it affected him. If that is not relevant, nothing else is."

"The Mark 12A isn't on trial," Salus said. "He is on trial for the charges which I indicated from the beginning of this trial. Those charges, of why he wanted to do it, he can perfectly well state it. He is entitled to. He indicated the threat he felt from this thing."

Glackin said, "And he wanted to give some reasonable basis for that, Your Honor."

Salus rejoined, "He doesn't have to testify as to Dr. Falk's theories. All he has to do is say, 'I believe in those theories. And on that basis of such-and-such, this is why I did it.'"

Crimson, Maas left the witness stand. Salus said, "I don't think he has ever gotten to what his individual thoughts and conscience was at this point."

"That is because you kept interrupting him," said Daniel Berrigan.

"No, that is not true," said Salus. "Mr. Maas, do you want to say why you did this on September ninth?" Eckel said he wanted to cross-examine Maas. "Yes, he has the right to cross-examine him," said Salus.

Dean Hammer said, "He states he's motivated by international law, but we have no idea what international law means."

"He can say what principle motivated him, not what international law—" said Salus.

"Well," said Hammer, "he said the Nuremberg principle—"

"I'm not going to argue with you, Mr. Hammer," said Salus. "Please return to the stand," he instructed Maas.

"Well," said Maas, "I don't plan to return to the stand until there is an opportunity for a full hearing of the issues of this case, that are based upon the kind of defense that is legitimate and available to us under the laws of this state and country."

"He was terribly frustrated at being stomped on at every word," said Molly later. "We were all disgusted."

Salus said, "That is *your* choice. I have given you the offer to continue to testify. If you don't so choose, that is your business and your responsibility."

Just as Salus declared a lunch recess, church bells across the street rang out, "Were You There When They Crucified My Lord?" Some of the spectators in the courtroom joined the bells, singing the words. Salus scolded, but he couldn't stop the singing.

"We said," Molly told me, recalling this point in the trial, "That's it! We'll take this trial where it belongs, to G.E.!" And therefore, after lunch, when court reassembled, only Molly, Dean Hammer, Anne Montgomery and Daniel Berrigan were present as defendants. The other four had gone back to King of Prussia to keep a vigil in the early March snow outside Building Number 9.

Salus tried not to notice their absence. "There's been some confusion amongst members of the press with respect to what my rulings were." The defendants, he said, could "explore justification, necessity, or individual conscience," so long as no information got into their testimony. "You don't need an opinion to indicate the atrocities of nuclear holocaust," he said. "That is not the issue here."

Molly stood to say that she would explain why four defendants were not present. She wanted to do so, she said, in the presence of the jury. Salus refused to call the jury in. Molly delivered a statement on behalf of all eight defendants. "In regard to the fact that the court has impeded jury selection by arbitrarily changing voir dire procedure at least three times; that the court has consistently refused to admit evidence on the Mark 12A missile, or the nuclear arms race, or our justification defense, or the question of the jury's conscience; that the court has interrupted and harassed defendants repeatedly, and has issued threats of contempt and made prejudicial judgments in the presence of the jury, including, for example, calling our action a pathetic mistake, and saying that if we were nonviolent people we wouldn't destroy property; in addition, the court has lied to us by saying that our justification brief could be argued in public court; in effect, Your Honor, we believe the court and you personally have displayed yourself as the legalized arm for genocide. For these reasons, our four brother defendants have returned to General Electric to stand vigil against crimes being planned there every day and to protest the multiplied injustices of this court against hundreds of others."

Salus insisted, "There was no hampering of what you wanted to say as to your own individual conscience, your own individual necessity, or your own individual justification. You could allude to the various people you have read. But you could not put forth what they had to say, other than the fact that you relied on that in arriving at your individual conscience."

Salus ordered the defendants returned, though he didn't say who was to return them. "The courts would be in complete anarchy if people chose to determine when they wanted to appear and when they didn't want to appear." He was flushed. "An ordered society is the only kind of society that can exist. Those who decide their own rules individually are pumping for anarchy. With anarchy, we would all be eating each other. We wouldn't have to worry about nuclear weapons."

It had snowed the night before, a heavy, picturesque nine inches that made Norristown look like a scene on a Christmas card. Salus called in the jury and did his best to be jolly. "Well, we have a nice day out there," he said. "The world's covered with a nice fresh layer of white snow." Trying to act as though nothing at all out of the ordinary had happened, he called on Molly to present her defense. She stood slowly, but instead of speaking and looking grave, she turned silently to face away from the bench. One by one, as they were called to present their defenses, Dean Hammer, Anne Montgomery and Daniel Berrigan rose, turned their backs and stood mute.

Without a word, the advisory counsel, Glackin, Shields, and Clark, walked out. As Ramsey Clark remembered it, the defendants had decided right after lunch not to cooperate with the trial any further. " 'We appreciate your help, but we don't want advisory counsel present. So please leave when we stand up,' they said. We did so," said Clark. "We left the courtroom and went across the street to Mike Shields's office. A while later, a call came from the court to Mike, asking him to return. The judge wanted to see him. I felt suspicious of that," Clark recalled. "I felt he might try to coerce Mike, as the only lawyer from Norristown. So the three of us went over. There was some give and take. He said we'd turned our backs on him. I made a little joke that, since the door was on the side of the room, we'd turned our *sides*. It was an icy situation."

Salus cited the lawyers for contempt. He ordered the record to show the following: "Defendants Molly Rush, Dean Hammer, Sister Anne Montgomery, and Daniel Berrigan are standing with their backs to the court, which I consider an act of arrogance and contempt and an element of delay, and a demonstration contrary to good proceedings and contrary to the orderly progress of the trial." He had issued bench warrants for the arrests of the other four, who were eventually brought into court by the police, to join their friends facing away from the judge for the remainder of the trial.

Salus meanwhile had called for public defenders and ordered them to defend the absent defendants. The public defenders demurred; they didn't know the defendants; they didn't know the case; they hadn't followed the trial. They could not, they said, provide a defense on such short notice.

Salus had revealed the limits of his power. He could issue orders, but he was dependent on the willingness of others to obey. He might have envied Judge Starling, who put those who defied him into a cage in the corner or sent them to the "stinking hole." Salus said that for the record, "Four of the defendants, Molly Rush, Dean Hammer, Anne Montgomery, and Daniel Berrigan are standing with their backs to the

Judge Samuel W. Salus II (left) and the Plowshares Eight as they faced away from him at the end of the trial. Back row: Molly Rush, Dean Hammer, Anne Montgomery, Father Daniel Berrigan. Front row: Father Carl Kabat, Elmer Maas, Philip Berrigan, John Schuchardt. Drawing by Bill Ternay.

bench." He called their posture "arrogant, disrespectful and disorderly, showing once again that this proceeding is a demonstration." Salus soothed himself, saying, "In an abundance of caution, I am going to let them stand there during the closing argument and the charge of the court."

Bruce Eckel made his closing statement. "It is," he said, "an unusual case, a very important case, a serious case. No one is above the law. It is the law on which our country rests. The defendants are not charged with protesting against nuclear war. They are charged with violations of the criminal code under which we all live. The defendants have admitted their guilt. I'm not here to quarrel with the beliefs and motives of these defendants. They firmly believe in what they did.

"None of us is *for* nuclear war. None of us is *for* the arms race." Eckel pointed out that the other protestors at the G.E. site had not been arrested, but the defendants "did more than protest. Of course there had to be a plan. There had been *discussion*. Clearly they knew they were not allowed to be there."

Judge Salus relaxed as Eckel spoke. "They knew they were going to be arrested. They wanted to be arrested. Their concern was, 'what will we say if we're caught with hammers and we haven't been able to use them?' They were very secretive about the hammers, very clandestine. They had the hammers hidden."

I noted that two of the jurors had begun to cry as Eckel spoke. As he went on, others fought their tears.

Private property, said Eckel, "is the cornerstone of democracy. There are peaceful means to change policy." Further, "For everyone who's against nuclear arms, there are just as many—more—who are *for* nuclear arms. But if this argument prevails, those people would be entitled to enter peace group premises, break their typewriters, scatter blood about." Eckel repeated all of his arguments several times, ending, "You must follow the law as it is given to you by Judge Salus. And you must not stray from that. The Commonwealth has proved its case beyond a reasonable doubt. You are the spokesmen for this county, the people in this commonwealth." The only issue for the jury, said Eckel, was "did they commit the charges brought against them?"

The judge instructed the jury at length, explaining the legal charges, which considerations were material, which not. "The defendants have been permitted to present evidence that their actions were taken pursuant to a good-faith belief in the evil and immorality of nuclear weapons. The defendants maintain because of their beliefs, their actions were justified. The defendants' motivation, in this case, the fact that they were engaged in a protest, in a sincere belief they were acting in a good cause, is not alone an acceptable legal defense of justification."

Justification, Salus explained, is "only a legal excuse for conduct that would otherwise be criminal." But such a defense "is not available where the harm to be avoided is not imminent. Likewise, the defense of justification is not available where there is an alternative method rather than violating the law in order to avoid the perceived evil. The defendants' conduct, likewise, must also be calculated to abate that evil. Since these and other elements of the defense of justification are without any support in the evidence in the case at bar, I instruct you that, as a matter of law, certain elements of the defense justification are absent. And, therefore, the defense of justification is not proper in this case."

One of the public defenders, who had been ordered—over his objections—to represent the defendants, spoke of the judge's charge out of the jury's hearing. "Your Honor, regarding instructions on justification, you have taken the defense totally away from the consideration of the jurors. The instructions are tantamount to directing a verdict of guilty. On that basis, I move for a mistrial." Salus refused.

As Salus finished his instructions to the jury, one of the spectators in the courtroom rose, in silence, and turned his back to the bench. One by one, others did likewise, until nearly all of the spectators were standing, facing away from the judge.

At points during the trial, I had felt sympathy for Judge Salus, thinking he had a difficult job to do. I hoped he would do it well. But, by refusing the justification defense to the Plowshares Eight, when he would have permitted such a defense in other criminal cases, I thought he had abused his position and lost his power to govern the courtroom. I sat there as he charged the jury and as, one by one, the people sitting all around me stood and turned away from the bench. I felt my heart beat faster, my breath come shallower, and my skin bead with sweat. And almost as if by some volition other than my own, I felt myself rise and turn my back. Eventually, as the trial transcript records, "Humming emanate[d] from the body of the court," and though I was not humming, I was removed by policemen with everyone else who was standing. The courtroom was left nearly empty of spectators.

After the trial, I wrote to Salus to explain my "gesture of disrespect." He answered me at length, angry at my letter as he had been at losing control of the courtroom.

It took the jury nearly ten hours to reach a verdict. The defendants refused to return to the courtroom to hear it unless the public were readmitted. The judge would not admit the public "unless the defendants will indicate to the court that there will be no outbursts, no desecration of this courtroom, or no outcry or any demonstration whatsoever—and no singing, either."

"Can't stop singing, Judge," Ramsey Clark observed mildly. "It's a free country."

"They can sing," said the judge, "but they don't have to sing in the courtroom."

"You can't compel defendants and the public about what to do," answered Clark. "They are free people." Clark understood that while commands can be issued, obedience cannot be compelled. It was a small instance of the larger point made by the trial itself. The nuclear arms race could go on only as long as people gave their consent, both active and passive, to the production and deployment of the weapons.

Judge Salus was incredulous. "Mr. Clark, are you insinuating that the audience is doing it of their own free will and not on cue of the defendants?" He was convinced that his loss of control could only be masterminded.

"Absolutely," said Clark. "I am not insinuating. I am telling you my opinion."

Judge Salus admitted the public. The defendants returned to the courtroom. The jury reported its verdict. Not guilty of simple assault, criminal trespass, and disorderly conduct. Guilty of burglary, criminal mischief, and criminal conspiracy.

An anguished voice from among the spectators cried out, "How do you find General Electric? They are building genocidal weapons that can destroy all life on earth. How do you find them? Guilty or not guilty?" Another voice shouted, "You hung Christ today!" Again, just what the judge feared happened. The court transcript records that again "singing emanate[d] from the body of the court."

The judge thanked the jury at some length and adjourned the proceedings.

Some months later, when I was able to return to Montgomery County, I found it difficult to interview the jurors. Shortly after the trial, in response to interviews various jurors gave the news media, Judge Salus wrote the jurors a letter telling them not to talk with reporters. Some understood that he had no authority to give such instructions. Others felt they should obey the judge. I interviewed as many of the jurors as I could find who would talk to me. I also relied on interviews reported in the Boston *Globe* (March 11, 1981) and *Fellowship* (April–May 1981).

Some of the jurors were deeply troubled by what they had observed, which was by no means everything that had happened. The jury were often sent out of the courtroom while points of law were offered and discussed. They did not, therefore, know how the judge had ruled on the justification defense. One juror, Michael De Rosa, told the Boston *Globe* he had been bewildered by the way the defense had suddenly halted its case. "We couldn't understand that. All through the jury selection, the judge told us that they would use justification. He even gave us the example of someone breaking into a burning house to save someone's life. We said, fine. And then, bang, nobody showed up. I didn't know a judge could do that. If they have a defense, why didn't they let them have it?"

Another, Daryl Saylor, told me, "The judge did a good job, keeping things we didn't need to know away from us." This juror took his task with the utmost seriousness. Because the judge had instructed the jury to concentrate on the witnesses, this man told me he had conscientiously refrained from looking at the defendants. He thought the jury had done a good job, too, debating for many hours, coming to its decision only when the judge sent word it would be sequestered for the night if it didn't decide speedily. "The law was trying to point one thing out, and they were trying to point out another. They never intersected," he said. Of the defendants, he concluded, "I can see why they did it. They were probably right in their beliefs, but wrong in their approach." He was perplexed, though. "When someone asks, 'How would *you* do it [prevent nuclear war]?' I don't know. But the law comes first in our country. Law is *the* most important thing in this country."

De Rosa told the *Globe,* "The judge's narrow charge to them made a conviction on some of the counts practically mandatory. 'We convicted them on three things, and we really didn't want to convict them on anything. But we had to because of the way the judge said the only thing you can use is what you get under the law.'"

Mary Ann Ingram told the *Globe,* " 'These people are not criminals. Here are people who are trying to do some good for the country. But the judge said nuclear power wasn't the issue.'" Her son served on a nuclear submarine.

Still another juror, quoted in *Fellowship,* said, " 'I would have loved to hold up a flag to show them we approved of what they were doing.'"

" 'I didn't think they really went to commit a crime,' said De Rosa. 'We discussed the Boston Tea Party and all kinds of things that happened in history.'"

Michael De Rosa's wife, Ellen, told me at some length about the toll the trial had taken on her husband. Making the decision about these defendants, who had brought the Boston Tea Party to mind, had been "emotionally trying," she said. She thought that for her husband to admit the stress he had felt was "a lot for a male." This had been "his first time on a jury, and what a beaut!" she said. He had understood the term *first-strike* even without Robert Aldridge's testimony. They were not talking about "retaliatory or interceptive weapons," she said.

Ellen De Rosa said that she was frightened about the prospect of nuclear war, but, she said, "I don't feel I have much company." She continued, "It's so difficult to convince people when they don't want to hear. The thought that we're living in proximity—people don't want to think about it." The defendants who had demanded so much hard work of her husband and his fellow jurors were, she thought, "very frightened. They're trying to convince people that something's wrong. I'm not so sure I like the idea of the way they did it. But then, sometimes you have to be obnoxious to be listened to. Radicals have to be crazy for anything sane to happen."

Her husband, she said, had stood "in awe of [Molly's] kind of commitment. There was some kind of balance that she and her husband have worked out." Little did either De Rosa suspect that Bill felt he had lost all his balance, the familiarity of his marriage, the very order of things. Perhaps Ellen De Rosa imagined what would happen if she did as Molly had done, concluding that circumstances must be special for such a woman, though they were not. As for General Electric employees, her husband had told a Boston *Globe* reporter that their testimony wasn't impressive, because they feared for their jobs. "'How could you work for the company for twenty years and not know what they were?'" he was quoted as saying.

Daryl Saylor was impressed by the defendants. "They were trying to fulfill a goal. But they can't take their beliefs over the law. Because then you're opening it to where anything could happen." What the Plowshares Eight had done, he feared, might set a precedent.

That, of course, was just what the Plowshares Eight hoped would happen, though they didn't count on it. They thought, with legal philosopher Ronald Dworkin, that there was sometimes "an inherent defect in the rule of law as conceived by those who now invoke it. They think that the ideal of legality is expressed in the proposition that everyone should obey the law. But they do not—in any event they say they do not—mean that everyone should obey the law in all kinds of society. Even Abe Fortas, who wrote a book in defense of the rule of law, argued that citizens had no such duty in Nazi Germany." Like historian Howard Zinn, the Plowshares Eight questioned whether "the idea of obedience to law *in general* [has] such a high intrinsic value that the law must be held sacrosanct even where it violates an important human right or protects an evil condition."

William Penn had said, when he established the Commonwealth of Pennsylvania, "The nations want a precedent." Molly Rush, who had tried to restore Penn's precedent, set one as well. This was a source of perturbation and discomfort to those who saw themselves as running the commonwealth.

9

"The Lord of Heaven and Earth will be judge"

ON JULY 28, 1981, four months after Molly and her colleagues were convicted, they were required to appear again before Judge Salus for sentencing. Most of Molly's family and many friends accompanied her. Now that the trial was over and the eight had been convicted, Salus permitted more latitude. Each could make a statement. In addition, two of the experts who had not been allowed to provide evidence during the trial were allowed to speak in mitigation of sentences.

"Judge, five of my children are in the courtroom," Molly began. "So, if you don't mind, I would like to direct my comments in their direction. That's why I'm here today." She had pondered about the legal events of February and March. "I said during the trial that I thought this courtroom was irrelevant. I have been reflecting about that. I said that because of [the court's] refusal to deal with the questions of genocide, and the questions of nuclear holocaust. On further reflection, I have decided that I was wrong, and that this court and all courts *are* relevant in matters of overriding substance, in matters of genocide.

"Slavery was not illegal," said Molly. "It was protected by law." So was "genocide against native Americans," and in that instance, "treaties were made and were broken by our government.

"Legal systems and governments bless power," she said. "They help define its victims as less than human. We therefore make it all possible. We maintain illusions of domination required to keep the system going. The effect on public consciousness is just overwhelming."

Molly pointed out, "We don't see slavery in the same way as people did a hundred and fifty years ago, when it was inevitable and when it was legal. Today we might be repelled to hear the phrase, 'Another one bites the dust,' referring to Indians, native Americans. Today we know that though we almost destroyed them all, we didn't win over the Indians." The consequence of that violent relationship, she said, was that Americans lost the wisdom of their native predecessors, which "was more consistent with the idea of an ecological principle, or what we might say is God's will on earth, than our principles that have been driven by the need for power and for money." Because of its deadly Indian policy, the United States had lost "some of the human values that we are going to need if we are hoping to survive. Unless we recover those values, we can't recover hope.

"I was ten years old at the end of World War II," she recalled, "and I remember very, very well the stories that came out of Auschwitz and the death camps. Even at ten, I could imagine and see the hollow eyes and the bodies that were victims of absolute inhumanity. When it came out, I read Anne Frank's diary. So I was able to understand the holocaust in very human terms. Since then, I have been reading about the death camps in terms of the occupants who couldn't see any hope. The best they could hope for was to make it through the day.

"Those that ran the death camps," she reflected, "I don't think that they understood that their so-called power over the occupants was going to lead to their own destruction. Of course we know now. We can look back and see it as almost inevitable in a way that neither the occupants nor the occupiers could imagine. What was there was an illusion of total power signified by legally operated gas ovens."

It had taken many years, Molly said, "before the other genocidal sin of World War II grew to full impact in my conscience." It was "perpetrated by the victors. It was twenty-five years before films that were initially made of the bombing of Hiroshima by our government were released by this country and I came to see the human face of those who died and those who survived that holocaust. I didn't understand that hideous reality, and I'm stunned when I look back and realize how much I understood about the death camps—at least in certain childish terms—and of how little impact Hiroshima had on me until years and years later."

She had thought about this difference and offered her thoughts with care. "I think the reason that I didn't really understand has to do with responsibility. Our government was responsible for the second holocaust. They defined reality for us. They gave us the picture. I bought it. I accepted it."

She spoke of the history of her family. "As the granddaughter of Irish and German immigrants, I don't think I felt a burden on [my] conscience regarding slavery and Indian genocide, despite the fact that I grew up near Fort Pitt [at the junction of the three Pittsburgh rivers], where blankets infected with smallpox were distributed to the Indians, nor despite the fact that I lived near a black ghetto in Pittsburgh, where those who lived [there] continued to suffer the consequences of slavery. Because after all, my own people, the Irish, suffered at the hands of the British during the potato famine. I think it was only [in] my German part that I remember trying to fathom the question of why the insanity of Nazism took hold there."

For Molly, the evolution of awareness figured centrally in the idea of legal justification. To have explained to the court the growth of her conscientious conviction that she should destroy warheads would have required an account of personal, family, regional, and world history, an account of what she had read, how she had lived. Hope had grown in her as she had become *aware,* as she had faced the reality of nuclear weapons. The same possibility that existed in her life existed for others. "What surprises me now," she said, "is how late and how little I came to consciousness. For years and years, I feared the bomb, but I accepted it as an unpleasant necessity, something for national defense, national security. It's taken a long time to get to the point of letting go of those illusions. Only in the past few years have the scales fallen from my eyes, and only very recently have I come to see the enormity of the lies that have been perpetrated on all of us, the lies that keep all of us going, that lead to possible total holocaust.

"What I've come to see is that, under the bomb, we are all vulnerable. The judge, the G.E. executives, the government officials, and my newborn grandson. They are all in the same boat. This ultimate instrument of power strips all of us bare of illusions that power maintained by force is effective or useful or wins. It never did win. Now, if we really look, we can see its true face, the face of death, the face of the death of all of us and all of life out there."

As in all of Molly's public speaking, she had thought about the ideas ahead of time, but she searched out her meaning as she spoke.

She had cherished one final illusion, she said, and wanted to speak of it. "That is the final lie of those who would keep faith [with] the use of force. We swallow it. We believe it, as the Nazi death camp victims and victimizers did. This is the lie that all of us are helpless in the face of the bomb. That the people can do nothing, that we must accept the death of the world for ourselves and for our children and for our grandchildren. That is the big lie that's being perpetrated. We are trapped in this death-camp mentality as long as we believe and as long as we act on that belief by going along.

"So," she concluded, "for my sake and for the sake of my chil-dren—Gary, Janine, Danny, Bobby, Gregory, and my daughter Linda, who is home with the new baby, Michael—for them I reject that lie. I believe in a God who is the spirit of truth and love. I am happy to go to jail if it means keeping that spirit of life alive on this planet." With this, Molly concluded her statement.

In addition to the other members of the Plowshares Eight, Judge Salus permitted two of the experts, barred from trial testimony, to speak. Robert Jay Lifton, the Yale University psychiatrist, explained his work. He had tried to understand the bombing of Hiroshima "in psychological and historical terms," he said. Such "great and threaten-ing events" cause "the exclusion of feeling," he said. "We don't like to think about [nuclear war]. Most of the time, we don't." The defendants, he said, had "a commitment to help the rest of us to *feel* what happens at the other end of the weapons. I take that to be a valuable contribu-tion to our culture. It takes psychic and moral courage."

Lifton, a large man, gestured with his big, blunt fingers as gently as if he were handling an injured bird. "We all live what I call a double life," he said, "because we know that, in a moment, everything could be destroyed by these nuclear weapons. But we go about business as usual, as though no such danger existed." What he thought remarkable about the defendants, he said, was "that they put themselves at risk in order to make known the destructive truth about these weapons."

Richard Falk, professor of international law at Princeton University, spoke of "the centrality of law as a dimension of our civilization." The law did not mean simply statutes on the books, he explained. "The first obligation is that the law do no harm." Falk, slight and rabbinical-looking with a neat, grizzled beard, laid out the constitutional su-premacy of international law. He spoke of the law in Nazi Germany. "One of the things that Germans said in that period was 'gesetzt ist gesetzt,' the law is the law. That was used to justify blind obedience to the law on the part of the judges, on the part of German citizens, on the part of everyone caught up in that Nazi experience. Even people of good will justified their behavior by that."

Since World War II, Falk explained, there had been a "great revival in Germany of thinking that says, 'You cannot divorce the law from human values. You cannot divorce the law from a moral purpose.' Individuals in a political order, particularly one that calls itself a democracy, can never separate their obligation to respect rules that have been enunciated by the government from their moral conscience or from their concern to make sure what they do is consistent with their understanding of fundamental human decency."

Salus was curious. Couldn't the eight who had been convicted in his court have protested without breaking the law? he asked.

Falk asserted that they had *not* broken the law, because "these treaties, which are the supreme law of the land, take quite literal precedence over state law, and to the extent that they are valid, Pennsylvania law is invalid, if there is a conflict between the two."

The judge tried the question another way. Surely the eight could have exercised their right of free speech "in a legitimate and appropriate way."

Falk thought the question was, more properly, "whether it was reasonable to engage in symbolic acts of nonviolence, given the failure of our official institutions to deal with these issues in a serious and direct way. Congress has never had a hearing on the legal and moral status of international law. No court has allowed these questions to be faced directly. How would you have defendants—on issues that are of such consequence to the future of humanity—how would you have them raise the question in a manner that would be effective for the American people?"

Salus grumbled, "They have certainly gotten all of the free publicity that they have sought." He was convinced that "you don't have to symbolic [sic] anything. All you have to do is express your views. You don't have to make a hollow gesture in order to be heard."

Falk responded, "The question is, where does one locate the hollow gesture at this time in history? In my opinion, it is at the core of what our official institutions are doing about the questions of this moment. They are trivializing these issues by putting the law that governs things like trespassing and property above the law that governs genocide. If we continue to do that, we will be doomed as a civilization, as well as violating our own obligations as members of the legal profession not to do harm."

As a preface to the sentences he was about to pronounce, Judge Salus spoke at some length. He took considerable issue with the substance of the eight's defense, even though he had not heard its substance, having excluded expert testimony. "In the future," he admitted, "the majority may confirm the eight's universal wisdom. History, in this sense, will be the ultimate judge." For the present, however, he said, "They fail to acknowledge the realities of the twentieth century, the past history of the world, the majority opinions and opposing points of view. They even ignore the human experience of perfection."

(Molly chuckled as she remembered Salus's remarks after the sentencing. "That was one of the moments I found myself feeling sorry for him, which I often did during the trial," she told me. "The others were gnashing their teeth, and I just thought, 'Oh, poor man.'")

"While no one wants nuclear holocaust," Salus said, "disarmament in any age is foolhardy and suicidal in the light of immediate past history. One has only to look at the Nazi invasion of Poland to see its ridiculousness." Those who supported the action of the Plowshares Eight, he asserted, "ignore and reject all the logical and intellectual positions which other reasonable people can take." Some of those to whom he referred, he said, wrote him letters, though they "know nothing of the legal ramifications and precedents in this case. It is clear that they have excused and ignored similar past indiscretions. They have sometimes knee-jerk responses to the isues akin to those responses scientifically recorded by Pavlov.

"Their letters of support and advice show signs of vocabulary similarities, the same propaganda, and even some thought control. They assert their position with an arrogance to the system, an intolerance to others, and an innate immutability which has been reserved heretofore for proven prophets." (In the transcript of the judge's remarks, the court recorder wrote "profits": it seemed a nice, if unconscious, pun. The judge seemed unaware of the status of prophets, who have rarely been on the side of profits, who have always offended the majority, which has never hesitated to call their prophecies madness, lunacy, and treason.)

The Plowshares Eight, Salus charged, had engaged in "symbolic crying of 'wolf' against the majority for at least two decades, and for various and sundry social issues, which diffuses and discredits the sincerity which we are expected to accept. It seems incomprehensible that such a selected few have an inside track as to the necessities for the salvation of society."

It seemed even more to infuriate Salus that several other Plowshares actions—the damaging of nuclear weaponry—had taken place since the Plowshares Eight had tried, from their perspective, to enforce the law and from his to break it. It seemed to him evidence of the contagion he was trying to stamp out. He had seen news stories about protest rallies directed at intervention in Central America, in which the presence of the Berrigan brothers was remarked. These events, said Salus, "show an intransigence and a penchant for professional protestations. These actions further show a desire to substitute their point of view for the majority, and it often conflicts with the majority view and makes them look like chronic curmudgeons, malcontents, and soothsayers of doom, that a free society not only allows but also promotes because of our extensive media coverage, which has been sought by them.

"This world is not a Hollywood production," he pronounced. "It is not an article in the newspapers. It is the approach, in a cool, logical manner, of what we must do in order to survive.

"To say that there has been a research beyond the bounds and issues in this case is a gross understatement. [My] receipt of mail from various states and various sectors of the community at various times points to and gives an uneasy sense of conspiracy and prompting by those herein involved. Such witch hunts and conspiracies have been condemned with respect to any individual in government, the majority, or in this case, any minority view espousing a particular cause."

All this was his explanation for his decision. "I have examined my conscience and have constantly ruminated about the best course to take in this particular case. In fact, it might be said that I have rattled about the pans on the scales of justice." (I recalled that Sir Samuel Starling and Thomas Howel, who had also rattled about the pans on the scales of justice, had longed for the Spanish Inquisition as a way of dealing with the troublesome Penn and Mead.) Judge Samuel Salus longed for "a complete panoply of choices." His personal choice, he said, "would be: one, to send all eight of these defendants to a leper colony in Puerto Rico and have them do service on a day-to-day basis to the human beings who suffer that terrible affliction; the second choice I would have and would exercise would be to send them to Soviet Russia, for them to make a similar protest to the one they made in King of Prussia, so that they might enjoy more fully the many freedoms, freedom of speech, and get a first-hand view of that repressive society. In truth, I believe that a protest of this sort, from what we know of that society, would certainly end up in a Siberian sentence."

His sentences were harsh: three to ten years in jail for the Berrigan brothers, John Schuchardt, and Carl Kabat; one and a half to five years for Dean Hammer, Elmer Maas, and Anne Montgomery. He said he regretted having to sentence Montgomery. "Of all the people that I met in the Plowshares Eight, your inner peace, your sincerity, your lady-like behavior, and your real conscience has struck me more than any-body associated in this very difficult trial. You are truly a person to be admired."

Judge Salus wasted no such regrets on Molly. Her sentence was two to five years in jail.

Salus revoked their bail and sent them packing back to jail, then and there, without allowing them so much as time to kiss family or hug friends. Thus ended the fireworks of the trial of the Plowshares Eight. The drama, however, though it became more convoluted and legalistic in the courts, was far from over. Nor is it over as this book goes to press.

A few days after Salus sent the Plowshares Eight to jail, a higher court reversed him and let them out pending appeal. The lawyers who had represented the Plowshares Eight in the courtroom, in addition to several others who found the legal problems interesting, continued to offer their services in the preparation of appeal briefs. They filed a lengthy and elegant appeal with the Pennsylvania Superior Court.

The superior court focused its attention on the issue of the justifica-tion defense, which Salus had refused to permit. They made a decision in the fall of 1982 in favor of the Plowshares Eight, but they did not make it public because another case, which presented similar issues but dissimilar judgments, was also moving through the court system. This case involved the trespass of protesters at a nuclear power generating plant, radioactive emissions from which, they argued, endangered the health of the surrounding community. The superior court, in that instance, had ruled, though with a powerful dissent, to uphold the trial court's conviction. Since appeals involve not only specific appellants in specific circumstances, but also precedents for future decisions, the president judge of the superior court ordered a rehearing of both cases before the full court of seven judges.

I found a copy of the superior court decision that was *not* issued in a wastebasket two years later when I went to Harrisburg, Pennsylvania, to hear the oral arguments for the two cases that had been linked by the president judge. It provided insight into the inclinations of the judges. This decision noted that the defendants in the trial court "offered evidence relevant both to their lawful intent and the factual reason-ableness of the beliefs predicating their conduct. Those conclusions, in turn, were drawn by them from the work of a variety of experts, each of whom was prepared to testify to the facts specifically predicating the defendants' beliefs so as to demonstrate their reasonableness." The superior court noted, "The trial court barred each of these seven expert witnesses from taking the stand, and drove from the witness box, by constant interruption and interference, the second [defendant-as-witness]. The charge to the jury on these issues also was entirely inadequate."

The discarded judgment continued, "The erratic and inconsistent rulings of the trial judge make it difficult to determine with confidence the basis of his refusal to permit the defense to go forward, but it seems to have been premised on several erroneous assumptions, some factual and some legal in nature. The cumulative effect of these errors was to prevent the jury from performing its lawful function of trying the facts of the case."

A footnote indicated, "The record is replete with emotionally charged remarks made by the trial [judge]. Also, during the voir dire period the trial judge granted an interview to the *New York Times;* he was quoted as having said of this case, 'It's a different kind of case. In any case of civil disobedience, the prosecutor, the judge and the jury are put on trial.' While we do not need to resolve the question of whether or not the court committed reversible error in so remarking, given our disposition herein, we recommend that, in the interests of the unquestioned appearance of justice, the trial judge excuse himself from any further participation in the proceedings."

In the several years during which the superior court was making and then reconsidering its decision, from 1981 to 1984, the apparent apathy and numbness prevalent in 1980 gave way to massive protests against nuclear weapons. Though little reported in mainstream media, incidents similar to the Plowshares Eight action, in which citizens attempted to enforce domestic and international law in matters of military and foreign policy—Nuremberg Actions, as they were sometimes called—proliferated. Community activists and interested lawyers paid attention to developments in this regard and refined justification or necessity arguments. The secretary-general of the United Nations received 90 million signatures petitioning for disarmament in June 1982. At the UN General Assembly, 122 countries out of 159 voted for a freeze of nuclear arsenals in December of that year. The Nonaligned Nations, meeting in New Delhi in March 1983, demanded a freeze on the testing, production, stockpiling, and deployment of nuclear weap-

Molly, early 1980s.

ons, as did hundreds of thousands of citizens, in town meetings and petition drives in the United States. City governments refused to implement procedures for the evacuation of their populations in the event of a nuclear attack. Women in England linked hands to form a nine- and then a fourteen-mile human chain in protest against the deployment of Cruise missiles in their midst. They also set up an encampment at the Greenham Common military base to dramatize their opposition to the missiles, an idea copied in Comiso, Italy, and in Seneca, New York. In Eastern Europe, many groups, particularly in the churches, defied repression to oppose nuclear weapons. The American Conference of Catholic Bishops called on a variety of experts, among whom Molly was one of three women to testify, as they formulated their pastoral letter, *God's Challenge and Our Response*. Notwithstanding Judge Salus's insistence on democratic mechanisms, the president of the United States said that protest would not affect him. The Congress went right on voting for expensive weapons of baroque complexity under pressure from such corporations as General Electric. But the public developed a nuclear weapons literacy that led to growing disenchantment with nuclear weapons policy.

The Plowshares Eight did not cause all of this change of awareness and attitude by any means, but they played a role. Molly, like her colleagues, was in great demand as a speaker among activist groups in the United States and Europe. Creativity and sophistication in peace and justice work flowered. In my judgment, it continues to do so. For many, Molly's action illuminated both the intransigence of institutions addicted to warfare and their fragility. The arms race could go forward only with massive cooperation and consent. The Plowshares Eight provided an instance in which citizens withdrew their consent. That instance was fraught with possibilities.

The rehearing by the superior court of oral arguments in the appeals of the two cases the president judge had decided to link, took place on May 10, 1983, in Harrisburg, the capital of Pennsylvania, in the chambers of the supreme court. The judges, seated behind an enormous mahogany bench, were surrounded by extraordinary frescoes depicting the evolution of legal principles. They were the work of Violet Oakley, who had also decorated the governor's reception room with paintings depicting William Penn's trial, and the senate chambers, depicting the evolution of unity in national affairs. Her style combined mystical elements in the manner of William Blake with the startling straightforwardness of WPA murals with memories of the Sistine Chapel. Above the judges were inscribed the Ten Commandments. To their left were the Beatitudes. At the back of the room, two gorgeously decorated inscriptions were, I thought, to the point. One said: "The civilized world will have to decide whether International Law is to be considered as a mere code of etiquette, or is to be a real body of law imposing obligations much more definite and inevitable." The other said: "The creator is not only of infinite power and wisdom but also of infinite goodness. He has so intimately connected the laws of general justice with the happiness of each individual, that the latter cannot be obtained but by observing the former, and if the former be punctually obeyed it cannot but produce the latter. In consequence of which mutual connection of justice and human felicity he has graciously reduced the role of obedience to this: that man should pursue his own

One of the panels on international law by Violet Oakley in the Supreme Court chambers, State Capitol, Harrisburg, Pennsylvania.

substantial happiness. This is the foundation of what we call ethics or natural law."

In this setting, in which the very walls cried out, Ramsey Clark seemed particularly soft-spoken. He quoted Hugo Grotius: "It is the care to preserve society that is the source of all law." He also quoted Blackstone to the effect that "an important exercise of public duty is the advancement of public justice." Justification in such instances as that before the court, said Clark, "is rarely invoked, rarely permitted, and never commended in the courts, though Pennsylvania statutes, allowing for justification, arose from the common law recognizing that the preservation of society is a legitimate public purpose."

One judge asked, "What do these people think they're doing? If Congress decides that missiles are necessary for defense, may members of the public decide they're not?"

Clark answered simply, "It is their duty," explaining that Congress, too, is bound by international law and the judgments rendered at Nuremberg. Further, he said, Congress could not redefine Pennsylvania law.

"Well, where do you draw the line?" asked one of the judges.

"Where there's only property damage, the line seems pretty clear," responded Clark.

The president judge inquired, "If we scrapped our weapons, would we be in a safer position?"

"I think so," said Clark, but he reminded the judges that the testimony of expert witnesses was necessary for the jury to determine whether the harm the eight had tried to prevent was real and imminent.

The decision of Pennsylvania Superior Court was not issued until February 17, 1984. It had caused more anguish than any decision in memory, one of the clerks of one of the judges told me. The primary issue, said the superior court, was "'Did the trial court err in so limiting appellants' evidence?' Because we believe that the court was so in error, we reverse the judgments of sentence and remand for new trial." They also decided, "Judge Salus may not participate further in this case."

Judge Edmund Spaeth, a Quaker, wrote an unusual concurring opinion in this case that, he said, "has given us such difficulty." His opinion was impassioned, personal, and literary. "Whenever a defendant pleads justification," he wrote, "the court should ask, 'What value higher than the value of literal compliance with the law is the defendant asserting?' The trial court failed to ask this question." Spaeth noted, "[The appellants] are pleading the danger arising from nuclear missiles.

One who does not understand that danger does not understand appellants' plea.

"I submit a 'public disaster' *is* imminent. By resorting only to our own Government's official publications, we may learn that the United States and the Soviet Union—without reference to Great Britain and France (and other? Israel?)—each has the capability of destroying the other within minutes and on command." He noted, "Appellants do not assert that their action would *avoid* nuclear war (what a grandiose and unlikely idea!). Instead, their belief was that their action *in combination with* the actions of others, *might accelerate a political process* ultimately leading to the abandonment of nuclear missiles."

Spaeth wrote, "No peril is greater—no peril approaches—the peril of nuclear war. It is in light of this peril that the reasonableness of appellants' belief must be judged." He said he was "skeptical of appellants' conduct. I believe there are better ways, the [Catholic] Bishops' among them." Nevertheless, Spaeth quoted Sigmund Freud's "fateful question for the human species," whether survival or the human capacity to "exterminat[e] one another to the last man" would be the outcome of the human project. "It is this question," Spaeth concluded, "that provides the context in which appellants' conduct must be judged."

The Commonwealth of Pennsylvania, which had prosecuted the Plowshares Eight in the first place, appealed the superior court decision to the Supreme Court of Pennsylvania, which reversed the superior court's decision on November 22, 1985. The supreme court did not respond to the reasoning of the superior court, but concluded, "Expert testimony that a nuclear weapon is capable of maiming or killing masses of people is no more necessary than expert testimony as to the manner in which people dial a telephone, chew gum, or tie their shoes." The convictions and sentences were reinstated.

Judge Salus, whose exclusion from the case the supreme court did not uphold, ordered Molly and her friends to report to Norristown for resentencing on the second day of the new year, 1986. He vacated this order shortly before it went into effect, because the eight had applied for either reargument before the supreme court or remand to the superior court. Two months later, the supreme court indicated that the superior court could look further into the Plowshares Eight case on issues that had not been addressed the first time around. Once again, the trial court was overturned. In February 1989, nine years after the Plowshares Eight had entered the G.E. warhead factory and eight years after the trial, the Supreme Court of Pennsylvania overturned the sentences but upheld the convictions, concurring that Judge Salus should involve himself no further in the case. A judge in Tunkhannock, in Wyoming County, Pennsylvania, was assigned to resentence the Plowshares Eight. He granted their motion for a delay pending their petition for certiorari to the Supreme Court of the United States, which was filed in May 1989. Certiorari represents a complaint from a party at law that she or he has not received a fair trial in a lower court. Knowing that the nation's Supreme Court can hear only a tiny fraction of the cases for which petitions are presented, the eight plan—if certiorari is denied—to take their case next to a federal district court, petitioning on a writ of habeas corpus. This proceeding would give them the chance for a much broader review of their claims, including the possibility of presenting, at last, the full justification argument.

It is, of course, unsettling for Molly not to know when the judicial axe, which has hung over her head for almost a decade, may fall. She has not, however, stopped what she was doing in order to worry about it. Nor has her world stood still. Her children have grown to adulthood. They have found jobs, begun college, married, had children, divorced. The lives of her siblings have changed. Two of their marriages have ended. The job of one has taken him out of town and back again. Their children have grown up, joined the army, gone to college, married, had children, found jobs. Bill, like legions of other Pittsburgh workers, lost his drafting job as the steel industry collapsed and ancillary industries declined. Sometimes he has found temporary jobs, sometimes not. Employers have often hired him for one day less than the period of time that would entitle him to unemployment benefits. He has occupied himself with softball and a newfound enthusiasm for videotaping events in which Molly is involved.

Molly thinks that, as time has passed, "Bill's come to see not only is he not going to change me, but has gained something of a respect." His videotaping and archival impulses are, she says, "something he could do to support me and something he could do for himself."

Bill says he isn't sure how he feels. "I go from day to day. I get a little bit upset about the way this trial's being run. You grow up under a criminal justice system where the bad guy's getting punished. But where's all this bail and money for fines going? I can't understand the [Pennsylvania] Supreme Court. I thought they took the case for publicity, to look good. And then they messed around. They paid no attention to the valid points, saying all these here legal things. They talk one way about justice and then they don't follow it. It surprised me a lot."

Sometimes, as Molly has contemplated and undertaken new acts directed against nuclear weapons, occasionally ending up in jail for brief periods, Bill has been suspicious and frightened. But over time, she says, the rupture in their marriage has healed. Bill has grown calmer and more trusting. Molly has given up the idea, which had at times seemed almost inevitable, of leaving the marriage. "He doesn't get nearly as hyper and nervous as he used to," Molly explained to me, but their perceptions continue to differ. "I think if you see something threatening your children's lives, you act to stop it."

"Things are pretty good right now," Bill says. "Not the best, but a lot better than it was. We tolerate each other now. I'm a person that's set in my ways. When I like something, I like it forever. It's when everything's changeable that I get upset." Bill thinks the ebb and flow of family events limit Molly's action and he is grateful for the increase in grandchildren. "She wants to be there when the kids and grandkids need her. The same thing for her brothers and sisters. Some of them are hurting and she wants to be there for them."

Molly is perfectly clear that she may have to serve a long jail term— "I'm willing to do that." She is also clear about the necessity for continuing resistance, which may mean other jail terms. "But hanging in there with Bill and hanging in there with the Merton Center are all of a piece. Bill's like the world—obtuse—and I keep trying to make him understand."

Molly has come to see Bill's softball connections as helpful to her. He schedules and umpires teams that include police, FBI, and jail employees. "They have trouble seeing me as the terrorist of Pittsburgh if I'm Softball Bill's wife.

"I went through a period when I asked myself, 'What next?'" Molly acknowledges. "Where do I go consistent with the truth of that Plowshares action? I was like a snake swallowing a rabbit—an elephant! That experience had to be digested and used to illuminate the work I'm doing now. It was a difficult process. It's made it necessary for me to look more deeply at the question of resistance."

Following the 1981 trial in the Montgomery County Court of Common Pleas, Molly and several associates began an extended and persistent campaign to resist the production of first-strike weapons by corporations headquartered in Pittsburgh. These were Rockwell International, the Westinghouse Corporation, and Carnegie Mellon University, whose military contracts multiplied—with provocative, destabilizing, and economically debilitating consequences, Molly thought. Every Wednesday, starting in 1982, Molly and her local associates leafleted, encouraged dialogue with corporate officials, and occasionally engaged in minor trespasses, trying in local courts, with mixed success, to argue the justification defense. She continued her work at the Thomas Merton Center, serving on board of directors of the Tri-State Conference on Steel, the American Civil Liberties Union, the Pittsburgh Peace Institute, and the Pittsburgh Rainbow Coalition, whose co-chair she became after the 1988 national election.

"Theorizing is one thing," says Molly. "Living it out is another, learning in the most important way, experientially. You can read, you can increase your information, and I continue to do that." Indeed, she has developed some expertise on nuclear weapons production cycles, has studied economic developments, and has thought at length about how social change takes place. "But there's something to living that *out* as a way of learning," she says.

"You think of a hammer as an educational tool?" I asked her.

Molly laughed. "Could be," she said.

"It's connecting what you've learned out of your living with other ways of knowing that's important," she ruminates. "That's what I've been doing for the last nine years, translating that [1980] action, explaining it to thousands of people. But if that's *all* I've been doing, I'd be frozen in the Plowshares Eight action.

"I've been learning in so many ways what that action meant to family, to friends, to co-workers—to people I don't even know, who've told me they've been moved into action themselves because of it.

"I can't begin to describe what I've learned. What is a nonviolent campaign? I'd already learned how to organize. Then I learned what it was to do a powerful symbolic action—far more powerful than I anticipated when I did it.

"In order to move on, I had two choices. I could have formed a small community like some of [the other Plowshares] have done. But there wasn't, in Pittsburgh, that kind of community. I could keep on leaving town to do actions. But it was important to me to connect the truthfulness of the Plowshares Eight experience to my life in Pittsburgh. That meant, sometimes, a very painful and lonely experience. I was feeling tension between what I know needs to happen in Pittsburgh—

growing resistance—and the fact that it wasn't happening. I could work to make it happen here."

Molly's reputation takes her around the country and around the world, but her work takes place largely in her own community, where her ancestors settled six generations ago.

Over and over she encounters the litany of standard responses. Nobody is *for* nuclear war, but. . . .

Molly keeps pressing. But what? And when? And who? It isn't enough, she thinks, only to have the opinion that the weapons are a threat. "Be doers of the word and not hearers only," Scripture says, an admonition that continues to reverberate.

"Perhaps," wrote an editor of the *Pittsburgh Post-Gazette* (April 10, 1982), "the futile hammer blows Molly Rush drove into a nuclear nose-cone had some cathartic power for confirmed protesters." Catharsis wasn't the point, Molly said. She intended to confront, to insist that those she confronted make deliberate choices.

Bill told the *Pittsburgh Press* (May 16, 1982), "Molly is a good organizer, but if she's away [in jail], she can't organize. She feels she's protected by some higher providence, but I know where higher providence gets you." But Molly's and Bill's fifteen-year-old, Bobby, quoted in the same story, understood. "No one's going to pay attention to somebody who's just passing out papers. If you see a lady with six kids taking action, you may start to wonder."

When the *Pittsburgh Press* featured Molly and her family on Mother's Day, May 16, 1982, Eugene "Jeep" DePasquale, president of the Pittsburgh City Council, wrote Molly a letter on official paper that carried the slogan "City of Champions."

"Dear Molly," wrote DePasquale. "I have only met you personally one time and that was at City Council. I was quite impressed with you at that meeting. I might add that I am not an activist and I don't demonstrate, I guess you could call me one of the silent moral majority. I have even looked down my nose at people who do those things, however, after reading the article in the Press this past Sunday, I couldn't help but think—I don't think that you, Molly Rush, are really that concerned about Molly Rush per se, or Jeep DePasquale, but you are concerned with mankind in general and this I must commend you for.

"I don't condone breaking the law, however I have bent the law myself. I just wonder Molly, if everyone realizes that a handful of people throughout the world control the destiny and could possibly trigger an atom bomb war that would destroy the world and all its people. It doesn't seem fair, but those are facts and why the rest of us, including I believe, the average Russian, Chinaman, or any person of any other nation, [would] like to see all weapons of this type be done away with. If enough people in enough nations force the issue, this would happen. To that respect, we probably need more Molly Rush's in the world.

"I have had a taste of warfare myself in World War II as a Marine who took part in three combat invasions. I have lived through the agony of a son who was almost killed in Viet Nam, yet compared to a A-bomb war, these were merely skirmishes.

"I wish you luck in you ventures in the future and hopefully you can work up enough people throughout the world to stop this nonsense."

Shortly thereafter, Pittsburgh became the first major industrial American city whose city council passed a resolution urging the super-powers to negotiate an end to the arms race. Pittsburghers voted to amend their Home Rule Charter in such a way as to instruct the mayor to inform Pittsburghers annually about the local economic and social impact of military spending. In Pittsburgh, corporate headquarters for some of the nation's biggest arms manufacturers, numbers of people grew who saw their beloved three rivers—namesake of stadium, sum-mer festivals, youth orchestras, piano competitions—in a new way. The rivers began to look less like the good place to situate a fort to compete for strategic advantage and more like the seven-river city of Hiroshima.

It grew clear that Pittsburgh, like Hiroshima, was utterly defense-less, no matter how many warheads taxpayers bought with their hard-earned money. As DePasquale understood, "a handful of people" had the power, without consulting anyone, to end the world. He saw a new form of tyranny. Though torn in his feelings, he looked to Molly for leadership.

Molly had felt that in much of her organizing and speaking, she was urging others to act. Her decision to walk into the warhead plant, with a hammer as an "educational tool," was the decision to "let go" of the demand for effectiveness, of the feeling of impotent fear. "I'm trying to deal with the possibility of a long jail term," she said during her three months in prison. "I'm not sure what it means. You just have to let go, take things as they come. I learned that from my mother."

She had had to relearn that lesson, she said, "coming from a very pragmatic, job-oriented viewpoint, looking for success. There's no way you can calculate ahead of time what something like this *might* mean, and if you try, you're likely to end up with an inflated notion of what it's about, or just miss the whole point of what you're doing."

Many people, including Judge Salus, thought the whole point had been to get attention. No, Molly said, "we were aware that we could do this in total obscurity. It might be quickly forgotten." She had, she said, "been a pragmatist all these years, a community organizer who tried to get the numbers out, get the votes out, get as many letters to Congress generated as possible and all that."

To one group, she explained, "I don't *know* if it's a futile gesture. For me, it was a way of making my own life whole, making my work for peace more than talk. I don't know if going into that G.E. plant is going to be a small step in the right direction in terms of turning it around, or if it's too late. People want a guarantee that their action's going to be effective. I've heard people say that. Why go to jail when you don't know if it's going to have an effect?"

The most common reactions, she said, were " 'If I knew it would really have an effect, I'd risk going to jail.' 'I want a guarantee that what I do is going to work, that any risk I take will solve the problem.' 'How do you know your action was effective?'

"I *don't* know. I don't *know*. I'm living in as much uncertainty as ever. But something has changed my life." She was such a small person, so rooted in the commonplace, that I marveled when she spoke with confidence to a room full of professors, with all their years of certified learning. She asked them the kinds of questions they were practiced in not asking. "What does it mean to be a human being? What does it mean to be a person who loves people? Who loves life and loves the planet? Who loves to go out in the country and take a walk? Who loves to go out for a few beers after a talk? I love all that, and I'm not going to give up on it. That's worth taking a risk for."

Letting go of the demand for assured results, for knowing the future with certitude, meant giving up one kind of imprisonment. "It was the most freeing act of my life," she said.

"I could have closed my eyes and hoped for the best," she wrote, and many would have been far happier had she done that. "But that hope would have been a blind hope based on refusal to see and refusal to act responsibly." On September 9, 1980, "I felt very clear that I had brought my concerns for my kids' lives and my hope in the future and my love of being a peace-maker all together. When we walked into that

G.E. plant, I felt no fear. I felt tremendous peace. [That act] freed me from the myth of my own powerlessness. I didn't end the arms race, but I certainly acted on behalf of life. And I certainly acted in a way that connected with a lot of people."

"Connected," she said. All around her were disconnections. The General Electric employees, whose work took them through a concrete maze of roads and shopping malls and industrial parks, away from their homes, past the old inn that stood preserved and forgotten, to work where they made objects whose names and uses they didn't want to know about; the weapons, whose appearance was so unindicative; the family, who wanted her to stay home and care for her children while not acting to keep them from destruction; the judge who didn't want to know what the defendants thought, what they knew, how they knew it, what the evidence was; and beyond community and courtroom, in the corridors of corporate and government power, the boards of directors who never considered whether it was ethical to make profit from megadeath; the strategists and planners who made up a new language to describe history, community, family, human beings—"collateral damage," "soft targets," "survivability."

Molly was an intersection where the history of her state, having gone full circle, arrived to join its beginnings; where the history of her warring species encountered the good sense of the founder of her religion; where her Catholic vision restored the vision of a Quaker; where her ancestors met her grandchildren; where the legal impulse to stand up for the species encountered the narrower but equally legal impulse to protect the status quo.

Molly thought the human race was almost out of time. The evidence the court wouldn't hear, that the existence of first-strike weapons was provocative and destabilizing, led her to think that the "last days" predicted by Isaiah and Micah had arrived. She thought that the habit of associating weapons with strength would not break itself. Having accepted the death of innocents at Hiroshima as justified because it saved American soldiers' lives; having accepted that the United States was justified in threatening to destroy entire cities in order to prevent enemy behavior; having accepted that therefore it was justified in preparing to strike first; having accepted that it was prepared to lose millions of the world's people—having accepted all this, political and corporate leaders and much of the population had accepted a theory of human nature that denied connections.

There was no choice, they reasoned. People had always fought. The

Soviets were inveterately evil and unjust. Individuals could do nothing. Only armies with mighty weapons could act. Deep currents of pessimism and despair ran through the renunciation of human allegiance. The possibility of the end of everything infected everything, added its proviso to every thought of the future: When I grow up, I'll be an astronaut (if I grow up); when we retire, we'll move to the country (if there still is a country); we'll fix that bridge three years from now (if we're still here three years from now).

So, the last days having arrived, as far as Molly was able to tell, and there being no one charged with making sure those days were never accomplished, and everyone around her waiting for someone else to take responsibility—she simply took the responsibility herself. There would never be a better time. There would never be a better person. She simply did what needed to be done, dismantling parts of two weapons, pressing the courts to look at legal precedents they preferred to ignore.

I came to think that when people protested that her act was ineffectual, they objected because it had affected them so deeply. I thought that perhaps people feared not ineffectuality, but power—the power to choose freely, to act, to connect with those who have set the most difficult precedents, to affirm those connections. Molly worried people because of the example she offered them.

Molly tied together some of the threads that connected her with her predecessors and successors. One ran from William Penn, who had furthered religious freedom and found security for his people in a disarmed state. Another ran from the stubborn juror, Edward Bushel, who had refused cooperation with an unjust legal proceeding. Another ran from Hugo Grotius, who had codified international law. Another ran from the ordinary workingman's voice telling homely stories in commonplace terms two thousand years earlier to his oppressed people, setting forth the practical wisdom of nonviolent revolutionary love for enemies. She wove together Old Testament prophets, modern scientists and engineers, doctors and psychologists, biologists and lawyers, children and grandchildren, parents and grandparents, Pittsburgh and Hiroshima.

It was as if hope flamed up and kindled hope. So well had psychic numbness done its protective job, that hope was foreign. It alarmed and even hurt. But like small signal lights in a dark night, one flame answered another.

"Molly Rush," said a woman, hearing her name for the first time. "That sounds like someone in history!"

Molly, 1989.

BIBLIOGRAPHY

Aldridge, Robert. *The Counterforce Syndrome: A Guide to U.S. Nuclear Weapons and Strategic Doctrine*. Washington, D.C.: Institute for Policy Studies, 1978.

———. *First Strike! The Pentagon's Strategy for Nuclear War*. Boston: Southend Press, 1983.

Alexander, James. *A Brief Narrative of the Case and Trial of John Peter Zenger*. Edited by S. N. Katz. Cambridge, Mass.: Belknap Press, 1972.

Barksdale, Brent. *Pacifism and Democracy in Colonial Pennsylvania (1682–1758)*. Ph.D. thesis, Stanford University, 1961.

Blackstone, William. *Blackstone's Commentaries with Notes of Reference to the Constitution and Laws of the Federal Government of the United States*. 1803. Reprint. 5 vols. South Hackensack, N.J.: Rothman Reprints, 1969.

Coke, Edward. *The Institutes of the Laws of England*. 1797. Reprint. Buffalo, N.Y.: Wm. S. Hein Co., 1986.

Dworkin, Ronald M. "What Is the Rule of Law?" *Antioch Review* 30 (1970), 151–55.

Dunn, Mary Maples. *William Penn: Politics and Conscience*. Princeton, N.J.: Princeton University Press, 1967.

Falk, Richard, Elliott Meyrowitz, and Jack Sanderson. "Nuclear Weapons and International Law." Occasional Paper #10. Princeton University: Center for International Studies, 1981.

Fantel, Hans. *William Penn: Apostle of Dissent*. New York: Morrow, 1974.

Frank, Anne. *Anne Frank: The Diary of a Young Girl*. Translated by B. M. Mooyaart-Doubleday. New York: Pocket Books, 1958.

Furfey, Paul H. *The Respectable Murderers: Social Evil and Christian Conscience*. New York: Herder and Herder, 1966.

Gandhi, Mahatma. *Gandhi on Non-Violence*. Edited by T. Merton. New York: New Directors, 1965.

G:oka O Mita. *Unforgettable Fire: Pictures Drawn by Atomic Bomb Survivors*. Translated by World Friendship Center in Hiroshima. New York: Pantheon Books, 1977.

Grannis, J. Christopher, et al. *The Risk of the Cross: Christian Discipleship in the Nuclear Age*. New York: Harper & Row, 1981.

Grotius, Hugo. *The Law of War and Peace*. Translated by F. W. Kelsey et al. Indianapolis: Bobbs-Merrill, 1962.

Hallie, Philip P. "From Cruelty to Goodness." *The Hastings Center Report* 11, no. 3 (June 1981).

———. *Lest Innocent Blood Be Shed: The Story of the Village of Le Chambon and How Goodness Happened There.* New York: Harper & Row, 1979.

Jungk, Robert. *Brighter Than a Thousand Suns: A Personal History of the Atomic Scientists.* New York: Harcourt Brace, 1958.

Merton, Thomas. *The Nonviolent Alternative.* New York: Farrar, Straus & Giroux, 1971.

National Conference of Catholic Bishops. *The Challenge of Peace: God's Promise and Our Response.* Washington, D.C.: National Catholic News Service, 1983.

Penn, William. *The Papers of William Penn.* Edited by M. M. Dunn and R. S. Dunn. 5 vols. Philadelphia: University of Pennsylvania Press, 1981.

———. "The Sandy Foundation Shaken." In *The Christian Quaker and His Divine Testimony Stated and Vindicated.* Philadelphia: Rakestraw, 1824.

———. *The Tryal of William Penn and William Mead for Causing a Tumult: at the Sessions Held at the Old Bailey in London, the 1st, 3rd, 4th and 5th of September, 1670.* 1719. Reprint. Boston: Marshall Jones, 1919.

Rogers, Rita. "On Emotional Responses to Nuclear Issues and Terrorism." *Psychiatric Journal of the University of Ottawa* 5, no. 3 (September 1980): 147–52.

Schell, Jonathan. *The Fate of the Earth.* New York: Knopf, 1982.

Thomas, Lewis. *Late Night Thoughts on Listening to Mahler's Ninth Symphony.* New York: Bantam Books, 1984.

Thoreau, Henry David. *Resistance to Civil Government.* [*Civil Disobedience*]. 1849. Reprint. New York: C. N. Patter, 1970.

Zinn, Howard. *Disobedience and Democracy: Nine Fallacies on Law and Order.* New York: Random House, 1968.

THE PITTSBURGH PEACE INSTITUTE

Since January 1984, the Pittsburgh Peace Institute has generated a momentum counter to the fears and forces that lead to war. PPI provides community-based education, teaching that conflict at every level—international, national, local, and domestic—can be conducted and resolved nonviolently. The use of nonviolent strategies can empower a broad range of citizens to bring about just and durable social change. Through its education offerings and publications, PPI teaches that:

- Nonviolent conflict resolution has a long and effective history.

- Ordinary individuals have power, and the nonviolent use of power can be learned.

- Evidence exists that a strong defense need not rely on warfare. With training and indoctrination equal to that promoting violent tactics, nonviolent measures can be as effective as violent ones.

- In our time, waging war can, in fact, mean the end of everything we have traditionally fought for.

- War and violence are not inevitable expressions of human nature.

ORDER FORM

HAMMER OF JUSTICE		Quantity	Total
hardbound	($24.95)	_____	_____
paper	($12.95)	_____	_____
STUDY GUIDE	($1.00)	_____	_____

6% tax in PA   _____
Handling and shipping
($2.50 first book + .50 each additional book)   _____

$\qquad\qquad\qquad\qquad\qquad$ **Amount enclosed** $ _____

Name: _____

Address: _____

City: _____ State: _____ Zip: _____

☐ Please put me on the Pittsburgh Peace Institute mailing list.

Other publications of PPI Books

First-Strike Weapons ($1.00)
Star Wars: Waking Up From the Dream ($1.00)
Simpleton Story: A Fairy Tale for a Nuclear Age ($3.00)
$\quad$ Study Guide ($1.00)

PPI Books
Pittsburgh Peace Institute
1139 Wightman St. #A
Pittsburgh, PA 15217
412-682-2600